Textual In

Widely encompassing in its examples and comprehensive in its theoretical coverage, this important book is full of insights, offers clear methodology, puts a coherent new position on text, and is, throughout, written in a most engaging manner.

> Gunther Kress, Institute of Education, University of London

Textual Interaction provides a lucid and cogent account of written discourse analysis.

Hoey clearly sets out his own approach, which focuses on the way writers and readers interact, and relates it to other approaches. Each chapter introduces key concepts and analytical techniques, describes important parallel work, and suggests how to apply the ideas to stylistics and to the teaching and learning of reading and writing.

In this book, Hoey analyses a wide variety of narrative texts: fairy-tales, novels, poems, short stories, jokes; and non-narrative texts: posters, timetables, till receipts. He shows how much these very different text types have in common with each other and argues that, in the interaction between writer and reader, the reader has as much power as the writer.

Written in a lively and accessible style, *Textual Interaction* is suitable for adoption on text linguistics, applied linguistics, critical discourse analysis, and stylistics courses.

Michael Hoey is Baines Professor of English Language and Director of the Applied English Language Studies Unit at the University of Liverpool. His books include *On the Surface of Discourse* and *Patterns of Lexis in Text*.

Textual Interaction

An introduction to written discourse analysis

Michael Hoey

London and New York

First published 2001
by Routledge
11 New Fetter Lane, London EC4P 4EE

Simultaneously published in the USA and Canada
by Routledge
29 West 35th Street, New York, NY 10001

Transferred to Digital Printing 2004

Routledge is an imprint of the Taylor & Francis Group

Typeset in Baskerville by
MHL Typesetting Ltd, Coventry
Printed and bound in Great Britain by
Biddles Ltd, King's Lynn, Norfolk

British Library Cataloguing in Publication Data
A catalogue record for this book is available
from the British Library

Library of Congress Cataloging in Publication Data
Hoey, Michael.
  Textual interaction: an introduction to written discourse analysis/
Michael Hoey.
    p. cm.
  Includes bibliographical references and index.
  1. Discourse analysis. I. Title.
P302 .H557 2000
401'.41–dc21   00-038252

ISBN 0-415-23168-X (hbk)
    0-415-23169-8 (pbk)

To Mum and Dad with love and thanks

Contents

Figures

Tables

Acknowledgements

I have been lucky in my life in both personal and academic terms. Academically this book has benefited greatly from excellent colleagues at each of the three institutions where I have worked over the years as well as an excellent supervisor and guide at the beginning of my career. Randolph Quirk, now Lord Quirk, was my supervisor and he instilled in me a real interest in the English Language and a respect for data that I have never lost. At the former Hatfield Polytechnic (now the University of Hertfordshire) I acquired from Eugene Winter an enthusiasm for discourse analysis and an independence of intellectual spirit; he reinforced also in me a belief in the centrality of data in any description. His death deprived me of a loyal friend and fierce critic; this book is the better for having been influenced by him and the worse for not having been read by him.

At the University of Birmingham I benefited hugely from the friendship and critical interest of Malcolm Coulthard, John Sinclair, David Brazil, and many other colleagues. I have sought to reflect their influence upon me in the body of my text. Again, a passionate commitment to investigating discourse coupled with respect for what the data were saying was what characterised these linguists. Malcolm Coulthard's influence went beyond this; it was he that gave me my first opportunity to publish on the subject of this book and he has been unfailingly supportive ever since. At one point we intended to write a book on narrative together: the comments on Borges' *Death and the Compass* scattered through this book are remnants of analyses done in preparation of that book and have in all cases been improved by our discussions together, to such an extent that I cannot promise that his ideas will not have crept in alongside mine (though defects in the analyses are indisputably mine alone).

My colleagues at the University of Liverpool, past and present, deserve the greatest thanks, however. Siobhan Chapman, Lewis Hall, Andrew Hamer, Carol Marley, Antoinette Renouf, Mike Scott, Nelia Scott, Celia Shalom, Karl Simms, Geoff Thompson, Sue Thompson and Sarah Waite-Gleave have all been supportive in every way possible, discussing my ideas with me on every available occasion, covering for me when I presented papers at conferences that helped me work through the ideas contained in this book, supplying the many gaps in my reading and, in Mike Scott's case, giving me free use of his WordSmith software. To all of them I convey my heartfelt thanks; they will understand, however, if I reserve still greater thanks to Maureen Molloy who valiantly fights to find me space to research and write, and unselfishly struggles to keep my working day in order; in the final days of this book, furthermore, she uncomplainingly responded to a myriad cries for help in tracing references, finding articles and collecting together essential information.

I have been greatly helped by staff at Routledge, notably Louise Patchett, Katherine Jacobson and Louisa Semlyen, and also by the project manager, Stuart Macfarlane, all of whom have been supportive and efficient in equal measure.

The greatest academic thanks must go to my students, both undergraduate and postgraduate. Indeed without them this book would have been markedly poorer. I have reluctantly decided that any attempt to thank by name every one of the students who has influenced this book would result in invidious and unintentional omissions. In very many cases, though, they will find their influence explicitly acknowledged in the bibliographical end-notes to each chapter, and their anonymity here is no measure of the importance I ascribe to their influence upon my thinking.

If I have been lucky in my academic life, still more so have I been in my personal life. The companionship and love of my wife, Sue, has ensured that I have been able to write my book in a happy and contented state, and no thanks could be great enough to her. The same goes for my (adult) children, Richard and Alice, who have allowed me to use their childhood jokes and writings as data in this book and have prevented me from taking myself too seriously. Likewise I was blessed with excellent parents, who ensured during periods of extended illness in my childhood that my studies never suffered and have given me encouragement and love at all times. To them this book is gratefully dedicated.

The author and publishers would like to thank the following copyright holders for granting permission to reproduce their material:

Extract from 'Quietly Vanishing' by Malcolm Smith reprinted by permission of Malcolm Smith and *The Independent on Sunday.*

The complete text of *Well Loved Tales: Goldilocks and the Three Bears* retold by Vera Southgate (Ladybird, 1971) Copyright © Ladybird Books Ltd, 1971. Reprinted by permission of Ladybird Books Ltd.

Extract from Lexmark advertisement reprinted by permission of Lexmark International.

While the author and the publishers have made every effort to contact copyright holders of the material used in this volume, they would be happy to hear from anyone they were unable to contact.

1 What to expect and what not to expect

Although it was still early morning, there was already heat in the air. The two aborigines, members of the Anangu people, had stopped in a patch clear of brush and the elder of them was crouching on the ground with a stick in his hand with which he drew in the sand. Behind them in the middle distance loomed the impressive brick-red shape of Uluru, or Ayers Rock as the Europeans rechristened it when they finally stumbled upon it. Up the side of it a thin line of climbers could be seen, like ants on the side of an ant-hill, proving their fitness and their insensitivity at one and the same time. For Uluru is a sacred site of the Aborigines and that was why Sue and I were here, bending over the older aborigine as he drew, trying to learn to see this huge wasteland through his eyes rather than our own, perhaps trying also, in a way, to atone for the thick skins of the hundreds on the Rock. As he drew he talked, clearly and loudly but in his own tongue – either Pitjantjatjara or Yankunytjatjara, I had no way of knowing which. That was also right. His tongue was here long before English, and we needed to know that we had no right to instant access to his thoughts. We waited expectantly. The drawing seemed to be a kind of diagram, a diagram to which we did not yet have the key. All we knew was that he was telling us a story, an ancient legend of his aboriginal tribe. At last he stopped and the younger man, possibly his son, translated for us in good English. This is what he said:

> In the beginning the Mala people come to Uluru from the north and the west to participate in an Inma, a religious ceremony. In preparation for that ceremony the young men, the old men, the young and unmarried women and the old and married women all set up separate camps. Some of the men carry a ceremonial pole, Ngaltawata, up to the top of Uluru where they plant it in the northernmost corner. This signals the beginning of the ceremony and everything they do from now on will become part of the ceremony; even the most menial tasks must be done in a manner appropriate to the ceremony.
>
> While the Mala are busy about their ceremony, happy in what they doing, people arrive from the west with an invitation to join another Inma. The Mala have no choice but to refuse as a ceremony once started cannot be stopped in the middle. This is, however, a great insult to the people from the west and they return home angry, determined to take revenge upon the Mala for the insult.

Accordingly they create an evil, black dog-like creature called Kurpany to destroy the Mala people's ceremony. As Kurpany heads for Uluru, Lunpa the kingfisher flies ahead and tries to warn the people but his warning is ignored. Kurpany arrives at the ceremony and destroys it, killing many of the Mala men, women and children. The survivors flee terrified to the south pursued all the way by Kurpany.

With that he fell silent. The story was at an end. He pointed to the line of tiny figures climbing Uluru, testing their fitness against the steepness of the Rock. 'We call them Minga – that is our word for ants', he said. 'Where they are climbing is where the Mala men climbed to put the ceremonial pole.' We nodded, ashamed but also a little smug. We had avoided a long and arduous climb in the heat and at the same time conformed with the religious sentiments of the people who were the traditional owners of Uluru.

Academic books are not narratives and they do not begin *in media res*. I have therefore broken a fundamental convention of academic textbook writing by beginning the way I just have, and my first purpose in so beginning was to draw attention to the existence of such conventions. Had this book been entitled *In Search of the Inner Australia*, there would have been nothing surprising about the first page at all. Travel books are characteristically narratives and may choose to begin wherever they like. Academic textbooks and travel books belong to different *genres* and a full survey of text analysis needs to take account of the conventions that govern such genres with varying degrees of rigidity. Key figures in such work are Swales (e.g. 1990), Hasan (e.g. Halliday and Hasan 1985) and Martin (e.g. 1997). It is not easy to define genre and some definitions would cover the academic textbook more readily than the travel book. But the existence of genre as a key feature of text can hardly be denied and affects little linguistic matters as well as large. So the beginning of this chapter is predominantly in the past tense, except where the translator of the story is being quoted, and is organised around time sequence. The remainder of the chapter on the other hand is overwhelmingly in the present tense and makes little use of time sequence.

You might imagine from the preceding paragraphs that this book was going to be about genre. But this book does not pretend to provide a description of genre structure, important though genre is. The above paragraphs were a confession of a failure to cover genre, not a promise to do so. Throughout the book references will be made to different genres and in a number of places an attempt is made to correlate these genres with some of the features found to characterise texts, but no theory of genre is outlined, nor are any connections stronger than correlations proposed. At the end of this chapter, however, will be found a bibliographical note in which some of the key works on genre are cited, and readers are invited to follow up these leads. Such bibliographical notes will be found at the end of each chapter; in this way the main text need not be encumbered with the machinery of extensive citations, but scholarly proprieties are properly maintained and my innumerable debts to other linguists can be paid.

Look again at the 'travel book' beginning and ponder for a moment what the discourse is saying. On the face of it, it is an account of an encounter in central Australia between the members of two cultures, one alien, one native, in which the visitors learn something of the native culture. But the story is less transparent than it seems. To begin with, as I have already noted, it conforms pretty closely to the norms associated with travel writing, which are, of course, norms associated with the alien culture, not the aboriginal one. In some sense, then, the aboriginal experience has simply been (ab)used as exotic fodder for an established western genre. There is no sense in which the cultural encounter has altered the discourse in which it is reported.

Secondly, although the visitors are reported as being sympathetic to and respectful of the aboriginal beliefs, the story begins and ends with the words of the narrator (me). It is the narrator who has the final word, not the Anangu translator. This is another way in which I have incorporated his words and world into mine. Look, too, at the distribution of grammatical subjects: one or other of the aborigines are the subject of thirteen clauses, my wife and I are subject of exactly the same number of clauses, once non-finite and coordinated clauses are taken into account. In other words the story is about us as much as them. In retrospect the story is as much about our giving them something – atonement, respect – as it is about their giving us something. It is not, as it could have been, a story about injustice and colonial oppression.

A vigorous branch of text linguistics at the present time is that devoted to what is termed *critical discourse analysis*. This approach to the analysis of text is concerned to unpack the political, social and cultural implications of the texts that we encounter (and produce). The traditional text linguist, in ignoring these implications, can be seen as conspiring to keep them hidden and thereby supports whatever status quo the texts are a cultural product of; the critical discourse analyst seeks to uncover such implications and thereby to make possible a challenge to the status quo.

As with genre, so with critical discourse analysis, as far as this book is concerned. On occasion, where appropriate, social/cultural implications are drawn out, particularly when correlations with genre are being made, and I have attended to any features of texts whose status quo positioning I am particularly anxious not to endorse; but in general this book does not offer critical discourse analytical insights in any systematic way, despite the current importance of this branch of text linguistics to the field as a whole. The bibliographical section of this chapter therefore offers a brief range of references for those who would like to explore further this aspect of text linguistics.

My third purpose in beginning the book the way I did was that I wanted you to read the aboriginal story. Although it is risky to make sweeping assumptions about reader reactions, I suspect that the story will seem strange to many readers, particularly those who have grown up or been educated within what might be termed the Graeco-Roman tradition that has so profoundly influenced the cultures of Europe and North America. It flouts our expectations about story-telling. It is, to begin with, told in the present tense, as if the events described are timeless or endlessly repeated. It also pays no attention to establishing a setting. We are not told who the Mala people were nor who the people from the west were. (Is it significant, for example, that some of the Mala also come from the west?) Key questions – or, more properly, questions that I deem key – are left unanswered, presumably because for the original audience the answers were already known or irrelevant. But my western mind wants, for instance, to know why the Mala's refusal to accept the invitation was such a deadly insult and in what way the people from the west were able to create Kurpany.

Then on a larger scale I am aware of what are (for me) unexpected plot features. The black dog-like creature Kurpany is described as evil and yet not only survives but wins. The Mala people are – in my reading – the ones with whom we sympathise; they try to do things right, there is no malice in their heart in refusing the invitation of the people from the west, they have done nothing to deserve a bad fate. The people from the west on the other hand do have bad hearts: they get angry at being insulted and seek vengeance. Yet it is the Mala who end the story destroyed, scattered and in terror of their lives. Such a story arising out of the Graeco-Roman tradition, told in any of the major European languages, might well have continued to describe how the Mala finally destroyed Kurpany either by their own devices or with outside help. Alternatively it might have had a different development, one in which Lunpa the kingfisher had some impact on their behaviour and they successfully defended themselves against Kurpany.

The point here is that the present book does not assume that the characteristics of English texts apply to other languages. In the course of the book a number of claims about text organisation will be made but no claim is made about their applicability outside the English language. It is likely, even probable, that many of the features described in this book do in fact apply to other languages, particularly those affected by the Graeco-Roman tradition. In the course of many of the chapters there is an attempt to apply the analytical features there described to a complex and endlessly fascinating story by Jorge Luis Borges, *Death and the Compass*, which was originally written in Spanish; there does not appear to be any obstacle to transferring the characteristics of English texts to this story (though, as we shall see, it challenges some of our assumptions about text organisation). But the aboriginal text above, and many others from a wide range of cultures, do not admit so easily of analysis in the same terms as apply to English texts. Accordingly another important branch of text linguistics is that devoted to comparing and contrasting the different strategies for organising texts employed by languages around the world; the term usually used to describe this field is *contrastive rhetoric*, following the pioneering work of Robert Kaplan (1966 *et seq.*).

Texts establish their own patterns as they develop and this one has already raised two important areas, only to dampen hopes that they will be covered in this book. So you will not be surprised to learn that, important as contrastive rhetoric is, this book makes no systematic attempt to note where the descriptions it provides apply to other languages nor where other languages would do things differently. Only in Chapter 7 are there any such comparisons and even here they are offered in passing. The bibliographical note at the end of this chapter, however, contains references to representative works on contrastive rhetoric.

So what does this book attempt to do, if it eschews the description of genre, makes no claim to offer critical discourse analyses and avoids contrastive rhetorical description? As mature and experienced readers, it is likely that you did one of two things when you encountered the travel experience with which this book began. You may have skipped it altogether to see whether you needed to read it, or you may have read it with mounting curiosity (or even irritation) at my ill-manners in not providing a focus for your reading. If you did not skip the first page, it is likely that you began to speculate on the uses I might be intending to make of my experience in Australia. Knowing that this book is about the analysis of text, you may for example have wondered whether the passage was going to be used as an example of some textual point. Identifying an unusual narrative as part of the account, you may have speculated that I was going to draw some conclusions about the nature of narratives. Noting the reference to the older aborigine having first told his story in one of the languages of the Anangu, you might have expected an observation of a comparative linguistic kind. The point is that you will have *interacted* with the passage. One of the aims of this book is to show the linguistic implications of the fundamental fact that texts gain their meaning from a reader's interaction with them. Had I been a co-operative writer and introduced the book in the normal way so that you knew what I was attempting to do and where I intended to go, that would likewise have been reflected in the wording of my text. The beginning of this paragraph starts with a question which I then attempt to answer – this, too, is a reflection of the interactivity of text. The whole of this book is concerned with this topic, but Chapters 2, 3 and 9 in particular focus on it.

As we shall see in Chapter 3, however, the interactivity just alluded to is not simple and linear. When I discussed the strangeness to the western mind of the Anangu story, I treated the story as if it were self-contained. Likewise when I discussed the critical discourse implications of my own text, I ignored the story as irrelevant to my purposes. In the latter case I treated the story as an unanalysable whole; in the former case I treated the surrounding commentary as if it did not exist. What this shows is that texts are in part hierarchically organised and that as readers we may attend to the outer or inner structures at will. Chapter 4 of this book concerns itself with the mechanics of this property, while Chapters 6 onwards seek to flesh out the implications in terms of the characteristic patterns of English texts.

Description of these patterns comprises a good proportion of the book. When I attempted to describe my sense of the oddity of the Anangu story, I made reference to questions that might have been answered in a western telling and to ways in which the story might have developed or changed in such a telling. In so doing I was presuming upon a shared understanding of what texts do, what they are like, within our culture. This shared understanding is another feature of interactivity in text and is, more than anything else, the subject of this book. The book attempts, indirectly, to offer a partial explanation of why the Anangu story seems unfamiliar by providing an account of what we tend to expect in narratives and other kinds of text. So in Chapters 7, 8 and 9, in particular, I attempt to outline some of the main ways in which narratives and other kinds of text come to feel familiar to us. Some non-narrative texts, however, are of a very different kind and Chapter 5 attempts to describe the characteristics of a special class of non-narrative texts which includes dictionaries, shopping lists and telephone directories.

At this point it is perhaps important to state explicitly something that is implicit throughout the book. Unlike some linguists, I do not hold that there is a great gulf fixed between narrative and non-narrative texts, and as the book develops I shall marshall evidence in support of this view. This in turn relates to my most important purpose in writing this book. I want to show some of the properties of texts written in English that underpin all the descriptions of genre and contrastive rhetoric and make critical discourse analysis possible. In a way, this is a book about the nuts and bolts of text, the characteristics of text that make them texts in the first place, and I hope it will find a place alongside the texts cited in the bibliographical end-notes. The next five chapters in particular describe these nuts and bolts, and the claims made in these chapters are very tentatively offered as operating beyond the confines of English.

Although there may be nut and bolt rules that ensure the coherence of text, beyond these there are, I have argued elsewhere, only conventions. For this reason, many text-linguists, this one included, seem better able to account for safe and ordinary texts rather than the ones that most excite. Perhaps that is one of the reasons why linguistic stylistics has never been seen as a major breakthrough in literary studies. Despite that, as an ancillary objective of this book, I have attempted in a few places to draw literary conclusions from text-linguistic evidence in order to show how a connection might be ventured between literary criticism and text-linguistics of the kind I advocate.

From the point of view of language learners, on the other hand, the safe and ordinary texts are likely to be the ones that they encounter first and indeed most wish to emulate. There are therefore also some language teaching and learning observations made in the course of each chapter, to indicate the ways in which the nuts and bolts might help, or be important in, the teaching of English.

I noted above that beyond the 'nuts and bolts' rules there are in my view only conventions. This leads me to my final reason for beginning this textbook with a travel experience – to show that it can be done. Text does have patterning, and genres do conform to conventions, but it is always possible to deviate from the expected, buck the convention. Text is one of the places where we can show most creativity. Every statement in this book should be taken as a statement of description of the norm, not necessarily (or indeed usually) a statement of what is possible. Nabokov's *Pale Fire* is a narrative written in the form of footnotes to a poem; likewise, one of the chapters of Julian Barnes' *Flaubert's Parrot* (a narrative or collection of essays, according to viewpoint) takes the form of an examination paper. (Of course, linguistic creativity with narrative may take non-discoursal forms; an example would be Georges Perec's *La Disparition*, translated, or, more accurately, re-created in English, as *A Void* by Gilbert Adair, in which the letter 'e' is avoided for 283 pages.)

Nor is it only the province of novelists to be innovative. When Martin Joos wrote his linguistic monograph, *The Five Clocks* (1961), on the styles of language, he gave it a title that sounds like that of a novel, not an academic monograph. If a novel-like title were all his innovation, it would not be worth remarking on here. But in fact Joos's daring runs deeper in that he introduces features of narrative into the monograph itself. In particular he objectifies a possible opponent to his views to such an extent that in the later stages of the book, this 'opponent' acquires a complete character and a voice of her own and interrupts Joos's monologue, thereby converting it into a dialogue. For this particular rather conventional reader at an early stage in his academic career, it was a little too much, as perhaps my own limited experimentation in this book may be for others. But it is a fundamental property of text that such experimentation is possible in a way that, for example, experimentation with grammar is not, except within strictly narrow bounds.

Whether writers experiment or not, their objective is to have an effect on their readers using their text. My title 'Textual Interaction' is chosen to reflect two perspectives. First, 'text' does not exist except as part of a commitment to interaction in which each contributor to the interaction has needs to meet at the same time as respecting the needs of the other. Second, interaction is necessarily personal and each person's experience of it will be different from everyone else's. It can be experienced as routine or found to be life-enhancing. This book is about such interaction; it may not be life-enhancing but I hope it will not be found routine.

As we walked back along the Anangu track afterwards, I had ceased to be an excited tourist and had become an excited linguist instead. 'I could use that experience in my book,' I said.

Bibliographical end-notes

Each chapter will end with a bibliographical end-note like this. The end-notes will be used to give the sources of texts quoted and of ideas used, as appropriate. I will also sometimes defer to the end-note the discussion of matters that might have led to the argument of the main chapter seeming misshapen. Sometimes, as in this case, the end-notes will be quite extensive; in other cases, they will be little more than a footnote to the chapter. In doing this I acknowledge my debt to Norman Fairclough, who adopts this practice, rather effectively to my mind, in his book *Language and Power* (Fairclough 1989).

The account of how I was told a story by members of the Anangu people is true and is partly constructed from memory. However, my memory was substantially aided by an invaluable booklet bought at the Uluru-Kata Tjuta National Park Visitor's Centre (Australian Nature Conservation Agency & Mutijulu Community Inc. 1990), the last sentence of which reads: 'Please keep [this brochure] and tell other people about what you have learned from it.' In a small way, I have now complied with their request.

There are two main schools of thought about genre. They differ somewhat in their theoretical formulations but they do not appear to be in fundamental conflict and there is much to be learnt from both. The leading figure in the first of these schools is John Swales, whose most influential books concentrate on academic genres (Swales 1981, 1990). His definition centres on the notion of a discourse community that has, in some sense, ownership of a genre. His analysis focuses on what he terms the *moves* that writers choose (and to some extent are required) to make in constructing their text. This notion is exemplified in detail by reference to article introductions. The structure of moves is similar in some respects to the description of Gap in Knowledge structures provided in Chapter 8 of this book. Vijay Bhatia takes Swales's ideas and shows their application to genres belonging to other discourse communities, most notably those associated with the legal profession (Bhatia 1983, 1993). From a slightly different perspective, Berkenkotter and Huckin (1995) examine genre knowledge within disciplinary communication. Tony Dudley-Evans (1994, 1995, with Hopkins 1988), on the other hand, stays with the genres belonging to the academic community, looking, for example, at article discussion sections. Their work suggests that moves do not apply as straight-forwardly to (some parts of) some genres. Kay and Dudley-Evans (1998) consider the implication of genre for ELT, as does Paltridge (1996).

The other major school of thought with regard to genre is that associated with Systemic-Functional linguistics and in particular with Australian linguists working in this tradition. A pioneer among this group was Ruqaiya Hasan (with Halliday 1985), though she has voiced some concern about recent developments (Hasan 1995). A rather different approach, though with some of the same theoretical underpinning, is adopted by Eija Ventola (1987), who follows the work of Martin (e.g. 1992). Ventola's work is primarily concerned with spoken genres but Martin's is directly concerned with written genres and, in part, with the impact on the child that distorted patterns of educational exposure to these genres have (Martin 1989). This educational perspective is continued in Christie and Martin (1997), where Martin's current position and how he arrived at it is economically expressed in the first paper. There are some thorny theoretical questions regarding the relationship of genre to register and language that are unresolved in the Systemic tradition (see Hasan 1995 and Bowcher in preparation; Martin 1997, addresses some of the theoretical concerns), and one could get bogged down in these, but the analyses of the texts these linguists produce are almost unfailingly interesting. Hon (1998), however, questions the emphasis on sequence of elements shared by both the Swalesian and Systemic-Functional approaches, providing analyses of advertising texts that derive from both approaches but assume no favoured order of elements except at the most general level. White (1999) also characterises newspaper stories in strictly non-sequential terms while remaining true to the Systemic theoretical position.

In addition to the above linguists, who place themselves within (or have created) a particular view of genre, there are a number of linguists who have, in effect, undertaken studies of particular genres without choosing to use the term or connecting what they have to say to either of the schools of thought I have mentioned. These include Torben Vestergaard and Kim Schrøder (1985) and Guy Cook (1992), who deal with advertising texts, and Teun Van Dijk (1988), Roger Fowler (1991) and Allan Bell (1991), who all deal with news stories in newspapers.

Biber (1988) seeks to relate variations in speech and writing to genre; he has, however, a loose notion of genre and his work is more revealing of the insights that corpus linguistics can bring than of genres *per se*. Lee (2000) in any case casts serious doubt upon his methodology. Mauranen (1998) argues that not only does future genre research need to be informed by corpus study but that corpus linguistics needs to become genre-oriented and that corpora need to be designed with specific genres in mind.

Roger Fowler, mentioned above in connection with genre, was also a leading figure in the field that came to be known as critical discourse analysis. He and Tony True, Gunther Kress and Bob Hodge argued that linguistic analysis of representative texts of official institutions (such as universities) could reveal the underlying positions of power and (avoidance of) responsibility being adopted on behalf of those institutions (Fowler *et al.* 1979; Hodge and Kress 1993). These analyses are not strictly textual – the focus is primarily grammatical – and are mentioned only because they are the starting point for the discourse-centred work that followed. Norman Fairclough (1989, 1992a) is the linguist who, with Gunther Kress (1991), can be credited with giving wide currency to the discourse perspective in critical linguistic analyses. Fairclough's check-list of analytical questions to ask of a text is exemplary (1989, pp. 110–11) and could usefully be put in the hands of every trainee analyst, but the analyses themselves do not always consider alternative positions. The analyses that critical discourse analysts produce are highly stimulating and contentious in equal proportions, and it cannot be said that there is yet any consensus of support for the arguments put forward. The problems lie in the impossibility of there being a single interpretation of any text. O'Halloran (1999) argues that critical discourse is working with outmoded theories of mental representation and that consequently the reading that one author comes up with may be challenged by other readers with different political points of view. The suspicion of only finding what one sets out to find always lingers in the air. Widdowson (1996, 1998) and Stubbs (1997) have both argued against critical discourse analysis, Stubbs putting the case against with deceptive charity. While some of the criticisms levelled against critical discourse analysis have yet to be answered, the general argument, that texts encode political/social/cultural positions of which the writers may be unaware and that these positions will somewhere be inscribed in the language, is a powerful correction to the empty formalism of some earlier work, and it is incumbent on any analyst to be aware of the way his/her analysis may be supportive of such positions. A useful collection of papers on critical discourse analysis can be found in Caldas-Coulthard and Coulthard (1996); see also Caldas-Coulthard (1993).

The classic contrastive rhetoric position was formulated a long while ago (1966) by Robert Kaplan in a now classic paper, 'Cultural thought patterns in intercultural education'. In this paper he notes that different cultures have different preferences for sequencing an argument; he presents each of the possibilities in terms of simple line drawings, with x culture favouring a spiral ordering, y culture preferring a stepping sequence and the Anglo-American culture going for the straight-line approach. Not unexpectedly he has been criticised for the anglocentricism of his representation of the options available to different cultures, the Anglo-American option manifesting suspicious simplicity, but the underlying insight has proved durable. Amongst linguists whose work has subsequently expanded upon Kaplan's original insight should be noted Connor (1996), Mauranen (1993a, 1993b), Salager-Meyer (1990) and Hinds (1983, 1987). Kaplan has himself done a great deal of work himself (e.g. 1972, 1977, 1987) as well as co-editing several collections of papers on the topic (e.g. Kaplan *et al.* 1982; Connor and Kaplan (eds) 1987); Purves (1988) collects some worthwhile papers on contrastive rhetoric and includes Kaplan's own theoretical overview of the field. A short but helpful account of the history of contrastive rhetoric can be found in Connor (1998).

Falling outside the contrastive rhetoric umbrella but nevertheless offering insights into the differing textual strategies used in other cultures/languages are Grimes (1972, 1975) who, amongst other matters, distinguishes outline and overlay languages (the former moving quickly from narrative point to point, the latter building the narrative by a process of accretion involving considerable repetition and paraphrase) and Longacre (1968, 1972), whose emphasis is on the underlying similarity of the varying languages with the focus instead being placed on the detailed and local differences among them. These books are now hard to get hold of, but they repay careful attention, particularly in respect of the claims Longacre makes (also with Ballard and Conrad 1971a, 1971b) about the apparent universality of certain textual features (discussed in Chapter 3).

2   Text as a site for interaction

Introduction

Before you read this chapter, try listing all the texts you remember reading in the past week. Your list is likely to include academic textbooks, newspaper articles, novels and advertisements. It may even include instruction leaflets and junk mail, neither of which look particularly like the text you are currently reading. But would you consider including store receipts, junction signposts, telephone directories, dictionaries, TV listings or library catalogues? You are likely to have encountered several of these at least in the past week, and they are texts as much as fictions or editorials, although their characteristics are in many respects markedly different.

Text can be defined as the visible evidence of a reasonably self-contained purposeful interaction between one or more writers and one or more readers, in which the writer(s) control the interaction and produce most of (charac-teristically all) the language. This definition excludes spoken language, though it is possible to modify it so that speech is included. The whole interaction can be referred to as a *discourse*, and here, of course, the overlap with speech occurs entirely naturally. As the subtitle of this book indicates, we are concerned here with *written discourse*, though occasional reference will be made to spoken data.

All the text types listed in the first paragraph fit the characterisation of text as the visible evidence of a purposeful interaction between writers and readers. Thus at one extreme an academic textbook is the visible evidence of an interaction between an academic and undergraduates, in which the academic seeks to encapsulate the state of knowledge in a particular discipline in order that the undergraduates may have a coherent overview of the discipline and be able to place any particular aspect of the discipline within the larger whole. At the other extreme a till receipt is part of an interaction between shop management and customers, in which a variety of purposes are served, some of which are discussed in the next section.

In both cases, one has to learn how to read the texts. One is not necessarily expected to read textbooks from cover to cover, and one has to learn how to interpret features like academic references, not to mention having to get used to academic prose (which, for example, will often start generalisations with 'one' and set them in the timeless present – look again at this sentence). In the same way, though perhaps less obviously, there is nothing self-evident about a till receipt. Consider Example 2.1 below:

2.1

B & M
SOUTHPORT

SALE	
OPAL DISH WASH/POWDER 3KG	£2.99
H/HOOCH 330ML/LEMONADE	
3 × £0.69	£2.07
TRICEL 1.2KG/B10	£0.69
CABIN BAG/ASS COLOUR	£1.99
H/HOOCH 330ML/LEMONADE	£0.69
TOTAL (7 items)	£8.43

* PLEASE KEEP THIS RECEIPT WITH YOUR
    PAYMENT SLIP *

12 FEB 99 17:15 0870101 002 08 53
    VAT NO. 673 5836 01
FAMOUS FOR SENSATIONAL PRICES

We have to learn to read such a text, and indeed there are elements on it that we never attend to and are unlikely to know the purpose of, such as the cryptic run of numbers following the date or the VAT number. Although we may regard such a text as extremely basic and straightforward, it is in reality the site of a number of discrete possible interactions.

There is nothing self-evident about a till receipt or about an academic textbook, but to a regular user of such texts there seems to be, simply because each new instance of the type conforms to expectations that the reader has formed on the basis of previous encounters with texts of the same type. Put simply, once you've seen one till receipt (or academic text) you've seen them all! When writers compose their texts, they draw upon models that have become normal within their culture; when readers process these texts, they do the same. It is this property of text that makes the study of reading and writing so interesting – and so complicated.

Another feature of text that makes the study of its production and reception complicated is that one text may appear inside another. To take an obvious example, the till receipt above is a complete text, albeit out of its proper context, and might be analysed either in its own terms or as part of the section or chapter within which it is embedded. More subtly, this can be said also of the sections and chapters themselves in a book like this: we can either look at how the section/chapter works in its own terms or we can look at its place in the larger scheme of things. I referred to this property of text in Chapter 1 when I noted that the

Anangu story was embedded within the larger travel account. Pike (1967) refers to the two perspectives as the *particle* perspective on language – what is this piece of language made of? – and the *field* perspective – what role does this piece of language play in its larger linguistic and non-linguistic context? Both perspectives are necessary for a full description of any linguistic phenomenon, and both have obvious implications for our understanding of reading or writing.

As the examples I gave above may suggest, texts divide into two broad classes. The first of these might be termed 'mainstream' texts. These are the kind of text you are likely to have included first in your list – novels, articles, editorials, and the like. Such texts share a number of important properties and are the main subject of the chapters of this book; when people say they can read or write a language, it is this kind of text that they usually have in mind. Nevertheless, the other kind of text – which for the moment I will not label – is very important and Chapter 4 is devoted to the character of such texts.

Text as a site of interaction amongst author, writer, audience and reader

For many purposes, we can think of a text as the site of an interaction between a writer and readers which the writer controls. Fictional works, for example, seem to fit this model of interaction quite well. In such a case there is a writer who has a certain kind of reader in mind and that kind of reader then comes to the text and accepts what the writer offers. But this model of reading and of the interaction that operates in text is very limiting if one looks at a wider range of texts. In the first place it treats writing as a proactive process and reading as a receptive process. Julian Edge (1986) represents such a relationship in the following way:

This picture shows lots of little worshipping readers coming to the feet of the great writer-idol in the hope for enlightenment. Such a relationship can exist but it is by no means certain that it should be normative of reading-writing relationships, and certainly does not reflect my relationship to minutes of a committee meeting or even, perhaps unfairly, to student essays (though enlightenment quite often comes from the latter willy-nilly). Edge suggests another image that empowers the reader and reflects much more accurately much that passes for reading:

In this image the reader is seen as striding over lots of little writers to get wherever s/he wants to go. This reflects the relationship I have to dictionaries, train timetables and sets of instructions but also (I am half ashamed to admit) to much academic writing. When students work on essays or dissertations, much of their reading is similarly driven by utilitarian objectives – this article is a good reference, that chapter will save them reading a book they can't get hold of, this paper nicely supports their argument, that one will serve as a good Aunt Sally at which to throw their critical weight. Even the fiction reader, in fact, has great control and may throw the book aside if it is found to disappoint.

There is a second respect in which we might find fault with the view of text as the site of an interaction between a writer and readers which the writer controls. It can be useful to see texts as the product of an interaction not between two participants but amongst four: the author, the writer, the audience and the reader. The first of these, the author, gives the text authority, authorises the text, takes responsibility for what the text attempts to do. S/he may be an individual or an organisation and is quite often the same person as the writer, though importantly s/he does not have to be. When a reader refers to a text, s/he will normally refer to its author. The writer on the other hand composes the text and is responsible for the language of the text; s/he is normally an individual, though occasionally writers work together in pairs or trios. In the case of a typical narrative, of course, the author and writer are normally the same, which is why the terms are usually confused.

The audience of a text is the intended readership, the imaginary person or persons whom the writer addresses and whose questions s/he tries to answer. Ultimately the audience is always a figment of the writer's imagination since no writer, however skilled, can ever get inside someone else's mind so completely as to know exactly what they want and need to learn. In composing his/her text, the writer makes assumptions about the state of knowledge of the audience and these are reflected in his/her grammar in quite subtle ways. For example, the complexity of nominal groups is a reflection, in part, of what the writer thinks the audience can be assumed to know. Consider Example 2.2 from a magazine on stamp collecting; the paragraph is the first in its section and begins an entirely new topic:

2.2 **Replacement MCA Crown**
The interest produced by recent research into the damage to the Crown Agents Script watermark, as illustrated by the varieties occurring on the Dominica 1951 King George VI definitive series, has led to much more attention being paid to watermarks on earlier issues.

The first nominal group assumes an immense amount of philatelic knowledge on the part of its audience. First, it assumes that the intended reader will know that watermarks can be categorised and that there are several kinds of Crown Agents watermark, one of which makes use of Script lettering rather than block lettering. It further assumes that the audience will know that damage can be done to the impression that makes the watermark in the paper, that some philatelists of a technical bent at the specialist end of the hobby like to investigate the effects (and causes) of such damage and that others are interested in their investigations. Morley (1998) has shown how this use of nominal groups to compress known or assumed-to-be-known information is used by newspapers to encode ideologically-loaded positions; here, of course, the only effect is to enshrine a view of the hobby.

To sum up, then, the audience is the ideal reader, the reader that the writer had in mind when s/he wrote and that the author wants to communicate with. The reader on the other hand is the person who actually encounters and processes the text. S/he may correspond quite closely to the image in the writer's mind or may be wildly divergent, since an author often has next to no control over who encounters a text. Some readers of the *Gibbons Stamp Monthly*, from which Example 2.2 was taken, buy the magazine just for the kind of technical material quoted above. The previous article in the same issue is, however, headed 'New Collector' and is part of a long-running series explaining technical matters to novice collectors; many of these will turn the page and encounter the 'Catalogue Column', and some at least of such readers will not have the knowledge that the Column assumes and may wonder what the innocent accumulation of stamps has to do with these arcane matters.

Purposes of the interactions amongst author, writer, audience and reader

The interactions amongst author, writer, audience and reader are complex. The author has a purpose in communicating to the audience and authorises the writer to produce a text that will achieve that purpose. The writer composes a text for an audience that may or may not match the description of the actual readers. The readers also have a purpose in reading the text which may not be the one that the writer had in mind and may not be congruent with the author's original purpose. An example may help here. Consider Example 2.3, a maximally simple advertisement for the RAC, an organisation one can join in the UK that will come to one's assistance in the event of car breakdown:

2.3

The author of this text is the RAC. The author's purpose is to increase membership of the RAC. The writer is likely to have been some advertising copywriter, whose anonymity is absolute, but s/he will have been instructed by a representative of the author to produce the text. The writer will have taken the decision to use the (unusually few) words that are in the text, a decision that the RAC will then have endorsed and given authority to. Although the writer was responsible for the wording, the author, the RAC, is responsible for the effect of the advertisement. If complaints are made against an advertisement in the UK, it is usually the advertiser, not the advertising agency, that takes the flak. The audience in the case of this particular advertisement is the car owner, and presumably in particular car owners who do not already belong to the RAC (though RAC members might take comfort from being reminded of their security on the road). Assumptions are being made about that audience; it is assumed, for example, that they are sometimes anxious while driving and that they know already what kind of organisation the RAC is. These assumptions may not always be correct. The reader is whoever chances upon the text and s/he may already be relaxed or alternatively be ignorant of the RAC's function. More fundamentally, s/he may not be a driver or possess a car. I, for instance, neither drive nor own a car. So I am the 'wrong' reader; I am a reader, for all that.

A similar analysis could be provided for every kind of text. In the UK, the author of a statute is Parliament and Queen. Every British statute begins with a statement of the authority of Parliament and monarch and the authorising of the law that follows. The writer, on the other hand, is anonymous, a legal drafts-person. Judges are capable of complaining of statutes that they are bad law (the author to blame) or badly drafted law (the writer to blame). The audience is not, as one might expect, the general public, but other lawyers, since both the language of the statute and the specialist knowledge of other legislation that it assumes in its cross-referencing preclude any possibility that anyone without specialist knowledge is being addressed, and the readers are characteristically these lawyers. There is therefore in this case a close match between audience and readership. The purpose of the author is (indirectly) to regulate the behaviour of the nation's citizens. The reader's purpose on the other hand, assuming that the reader is a lawyer, is likely to be to discover whether a client is covered by the provisions of the statute or not; such a reader's interpretation may not always be a co-operative one.

Natural science articles are different from advertisements and statutes in having personal authors. Normally in fact they list a number of authors, all of whom will have participated in the research reported, but only one of whom will normally have played a significant part in the drafting of the article. Thus the authors in the case of such articles are all those listed under the title and the writer is (typically) the first-named of these, though the first-named may be the lead investigator rather than the writer. The audience is made up of fellow scientists with a specialist knowledge in the field, as again a glance at the nominal groups reveals. As with the statute, there is little chance that the actual readers will differ much from the ideal reader that the writer had in mind. The author's purpose is to lay claim to an advance in the field; the reader's purpose is likely to be to keep abreast of developments in the field and to assess critically the work reported.

News stories these days often have by-lines but if you have read a newspaper in the past day I challenge you to remember having noted any of them. (Comment articles in newspapers are a different matter; figures such as Bernard Levin, Polly Toynbee and David Aaronovich have a celebrity within the UK independent of the paper in which they write; the same is true for many other countries.) The author of any news story is the newspaper; one would always say 'Did you see that story in the Times?', not 'Did you see that story by John Turner?' John Turner (or whoever) is the writer. The audience for a political news story is expected to have been following the story, to recognise the names of the main participants and to know roughly where they stand on certain issues; in other words, they are expected to be informed nationals. Trying to read lead stories in foreign newspapers is a fruitless business if they relate the political events of the day; it is not even always straightforward if one returns to one's own country after a short absence. So readers and audience in this case do not necessarily match. The author's purpose is to inform and (indirectly) persuade. The reader's purpose only partly matches the author's; he or she will want to be informed but probably not to be persuaded.

To take a final example of the delicate interaction amongst author, writer, reader and audience, the minutes of a meeting have as their author the committee whose deliberations they record; one would always refer to 'the minutes of Faculty Committee' not to 'the minutes of Gill Lester' (or whoever). The writer is the minutes secretary. The audience is in the first place the committee itself, so in this unusual case author and audience are the same; indeed the first or second act of most committee meetings is the approval – the authorisation – of the previous meeting's minutes. The audience may also be other committees and the actual readership will almost always match the ideal readership exactly. The author's purpose is to record decisions; the reader's purpose will vary but will often be to refer to decisions made.

Sometimes there is more than one audience intended for a text. It is worth looking more closely at the till receipt reproduced as Example 2.1. Although it is a single text, it has been constructed to meet a variety of reading purposes fulfilled at a variety of times and for a variety of audiences. In the first place, of course, the reader is expected to be the purchaser and the moment of reading is the moment of purchase or shortly after. The purpose is to allow the reader to check that the prices – and the total – are as expected. This accounts for the prominent position and tabular presentation of the purchases and their prices (note how natural tabular presentation seems; any other means of presentation would seem perverse). The purchaser-reader certainly does not need to be told that B & M, Southport, is the store where the purchase was made since s/he is likely to be in the store at the time of reading! Nor is it likely that the reader will want to check his/her watch against the time printed on the receipt or confirm the date. These elements, as well as the VAT number, brief advertising slogan and mysterious numbers, are simply ignored and indeed not noticed.

As it happened this purchaser/reader was happy with the products bought. But imagine that there had turned out to be a problem with the cabin bag. Then the text would be pulled out of whatever pocket it had been stored away in and re-read. Now of course quite different parts of the text are attended to. The table is scanned for the particular product, to check that the receipt is the correct one, but the other products and their prices will not be looked at; the hitherto ignored heading – B&M Southport – now proves important as a way of identifying the relevant text amongst all the others in one's pockets. The audience for this bit of the text is a purchaser needing to check a purchase, not the satisfied purchaser on the point of leaving the store. The price is unlikely now to be in focus.

Armed with the receipt, the purchaser then returns to the store and takes the unhappy bag to the store complaints officer. This officer then in turn becomes the reader of the receipt. First, s/he will look at the heading to check that the responsibility for replacing the bag lies with the Southport store; then s/he will check the date to make sure that the offending object is still within guarantee.

I was happy, as I say, with the bag and only pulled out the receipt in order to throw it away (and then to use it as an example for this chapter). At that point, and not before, I noticed the advertisement at the bottom; the purchaser at the till does not need to be told and the disgruntled purchaser with a defective bag will not be interested, but the former purchaser may be pleased to be reminded of the bargains earlier achieved (and of course may be encouraged to return to the shop in the hope of further such bargains).

There are parts of the till receipt that this reader could never attend to: an unidentified number and a VAT number. The former is a till number and has as its reader the company auditor; the latter is of importance to purchasers from overseas who may show the till receipt to a customs official in order to recover tax paid on the items. Thus the single text is so composed that it has variously purchaser, store manager, auditor and customs official as audience.

One of the odd things about a till receipt is that it is automatically composed. It certainly has an author – in the example above, authorship was stated to be B & M's – but it has only indirectly got a writer in that it is produced as a result of actions performed by a check-out operator. Most texts are more consciously constructed and it is the writer's role in doing so that we now turn to.

The writer's desire to meet the audience's needs

Writers have a delicate task to perform. On the one hand they must meet the requirements of the author or, if author and writer are one and the same, they must fulfil their own objectives. On the other hand they must remember that readers have power too and can drop the text at any time if it does not meet their needs. Accordingly if the writer is to fulfil his/her own needs, s/he must meet the audience's needs too. The audience's needs can be formulated as questions that they want answering. This can be seen clearly in some children's writing. Consider Example 2.4, a complete short text written by a ten-year old boy reporting on a simple investigation of the heat-retaining properties of a particular kind of container; spelling, punctuation and grammar are as in the original:

2.4   We first heated up the water and measured the tempeeture. We poured in the tomatoe soup and put the soup and put a lid on one of them and waited for a boute seven minnits and then took the tempreture and the one with the highest reecordung was the lid one. So the shop was right.

Despite grammatical infelicities and spelling mistakes, this text achieves the objective of reporting with some clarity the procedures adopted in the course of the experiment being reported. The final conclusion, however, throws most readers completely. For an explanation, one needs to look at the instructions that the teacher gave the pupils prior to carrying out the experiment with containers (not, you will note, the instructions for writing the report). These instructions began as follows:

2.4a   This advert was seen in a shop.

> 'TAKE HOME OUR SOUP – IT STAYS HOT FOR HOURS IN OUR SOUPER CONTAINERS'

> You are going to check whether the advert is really true.

We can now see that the boy was answering the teacher's question 'Is the advert really true?' to which the boy replies, with impeccable scientific logic, if imperfect understanding of the rules of text construction, 'The shop was right.'

A still more compelling piece of evidence for the fundamental interactivity of children's factual writing is Example 2.5, a complete text from a girl of approximately the same age, reporting on an experiment with vacuum creation; as before, the grammar, punctuation and spelling have been left as in the original:

2.5   When you hold your hand over the flask bubbles come out of the bottom of the tube the air comes out and we're making vacume. When the bunsen burner flame is held over the flask the flame makes lots of bubbles. The air has come out and vacume is left. The water rises up to the tube and down. The water travels up and comes out of the tube at the top. All the water from the beaker travels up the tube and ends up filling full the flask at the top.

I imagine that if I asked you to re-do the experiment following the girl's instructions you would feel at a loss as to where to start. This is clearly an incoherent text and, like the teacher who first received this piece of work, we are inclined not to value it much. However, a hidden coherence in the text comes to light when we again look at the teacher's instructions for carrying out the experiment. This time the instructions took the form of three numbered steps, thus:

2.5a   1. Put your hands around the flask. What happens?
2. Now warm the flask more with the flame of a bunsen burner.
3. Now let the flask cool while the glass tube is still below the surface of the water – what happens now?

We are now in a position to see what governed the girl's choice of sentences. She was simply answering the teacher's questions in the order they were asked. This can be seen clearly if the instructions and the girl's report are interleaved as follows:

2.5b   Teacher: Put your hands around the flask. What happens?
       Pupil: When you hold your hand over the flask bubbles come out of the bottom of the tube the air comes out and we're making vacume.
       Teacher: Now warm the flask more with the flame of a bunsen burner.
       Pupil: When the bunsen burner flame is held over the flask the flame makes lots of bubbles.
       Teacher: Now let the flask cool while the glass tube is still below the surface of the water – what happens now?
       Pupil: The air has come out and vacume is left. The water rises up to the tube and down. The water travels up and comes out of the tube at the top. All the water from the beaker travels up the tube and ends up filling full the flask at the top.

Suddenly the text seems explicable. The girl is simply answering the questions of the only reader she ever thought she would have.

These texts teach us two things. First, texts are indeed the product of an interaction between their author and their audience, and, second, adults manage the interaction differently. Let us look at the way this interaction is managed from the point of view, first, of the reader. At any point in a text a reader has expectations about what might be going to happen next in the text. Sometimes these expectations are precise and strong; sometimes they are vague and weak. But a text which left us with no idea of how it might develop would be a text with which we were not properly engaging or from which we were gaining little. Even experimental fiction hopes that we will have expectations – how else could it thwart them? Part of the difficulty you may have had in reading the 'vacuum' text above is that your expectations after a first sentence like

2.5c   When you hold your hand over the flask bubbles come out of the bottom of the tube the air comes out and we're making vacume.

might include details of what the author did next or some characterisation of a vacuum or possibly what the purpose/usefulness of making a vacuum might be. Self-evidently none of these expectations are remotely met by the actual next sentence and the reader is left trying to work out what unanticipated question was actually being answered by the writer.

As evidence of the operation of expectations in the average reader, consider Example 2.6, a sentence from M.A.K. Halliday's *Introduction to Functional Grammar*. It comes from the introduction to the Introduction (!) and is the first sentence in a section headed 'Theories of language'. In the terms I have just been using, you might pause for a moment to work out what expectations you have of the way this section might develop; I have numbered this and subsequent sentences for ease of later reference:

2.6   (1) The basic opposition, in grammars of the second half of the twentieth century, is not that between 'structuralist' and 'generative' as set out in the public debates of the 1960s.

Your expectations may well include the following:

(i)   a reason why this is not the basic opposition
(ii)   a statement of what the basic opposition *is*
(iii)   a characterisation of the opposition between 'structuralist' and 'generative' grammars, e.g.'This is a minor opposition of little importance, etc.'
(iv)   another opposition that does not count as the basic opposition, e.g. 'Nor is it that between . . . .'

Of these the first two are very much more likely to have been expected than the third or fourth.
    The actual next sentence was the following:

2.6a   (2) There are many variables in the way grammars are written, and any clustering of these is bound to distort the picture; but the more fundamental opposition is between those that are primarily syntagmatic in orientation (by and large the formal grammars, with their roots in logic and philosophy) and those that are primarily paradigmatic (by and large the functional ones, with their roots in rhetoric and ethnography).

As you will see, it is the second of the expectations listed above that is actually met. Of course the first and third expectations could still be met, though they will probably be felt to be weaker now than before; the fourth expectation will disappear, since it would not be natural to return to something that was not the basic opposition after outlining something that was.
    The second sentence, however, gives rise to expectations of its own, which are likely to include one or more of the following:

(v)   an explanation of why this is more the fundamental opposition
(vi)   more details on the nature of the opposition
(vii) some characterisation of syntagmatic grammars followed by a similar characterisation of paradigmatic grammars

Obviously the sixth and seventh expectations are entirely compatible and could be seen as different ways of doing the same thing.
    The sentence that Halliday actually wrote next was the following:

2.6b   (3) The former interpret a language as a list of structures, among which, as a distinct second step, regular relationships may be established (hence the introduction of transformations); they tend to emphasize universal features of language, to take grammar (which they call 'syntax') as the foundation of language (hence the grammar is arbitrary), and so to be organized around the sentence.

You will see that expectation (vii) is the one that is most directly met.

I suspect it is obvious that at this juncture in the text what is now expected is:

(viii) an equivalent characterisation of paradigmatic grammars

not least because of the way Halliday refers to the syntagmatic grammars as *the former*, a characterisation which reminds us that two kinds are in play; I will return to the writer's use of this phrase shortly. Predictably, then, the next sentence reads:

2.6c   (4) The latter interpret a language as a network of relations, with structures coming in as the realization of these relationships; they tend to emphasize variables among different languages, to take semantics as the foundation (hence the grammar is natural), and so to be organized around the text, or discourse.

One might even have predicted the parallelism between the two sentences, so strongly does this sentence fulfil (most people's) expectations.

The picture changes, however, with the next sentence. Were I at this point to invite you to consider what your expectations would now be of the text, I suspect you would be hard pressed to say. Predictions might include:

(ix)   further information on the ways in which the two types of grammar are alike
(x)   further ways in which they are different
(xi)   more detail on the paradigmatic grammars (the category into which Halliday's own grammatical proposals would fit)
(xii) something on the text/discourse foundation of paradigmatic grammars.

But the truth is that at this point in the text there is no compelling reason for the text to go one way rather than another. Most readers have no precise expectations.

Halliday's actual next sentence, the last in the paragraph, is as follows:

2.6d   (5) There are many cross-currents, with insights borrowed from one to the other; but they are ideologically fairly different and it is often difficult to maintain a dialogue.

I think this is, as near as makes no difference, unpredictable. Certainly in the act of reading it would be near chance whether a reader expected such a sentence or not.

The paragraph we have just been looking at illustrates the way a reader's expectations work. Whenever we read a sentence it sets up expectations in our mind and those expectations shape our interpretation of what comes next. We do not of course formulate these expectations as questions; these are the product of slowing up the reading process until it becomes observable. But that we do have expectations is demonstrated every time we are surprised or disconcerted by the direction a text takes.

Expectations operate at more than one level. The higher levels of expectation will be considered in the next chapter. At the lower level, which is the one we have been considering, they function on a moment-by-moment basis, a series of tiny hypotheses that are immediately supported or refuted. We anticipate what the writer is going to do in what Kenneth Goodman (1967) has called 'a psycholinguistic guessing game'. This can be represented diagrammatically as in Figure 2.1. What this diagram seeks to represent is that on the basis of reading a sentence, a reader forms expectations about how the text may continue. S/he then matches those expectations against the next sentence. If this sentence appears to match one of his/her expectations more than any of the others, it will be interpreted in that light. So, for example, in the Halliday text used above, suppose that as a result of reading the first sentence you had formed one of the following expectations:

(a) The text will continue with a statement of what the basic opposition actually is in grammars of the second half of the twentieth century;
(b) The text will say why the opposition between 'structuralist' and 'generative' grammars is not the basic opposition;
(c) The text will characterise the opposition between 'structuralist' and 'generative' grammars, e.g. 'This is a minor opposition of little importance, etc.'

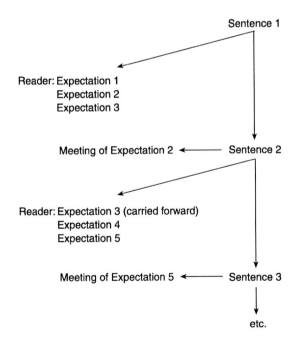

Figure 2.1 A representation of the interaction of a reader's expectations and a writer's sentences.

The next sentence:

2.6a   There are many variables in the way grammars are written, and any clustering of these is bound to distort the picture; but the more fundamental opposition is between those that are primarily syntagmatic in orientation (by and large the formal grammars, with their roots in logic and philosophy) and those that are primarily paradigmatic (by and large the functional ones, with their roots in rhetoric and ethnography).

would probably be felt not to match expectations (b) and (c) particularly well. If, though, (b) was the only expectation you formed, you could interpret this sentence as an answer to the question why the structuralist/generative opposition is not basic, i.e. it is not basic because something else is more fundamental. Again, if your only expectation had been (c), you might have tried to make sense of the sentence as an oblique answer to the question 'How would you characterise the opposition between 'structuralist' and 'generative' grammars?', i.e. it is less fundamental (which is, of course, a restatement of the previous sentence's message). In other words, you might have tried to interpret the sentence in the light of the expectation(s) you formed even though the sentence could not be said to match those expectations closely. If, on the other hand, your expectation had been (a), then the match would be exact. The question 'What then *is* the basic opposition?' is directly answered in the second half of the sentence: the basic opposition (the more fundamental opposition) is between syntagmatic and paradigmatic grammars.

The point is that our understanding of a text is partly governed by our ability to generate sensible hypotheses about what is going to happen in the text that we are reading and by the attempts we make to find those hypotheses fulfilled. Our understanding is fortunately also partly governed by our ability to interpret the juxtaposition of sentences in such a way that we can see how they are related *after* the event; otherwise a lazy reading would regularly result in non-comprehension. Whether or not we have accurately anticipated what question will be answered next, we attempt as good readers to assign a significance to the juxtaposition of sentences. Something similar happens within nominal groups. If we encounter the nominal groups *bird table, bird call* or *bird spider* we interpret them as we encounter them in accordance with our previous encounters with such expressions and in line with the demands of the context in which we have encountered them. Thus we interpret one as 'a small *table* built to allow a *bird* to feed from it', the second as 'the *call* made by a *bird*' and the last as 'a *spider* capable of catching and eating a *bird*'. It does not throw us as readers or listeners that the juxtaposition of *bird* as noun modifier with a variety of noun heads results in a multiplicity of meanings; we accept it as a simple necessity that a single grammar can be used to convey a wide range of semantic relationships. In the same way we are not thrown by the juxtaposition of sentences in a text. We take it for granted that the juxtaposition may have a range of meanings and normally have no difficulty in interpreting the juxtaposition, even if it happens that we have not accurately anticipated what will come next. In the case of *bird spider* it is at least possible that the juxtaposition of nouns will seem novel and in such a case we will look to the context to make the meaning clearer or will guess at an interpretation based on our knowledge of spiders and birds (which may of course be wrong). The same is true of juxtaposed sentences; we look to the context or our world knowledge to clarify the relation in places where the juxtaposition is not expected. The processes whereby this is achieved are by no means straightforward; the bibliographical end-notes mention some works that have sought to account for how this is done.

So far in this chapter we have only considered non-narrative texts. Narrative texts are much the same with regard to the matter of answering the reader's questions except that, in principle, they are easier to process. Underpinning much narrative is the iterative question 'What happened next?' or, only slightly more precise, 'What did s/he or they do next?' This partly explains the universal attraction of narratives for children; in their most basic forms they do not require the reader to remain at the same level of alertness throughout. Likewise many young children find narratives easier to write; their greater exposure to narratives is probably sufficient to explain this, but a secondary factor is likely to be the reduced advanced planning that the simplest kind of narrative requires.

As we shall see below and in later chapters, there are more complex questions that are being answered in both adult and children's narratives, but it is not difficult to find passages in most narratives where the reader can relax and watch the repeated 'What happened next?' question being answered, usually interspersed with questions relating to the description of the scene or the thoughts of the characters. Consider the following passage, for example, from a minor Dickens story:

2.7   (1) Will, whose self-possession was now quite restored, needed no second bidding, but with his drawn sword in his hand, and his cloak so muffled over his left arm as to serve for a kind of shield without offering any impediment to its free action, suffered them to lead the way. (2) Through mud and mire, and wind and rain, they walked in silence a full mile. (3) At length they turned into a dark lane, where, suddenly starting out from beneath some trees where he had taken shelter, a man appeared, having in his own charge three saddled horses. (4) One of these (his own apparently), in obedience to a whisper from the women, he consigned to Will, who, seeing that they mounted, mounted also. (5) Then, without a word spoken, they rode on together, leaving the attendant behind.

Although there are more interesting ways of projecting this passage into dialogue, it is possible to see each of the sentences as answering the questions 'What happened next?' and 'What did he/they do next?', as Example 2.8 shows:

2.8   (1) Will, whose self-possession was now quite restored, needed no second bidding, but with his drawn sword in his hand, and his cloak so muffled over his left arm as to serve for a kind of shield without offering any impediment to its free action, suffered them to lead the way.

What did they do next?

(2) Through mud and mire, and wind and rain, they walked in silence a full mile.

What did they do next?

(3) At length they turned into a dark lane,

What happened next?

(3a) [where], suddenly starting out from beneath some trees where he had taken shelter, a man appeared, having in his own charge three saddled horses.

What did he do (next)?

(4) One of these (his own apparently), in obedience to a whisper from the women, he consigned to Will,

What did he do next?

[who], seeing that they mounted, <he> mounted also.

What happened next?

(5) Then, without a word spoken, they rode on together, leaving the attendant behind.

It will be noticed that in several cases the question interrupts what Dickens has presented as a single sentence. Halliday (1985) notes that non-specific clauses such as the ones beginning *where* and *who* above are hard to distinguish from co-ordinated independent clauses. In other words, sentence 3 from Example 2.7 can be rewritten as:

2.9   At length they turned into a dark lane; *there*, suddenly starting out from beneath some trees where he had taken shelter, a man appeared, having in his own charge three saddled horses.

Likewise sentence 4 can be rewritten as

2.10   One of these (his own apparently), in obedience to a whisper from the women, he consigned to Will; Will, seeing that they mounted, mounted also.

The same can be said of non-narratives. As a general truth, text is not built up with sentences as building blocks; sometimes the building blocks of text are smaller (as here), sometimes much larger, as we shall see in subsequent chapters.

Signals from writer to reader: moment-by-moment guidance

It will be remembered that at one point in Example 2.6 there was a sentence the predictability of which was particularly strong. I noted at that point the phrase *the former* and commented that it provided compelling grounds for supposing that the following sentence would begin *the latter* and deal with the second member of the pair. The phrase is a signal from the writer to the reader. In effect the writer is saying: 'Don't bother guessing, I'm *telling* you what's coming next.' If the writer is accurately anticipating the reader's questions, this will not be necessary all the time, but it is certainly helpful on occasion to be nudged in the right direction by the writer. Again, this is paralleled by what happens when we encounter nominal groups. The nominal group *bird call* could be read as either 'call of a bird' or as 'imitative call made to birds in order to catch them'. If a writer chooses the wording 'call of a bird', s/he is using the preposition *of* as a signal, in order to disambiguate the relationship between the words.

Signals at the level of the text are of a different kind. They vary in nature and will be discussed in more detail in later chapters. For the moment, I note only that they may take the form of specialised nouns (e.g. *consequence*), verbs (e.g. *differs*), adjectives (*contrasting*) and adverbs and prepositional phrases (e.g. *therefore, as a result*), the last being enshrined in grammars as 'conjuncts' or 'sentence conjunctions'. Some texts use signalling a great deal. In such circumstances the interaction between writer and reader can be modelled as Figure 2.2.

Just as a reader may either anticipate what question may be answered or work out what question was in fact answered, so a writer may signal in advance or

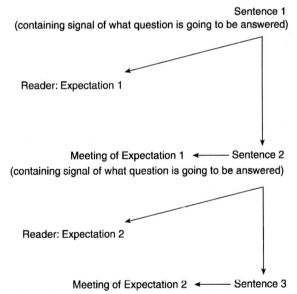

Figure 2.2 The interaction of reader's expectations and writer's sentences where the writer has used some form of prospective signalling.

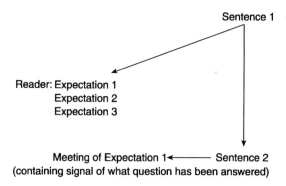

Figure 2.3 The interaction of reader's expectations and writer's sentences where the writer has used some form of retrospective signalling.

provide a retrospective clue. In such circumstances the model of interaction might be represented as in Figure 2.3.

As an example of the way signalling works in practice, consider the following passage from *Good God* by Jonathan Clatworthy:

2.11   (1) Our values, like the values of the islanders, are full of contradictions. (2) But we do not laugh at them, because they are our own. (3) Instead we live with the contradictions and accept them as normal. (4) With our public values we applaud the new motorway; (4a) it will save travelling time and help the economy. (5) With our private values we lament the new road widening; (5a) it will mean more pollution and noise and the neighbours' children will not be able to cross it on their own. (6) With our public values we are pleased that the price of components is going down because of new technology; (6a) with our private values we feel sorry for our friend whose business is closing down because it cannot compete. (7) With our public values we are pleased to hear that people are spending more money, because it helps get the country out of recession; (7a) with our private values we do not intend to waste our own money on things we do not need.

(8) We are proud of our modern civilization because, it has been drummed into us, we have advanced much further than any previous age. (9) On the other hand the crime rate, the suicide rate, drug addiction and alcoholism, homelessness and poverty, keep telling us that we have got our priorities very wrong. (10) To add to all of these, scientists now warn us that the world is finite and we cannot carry on demanding more and more from it.

This passage is a key one for the book – if the reader does not accept the argument at this point, the rest of the book's argument will also be lost. The writer therefore needs to take particular care that the reader does not (in his terms) misread the passage. He therefore uses a variety of signalling devices that render the connections between his sentences effectively unambiguous.

His first signal is one of the subtler ones, namely the word 'contradictions' in the first sentence. This is what Winter (1986) terms an 'unspecific' noun, noting that such nouns are informationally insufficient and lead the reader to expect informational specifics to be provided subsequently. Here then the author signals, by providing an unspecific noun without its specifics, that he will follow with specifics. However, he does more than that. He also signals that the specifics will be internally in a contrast relationship – because it is part of the meaning of the word 'contradiction' that an extreme contrast exists between two propositions. Further, he signals there will be more than one set of contrasting specifics, because he has used the plural form of 'contradiction'. He is saying in effect that the question he commits himself to answering is 'Give us several examples of contradictions/sharp contrasts relating to our values.'

But the writer does not want to leap straight into the specifics. He has more to say about the contradictions first. This means that readers are likely to be wrong-footed unless he handles the situation adeptly. Consequently he immediately signals that sentence 2 does not yet provide the looked-for specifics with the conjunction 'but', which is incompatible with the fulfilment of the expectation. Sentence 2 warns of a further delay in our getting the specifics because it contains a denial ('we do not laugh at them') which provokes an expectation that the next question to be answered will be 'If that is not the case, what *is* the case?' Sentence 3 answers just such a question, and the writer starts sentence 3 with the sentence conjunction (or conjunct) 'instead', which serves to signal that the denied statement is going to be replaced with one that the author can confidently affirm.

With the denial and its correction out of the way, it is time for the specifics of 'contradictions' and after the delay their arrival has to be signalled to the reader. The way the writer does this is by using the fronted prepositional phrase 'With our public values' at the beginning of sentence 4, which is grammatically a less common choice of sentence beginning (technically, a marked Theme; see Halliday 1994) and draws attention to itself. Within the phrase is a repetition of the word 'values' from sentence 1 and – importantly – the use of 'public'. 'Public' is one of a relatively small set of psychologically prominent antonyms (opposites) in the language (Jones 1998, 1999) and immediately opens the possibility of the opposite of 'public values', namely 'private values'. When the latter phrase occurs in a similarly fronted position in sentence 5 the author is, therefore, signalling a strong contrast and the completion of the first set of specifics of 'contradictions.'

The first sentence forewarned us that there were to be more than one set of specifics. The use again of the fronted 'With our public values' and 'with our private values' in sentences 6 and 6a and 7 and 7a are the writer's signals that the promise of plurality of specifics is being fulfilled. The relation of sentence 8 could be interpreted in several ways – as further specific or as generalisation from the previous specifics. To avoid the latter interpretation, and to retain the contradictoriness apparent in earlier specifics, the writer signals a further contrast with the fronted conjunct 'on the other hand'. The contrast with sentence 8, however, is not finished yet and to make sure the reader recognises this the writer inserts the clause 'to add to all of these' at the beginning of sentence 10; this clause is a paraphrase of 'moreover' or 'furthermore'.

The passage above is not unusual in the degree to which it signals, though certain types of writing (e.g. narrative, news stories) would be likely to signal less. Most writers mix sentences containing signals and sentences without signals, much as happened in Example 2.6. Too few signals can be exacting on the reader; too many can be boring.

Clause relations as a reflection of a text's interactivity

The questions we have been looking at throughout this chapter are just a way of talking about the inferences that readers need to make to connect sentences in text, and the signals that writers use are a way of reducing the amount of inference necessary in any particular case. We interpret the second half of Example 2.11a below as providing either a reason or particulars of the lament in the first half.

2.11a   (5) With our private values we lament the new road widening; (5a) it will mean more pollution and noise and the neighbours' children will not be able to cross it on their own.

In arriving at either of these interpretations, we are attending to the linguistic evidence (e.g. the pronoun 'it' connecting with 'the new road' and the future modal 'will' connecting with the 'new' of 'new road') and we are recognising characteristic combinations of propositions; after an expression of opinion ('lament') we anticipate, for example, some justification for the view held. Signals sometimes eliminate the need for such inferences, but few texts do not require some inferencing on the part of the reader.

Winter (1974) identifies two kinds of relation between clauses or sentences: Sequence relations and Matching relations. Sequence relations are relations in which one clause/sentence answers a question such as 'What happened next?', 'What happened as a result?' and 'What do you infer from this?', all of which involve putting propositions in some order of priority in time, space or logic. The ability to connect and logically sequence events is apparently acquired in a baby before the onset of language; every parent learns early to distinguish the distress signal from the cry designed to capitalise on the parent's loving nature. The latter cry seems to grow out of a connection the baby has made between its noise and comfort. We should not therefore be surprised that such logical sequencing appears to be one of the motors of discourse organisation all around the world (Ballard *et al.* 1971a,b).

Typical sequence relations are time sequence, cause-consequence, means-purpose, and premise-deduction. They are signalled by a variety of means; a fair number of subordinators and sentence conjunctions are dedicated to telling the reader that there is a sequence relation and what its nature is, e.g. because, if, after, before, when, as, (amongst the subordinators) and then, therefore, thus, thereby, afterwards, later, previously, consequently, as a result, as a consequence, in consequence, thereafter, finally (amongst the sentence conjunctions).

Matching relations, by contrast, do not involve putting things in any order; instead statements are brought together with a view to seeing what light they shed on each other. They occur when a clause, sentence or group of sentences answer questions such as 'How does x compare with y?', 'How does x differ from y?', 'What is an example of that?'. This paragraph for example answers the question 'How do Matching relations (x) differ from Sequence relations (y)?' As with the Sequence relations, there are reasons to suppose that a baby learns to match for compatibility and contrast before it learns to speak. Watch how a baby's face crumples in dismay when the appearance and smell of the loving adult that picks it up fails to match that of the parent's. With such a basic grounding in matching, it is unsurprising that Matching also appears to be a universal feature of discourse organisation (Ballard *et al*. 1971a, b).

Matching relations include relations such as contrast, similarity, exemplification, preview-detail, and exception. They also may be signalled by subordinators (e.g. while, whereas, although) and sentence conjunctions (e.g. however, moreover, nevertheless, furthermore, too, also). However, a major signal is repetition and parallelism, as illustrated in the passage above, which is largely organised around answers to the questions 'How do public values (x) differ from private values (y)?' and 'How does one contradiction in our values compare with another?' Table 2.1 demonstrates clearly how repetition and parallelism may signal Matching relations. The same is true of Example 2.6 that I used to illustrate interactivity; parallelism is used there to reinforce the relationship between sentences 3 and 4, a relationship already strongly signalled in the phrases 'the former' and 'the latter'.

Implications for the language learner

The key implication for the language learner of what we have been considering in this chapter concerns the claim that as readers interact with a text they formulate hypotheses about how the text will develop, and that these hypotheses help them understand and interpret the text as they continue reading. Clearly, the language learner needs to transfer the hypothesising skill s/he has in the first language to the second language.

Experience, however, suggests that many learners do not in fact make the transfer (and others may not have fully developed the skill in the first language for it to be available for transference). The decoding task is so exacting for some language learners – the unravelling of the grammar, the lexical recognition and/ or guesswork – that little energy is left for the crucial task of hypothesis-creation in the course of reading. But, according to the argument offered here, if the learner does not have expectations about the way a text might go, how can s/he interpret what s/he goes on to read? Learners need therefore to be encouraged to develop the appropriate hypothesis-forming skills and not to treat reading as an exercise in language practice only.

Table 2.1 Repetition and parallelism in passages from *Good God*

(4) With our public values	we applaud the new motorway	– [because] [implicit]	(4a) it will save travelling time and help the economy.
(5) With our private values	we lament the new road widening;	– [because] [implicit]	(5a) it will mean more pollution and noise and the neighbours' children will not be able to cross it on their own.
(6) With our public values	we are pleased that the price of components is going down	because	of new technology
(6a) with our private values	we feel sorry for our friend whose business is closing down	because	it cannot compete
(7) With our public values	we are pleased to hear that people are spending more money,	because	it helps get the country out of recession;
(7a) with our private values	we do not intend to waste our own money on things we do not need.		

The second implication for the learner concerns the signalling systems that a writer may make use of. Accurate recognition of the signals and their significance for the text's development can greatly ease a reader's processing burden in that it lessens the need for large-scale hypothesis-forming at the same time as all that detailed micro-processing is going on. It can also aid guesswork about the meanings of unfamiliar words if the reader knows what question a sentence is meant to be answering. The same goes for parallelisms. Non-native readers that identify parallelisms are likely to guess more accurately the meanings of unfamiliar words in those sentences; they are also likely to see the larger meaning relations more clearly. On the other hand non-native writers who make use of such parallelisms may maximise their sentence-constructing abilities as well as giving themselves a global structure for their text, as long – an important qualification, this – as the parallelism reflects what they actually want to say.

Bibliographical end-notes

The sources of the texts used are as follows. Example 2.1 is a receipt from the B & M store, Southport Branch, produced on 12 February 1999. I am grateful to the accounts manager at the Southport Branch, for information about the till number and VAT number on the receipt. Example 2.2 is taken from 'Catalogue Column' by David Aggersberg, *Gibbons Stamp Monthly*, March 1998, p. 112. The RAC advertisement given as Example 2.3 was current in national newspapers in the late 1990s. Examples 2.4 and 2.5 are drawn from data collected by the Open University in 1979 and made available to consultants. Example 2.6 and the sentences that follow begin the section headed 'Theories of language' on page xxviii of M.A.K. Halliday's *Introduction to Functional Grammar*, 1985, London: Edward Arnold. Example 2.7 is taken from 'Mr Pickwick's Tale' in *Master Humphrey's Clock* by Charles Dickens. Example 2.11 is taken from *Good God: Green Theology and the Value of Creation* by Jonathan Clatworthy, Charlbury: Jon Carpenter Publishing.

The interactivity of text has become a common-place, though it was not always thus. Early proponents of this position within reading theory included Goodman (1967, 1973) Smith (1978) and, in the context of applied linguistics, Widdowson (1979). Nystrand (1986, 1989) gives a central place to interaction within his description. Myers (1999) discusses some of the implications and problems of handling interaction in text and Al-Sharief (1998) provides a useful synthesis of the ways in which different types of interaction are interlinked. Goffman (1981) does not use the terms author, writer, audience and reader but must take credit for the insight; my reasons for not following his terminology are given in Hoey (1996a). Literary theory has laid stress on the autonomy of the reader's interpretation, sometimes going so far as to imply the redundancy of what has actually been written; key figures are Iser (1978), Eco (1979), Suleiman and Crosman (1980) and Freund (1987). Useful accounts of the viewpoint can be found discussed in Rimmon-Kenan (1983), Emmott (1997) and Scott (1998). Morley (1998) discusses the effect of a writer's assumptions on his or her nominal groups, looking at the ideological implications of such assumptions in newspaper writing. Schema theory also places great stress on what the reader brings to the text; for references to their work see the bibliographical end-note to chapter 7.

The ways in which a lawyer's purpose in reading a statute may differ radically from the author's purpose are discussed in Hoey (1985a) and the interactivity of children's writing is discussed in Hoey (1986a) and Bourne (1998). Thompson and Thetela (1995) show how advertisers exploit the essential interactivity of text by constructing positions for readers. Myers (1999) discusses some of the implications and problems of handling interaction in text.

The way in which readers (or listeners, come to that) attempt to make sense of what they have read or heard in the light of what they already know and expect is discussed in Grice (1967, 1975, 1978); another perspective on the same topic can be found in Sperber and Wilson (1995). A useful discussion and defence of Grice's approach can be found in Levinson (1983). Grice argues that there are a set of assumptions that underlie and control conversation; these assumptions he formulates as maxims, which include 'Do not say what you believe to be false' (part of the maxim of Quality), 'Make your contributions as informative as is required for the current purposes of the exchange' and 'Do not make your contribution more informative than is required' (together forming the maxim of Quantity), 'Make your contribution relevant' (the maxim of Relevance) and 'Avoid ambiguity' (part of the maxim of Manner). Pratt (1977) shows that these observations about conversation can be successfully applied to narrative, and indeed it is probably apparent that at one time or another all the maxims listed are broken by mystery writers. The maxims can be seen as being part of a more general rationality principle (cf. Brown and Levinson 1987; Kasher 1991), which, however, has been criticised by Kopytko (1995, 1998) as not contextualised.

The model developed in this and the next chapter draws heavily on the work of Eugene Winter. From him comes the idea that the sentences in a text can be seen as answering questions that the reader wants answered, and from him comes the notion of clause relations, with the major division being that between Matching and (as he would term it) Logical Sequence. His work is now largely inaccessible but reference may be made to Winter (1974) and particularly (1977) and (1979), where the notion of lexical signals and repetition patterning are spelt out in some detail. His book (Winter 1982) concentrates on the grammatical implications of his work, but Winter (1994) is a useful and accessible introduction to his clause relational work, as are Hoey (1983) and Crombie (1985). Michael Jordan has developed a distinctive version of clause relations; see for example Jordan (1985, 1988, 1990, 1992). Others who have worked with a similar notion of text structure and have attempted to provide a typology are John Beekman and his associates (Beekman 1970, with Callow 1974, with Callow and Kopesec 1981), Robert Longacre (1979, 1983, 1989, 1992), with Ballard and Conrad (1971a, 1971b), Bonnie Meyer (1975, 1992, with Rice, 1982, 1984) and Graustein and Thiele (1979, 1980, 1981, 1987). A more recent – and influential – synthesis of some of these positions, under the label of Rhetorical Structure Theory (RST), can be found in Mann and Thompson (1986, 1988) and Mann, Matthiessen and Thompson (1992). Maier and Hovy (1993) provide a useful résumé and classification of the relations used in RST. A useful and thorough introduction to relational description, though oddly without reference to Winter's work, can be found in Georgakopoulou and Goutsos (1997).

The concept of lexical signalling originates with Winter (1977) and is discussed in Hoey (1979, 1994a) and in Jordan (1984), as well as in Winter (1992). Carter (1998) provides a useful overview of the notion and contextualises it within a larger account of lexis. McCarthy (1991) provides a helpful introduction both to the notion of signalling and to the larger discourse description, oriented helpfully to language teachers. The syntactic and collocational limitations upon the functions of clause relational signals are discussed in Hoey (1993, 1996b). Rather different approaches to the description of signalling in text, though growing out of similar concerns with the interactivity of text, are those of Francis (1986, 1989, 1994) and Tadros (1985, 1994).

3 Interaction in text – the larger perspective

Introduction

In the previous chapter we saw that text could be conceived of as a dialogue between author and audience, writer and reader. The metaphor of dialogue and the conceptualisation of the reader's expectations as questions only takes us so far, however. The problem with the metaphor is that real-time interaction is a moment-by-moment affair in which speakers respond to what their interlocutors have just said. While much of the interaction cited in the text is also of this moment-by-moment kind, not all of it is. At the same time that we formulate expectations about the immediately unfolding text, so also we formulate larger-scale hypotheses about the text as a whole, and the text will be written with these larger hypotheses in mind as well as the local ones that could be modelled in terms of a question-answer dialogue. The questions a reader expects the text to answer need not be met immediately.

Questions that receive a deferred answer

The way questions may receive delayed answers can be illustrated from Example 3.1, an extract from an *Independent on Sunday* article about dormice; the sentence numbering is for ease of reference and takes into account where the quoted sentences appear in the full text.

3.1   (7) Only two scientific studies appear to have been published about British dormice this century.

(8) Unfortunate though it is, the dormouse is one of nature's ready-made victims. (9) It has exacting ecological requirements which make it vulnerable, particularly to habitat change, as well as to climatic variation. (10) It lives at a low population density and has a very low rate of population increase. (11) And because it hibernates for half the year (from October to at least April, depending upon the weather) and is mainly nocturnal, it is not an easy creature to study.

A reasonable question for the reader to ask on reading sentence 7 would be 'Why have only two studies been published this century?' This question is not answered by sentence 8 – indeed the two sentences are barely connected – nor by sentences 9 and 10, which spell out in what respects the dormouse is a ready-made victim. It *is* however answered in sentence 11:

3.1a　Reader:　Why do only two scientific studies appear to have been published about British dormice this century?

　　　Writer:　... because it hibernates for half the year (from October to at least April, depending upon the weather) and is mainly nocturnal, it is not an easy creature to study.

The possibility of carrying an expectation forward was in fact included in Figure 2.1 in the previous chapter.

　　There is nothing unusual about the answer of a question being deferred. Indeed it is a common phenomenon, particularly in non-narrative text. Let us look at the full text from which Example 3.1 was drawn:

3.2　SCIENCE
　　QUIETLY VANISHING
　　(1) Two new studies of the elusive dormouse have revealed that it has disappeared from several counties in England. (2) **Malcolm Smith** reports on why its geographical range is shrinking

(3) LEWIS CARROLL could not have been more accurate. (4) In *Alice's Adventures in Wonderland* he wrote: (4.1) 'There was a table set out under a tree in front of the house, and the March Hare and the Hatter were having tea at it. (4.2) A dormouse was sitting between them, fast asleep, and the other two were using it as a cushion, resting their elbows on it, and talking over its head. (4.3) "Very uncomfortable for the dormouse," thought Alice, "only as it's asleep, I suppose it doesn't mind." '

　　(5) This picture of a languorous dormouse, snoozing its time away and looked down on by everyone around it, sums up the life of one of our most engaging little mammals. (6) Attractive, with its golden brown fur and long, bushy tail and well known from stories such as Carroll's, it is nonetheless rarely seen and understood. (7) Only two scientific studies appear to have been published about British dormice this century.

　　(8) Unfortunate though it is, the dormouse is one of nature's ready-made victims. (9) It has exacting ecological requirements which make it vulnerable, particularly to habitat change, as well as to climatic variation. (10) It lives at a low population density and has a very low rate of population increase. (11) And because it hibernates for half of the year (from October to at least April, depending upon the weather) and is mainly nocturnal, it is not an easy creature to study.

　　(12) Nevertheless, two studies, one on the distribution of the dormouse, the other about its ecological needs, have been published recently. (13) Both are by Dr Paul Bright and Dr Pat Morris of Royal Holloway, University of

London – with the collaboration of Dr Tony Mitchell-Jones of English Nature on the distribution survey – and manage finally to shed some light on why the dormouse is so rare.

(14) To plot the distribution of the dormouse, it is no use relying on sighting these six-inch long (from nose to tip of tail) squirrel-like mice. (15) The more productive way is to search for opened hazelnuts in woodland. (16) Dormouse gnawed nuts have a different pattern of marks from those opened [by] other creatures. (17) As a result, the Great Nut Hunt was launched in 1993, with the help of the Countryside Council for Wales and English Nature, and attracted no less than 6,500 participants (people, not dormice). (18) Out of more than 172,000 gnawed nuts, 1,352 were confirmed as dormouse-nibbled, identifying 334 dormouse sites in England and Wales. (19) They have never been known to occur in Scotland.

(20) What the results of the Great Nut Hunt show is how confined to southern Britain this mammal now is. (21) A quarter of its known sites are in Devon and 12 per cent in Dorset, the two counties in which the dormouse is most abundant. (22) Other southern English counties have a scattering, as do the Welsh borders and a few woods in the north, west and south of Wales.

(23) The survey clarifies the extent to which the dormouse's range has contracted. (24) According to the naturalist and illustrator, Archibald Thorburn, writing in 1920, the dormouse was 'fairly plentiful in the southern and western counties of England, though rare in the Midlands and Norfolk'. (25) It was, he wrote, abundant in parts of Surrey. (26) Not now. (27) It is seemingly extinct in several counties where it was found late last century. (28) Understanding why is the key to trying to hold on to the populations that remain and, maybe, even help them expand.

(29) First, we need to look at its habitat requirements. (30) The three plant species most associated with dormice – hazel, honeysuckle and bramble – are widely distributed throughout Britain in woods, copses and hedgerows. (31) Hazelnuts are the main fattening-up food consumed prior to hibernation. (32) Honeysuckle offers flowers in springtime, with fruits later in the summer, and finely shredded bark which is the favoured nesting material. (33) Bramble is valuable for its late summer and early autumn fruit supply.

(34) 'None of these three species is absolutely vital,' argue Bright and Morris, 'provided suitable substitutes exist, but few very good dormouse sites are without more than one of them.' (35) The problem is that in many woods managed primarily for timber, hazel can take up unproductive space while bramble is a nuisance and climbing plants such as honeysuckle are sometimes cut down. (36) In woods grazed by sheep – common in Wales and the north of England – such shrubs struggle to survive.

(37) The structure of a good dormouse wood is important. (38) It needs to have a well-grown, unshaded understorey of shrubs and small trees so that the sunlight encourages plenty of flowers and fruits. (39) Dense woodlands, or planted rows of trees, are anathema for such frugivorous fantasies. (40) Equally important is a variety of shrubs; a wide range of flowering and

fruiting times is more likely to offer a suitable menu. (41) Dormice are unable to digest cellulose-rich foods easily, such as leaves, because they lack a large intestine, yet another restriction. (42) Furthermore, the shrub- and small-tree-rich understorey needs to be physically continuous so that dormice can move in the dark from branch to branch without having to touch the ground. (43) Simple really.

(44) For nesting, they often use tree holes and hollows, but sometimes they take over old squirrels['] dreys or birds' nests. (45) So, an understorey-rich wood, with not too many larger, shade-bearing trees, still has to possess older trees because these are most likely to have natural holes.

(46) The hibernation spot is different again – a cool place on the ground, often in a rock crevice, tree stump or rodent burrow. (47) Surprisingly, for such fussy fellows, dormice take avidly to nest boxes which can mimic the tree holes they need for summer nests. (48) In woods short of natural holes, but endowed with the structure and variety of shrubs required, putting up nest boxes could bolster flagging populations.

(49) But, back to the limitations. (50) Dormice don't move over long distances, but exploit food supplies in perhaps one hectare of woodland over a year, harvesting different spots and shrubs as the seasons change. (51) In one night, radio tracking has shown that they may travel between 150 and 300 metres, but no more than 70 metres in a straight line from the nest, relying on the local knowledge they build up of which shrubs have food and which branches interconnect.

(52) Little wonder, then, that woodland loss and the fragmentation of what native woodland remains have reduced substantially the number of dormouse-suitable habitats. (53) A couple of thousand years ago the bulk of lowland Britain was wooded and one can only assume that dormice were much more commonplace.

(54) Today, remnants of this ancient wildwood cover no more than a small percentage of land. (55) Recent plantations of conifers or broad-leaved trees are usually unsuitable for the dormouse which hasn't adapted to the changes we have wrought. (56) The one exception is that they have moved into some hedgerows, especially older ones with a variety of fruiting shrubs and a dense structure. (57) But hedgerows are in decline too; 150,000 kilometres have been lost since 1945. (58) Hedgerows are also often the only physical link between one isolated wood and the next.

(59) Apart from habitat, its other major drawback is the dormouse's population dynamics. (60) According to Bright and Morris, the best sites support up to eight dormice per hectare, compared, for example, with a minimum of 130 bank voles. (61) So small woods have few dormice, making them highly vulnerable if, for instance, woodland management is altered or there is a succession of poor summers for fruit supply. (62) As only one or two youngsters per female are successfully reared each year, the population rises slowly. (63) Perhaps to compensate, dormice can live up to five years – much longer than, say, bank voles, half of which die before they reach four months.

(64) Relatively untouched by predators – probably because they spend their lives in branches and bushes – the dormouse's lifestyle strategy of a long life, low production of youngsters and low population densities is fine in large areas of suitable habitat under stable conditions. (65) But it is the opposite of what it needs to succeed in today's sparse woods, many of which don't provide the structure and menu these fussy animals need.

(66) One thing it does get right is its lengthy hibernation – a strategy which overcomes winter food shortages. (67) But, ironically, mild winters are probably more of a threat than cold ones, simply because its fat reserves are deleted faster as its metabolic rate rises. (68) Long, mild British winters, albeit with cold spells, may not be in its favour.

(69) More research on the ecology of dormice is going to be necessary. (70) In the meantime, this mammal is starting to get the attention it deserves, courtesy of an action plan agreed by the government and its conservation agencies. (71) The objectives are to maintain and enhance existing populations, improve woodland management to encourage them, and reintroduce them to suitable woods in at least five counties in which they have been lost.

(72) No longer is the dormouse being ignored. (73) Alice would be ever so pleased.

As an example of the way in which an expectation raised by a sentence may be deferred, consider sentence 9. This sentence raises the obvious expectation that the text will somewhere describe how habitat change might make the dormouse vulnerable. This expectation is met indirectly in a number of places in the text but one sentence where the expectation is directly met is sentence 61:

3.2a   (9) It has exacting ecological requirements which make it vulnerable, particularly to habitat change, as well as to climatic variation.

(61) ... small woods have few dormice, making them highly vulnerable if, for instance, woodland management is altered or there is a succession of poor summers for fruit supply.

It will be noticed that, with 'So' omitted from the beginning of sentence 61, sentences 9 and 61 are almost as coherent together as if they had been juxtaposed by the writer. This coherence arises out of the fact that the writer is picking up an earlier point and adding to it and is reflected in the language that connects the two sentences. In the first place, the sentences are connected by repetition: 'make ... vulnerable' in sentence 9 is repeated as 'making ... vulnerable' in sentence 61. Then they are connected by a complex paraphrase: the noun 'change' in sentence 9 becomes the verb 'altered' in sentence 61. Finally they are connected by items that refer out of the text to the same entity (co-reference): the pronoun 'it' in sentence 9 refers to 'the dormouse', the same entity referred to (in plural form) in sentence 61. In this way the writer both reflects and signals to the reader the coherence to be detected between these sentences.

Another instance of the same property of the text can be found in sentence 10. Sentence 10 sets up an expectation, in the light of the previous sentence, that one of the questions that will be answered later will be: does the dormouse's low population density and rate of population increase make it vulnerable? This expectation is met in sentence 64, where, perhaps surprisingly, we are told that the answer is no, given stable conditions:

3.2b   (10) It lives at a low population density and has a very low rate of population increase.

(64) Relatively untouched by predators – probably because they spend their lives in branches and bushes – the dormouse's lifestyle strategy of a long life, low production of youngsters and low population densities is fine in large areas of suitable habitat under stable conditions.

Again, the two sentences are so coherent that they read quite naturally together, even though they are separated in the original text by 53 sentences. Again, the coherence arises out of the fact that the latter sentence does indeed meet a long-deferred expectation, and, again, this coherence is reflected in the shared vocabulary: 'low' and 'population'. There is also more complex connection in the repetition of the verb 'lives' as the noun 'lives' and, as before, in the co-reference of 'it' and 'the dormouse'.

As a third example, to show that this is no isolated phenomenon, take sentences 11 and 66.

3.2c   (11) And because it hibernates for half of the year (from October to at least April, depending upon the weather) and is mainly nocturnal, it is not an easy creature to study.

(66) One thing it does get right is its lengthy hibernation – a strategy which overcomes winter food shortages.

As a fairly weak expectation, we might hope for more information on the dormouse's hibernation pattern. This is supplied in sentence 66 and as before the connection is pointed up by the presence of the complex repetition 'hibernates/hibernation', the two instances of the pronoun 'it', in both sentences referring to the dormouse, and the generalisation 'lengthy' in sentence 66 which summarises the period of time 'half the year (from October to at least April)' mentioned in sentence 11. The coherence of the sentences is less pronounced than in previous examples, but is still there as can be seen if we juxtapose the first clause of sentence 11 with sentence 66:

3.2d   (11, 1st clause) It hibernates for half of the year (from October to at least April, depending upon the weather). (66) One thing it does get right is its lengthy hibernation – a strategy which overcomes winter food shortages.

The various kinds of repetition that link sentences across a text – grouped together along with other text-connecting features under the general heading of *cohesion* – have been much studied; key references will be found in the bibliographical end-notes. Here I will simply note that they are part of the signalling that a writer, consciously or subconsciously, supplies to enable a reader to detect places where expectations are to be met – or at very least connections to be made. Repetitions may be of a number of kinds as we have seen. The following seem the most important in written text:

(a) simple repetition   *low – low*
(b) complex repetition   *hibernates – hibernation,*

where there is morphological variation (other than that caused by normal grammatical variation, such as singular-plural: *dormouse – dormice*)

(c) pronouns   *dormouse – it*
(d) unspecific nouns   *dormouse – mammal*
(e) simple paraphrase   *change* [noun] *– alteration*
(f) complex paraphrase   *change* [verb] *– alteration*

where one word has a complex repetition that is a simple paraphrase of the other. Thus in the text we have been considering, 'alteration' is capable of being a complex repetition of 'alter' and 'alter' is capable of being a simple paraphrase of 'change' used as a verb, which allows us to see 'change' [verb] and 'alteration' as a kind of paraphrase. Antonyms are picked up under this category.

(g) co-reference   *it* [referring to the dormouse] *– dormouse*
(h) ellipsis   *Two studies – Both*

Ellipsis occurs when words are omitted from a later sentence and have to be supplied from an earlier sentence. An example is to be found in sentence 13 where 'Both' is missing its noun (Both what?) and sentence 12 supplies the missing information.

(i) closed sets   *Devon – Surrey*

Members of closed sets contain within them a shared meaning component. Thus 'Devon' in sentence 21 and 'Surrey' in sentence 25 share the meaning component 'English county', and the reader would be expected to see the connection. One technically unclosed set which is nevertheless linguistically closed that comes under this category is the number system.

These strategies for repetition – often termed *cohesive ties*, along with other connecting strategies not discussed here – can be noted for their own sake, but their real significance lies in their availability as means for connecting sentences, both close to and far off.

We have just been looking at the way repetition can be used by a writer to signal that an expectation is being met. But how real are these expectations? Do readers really have the capability of forming expectations that will be met much later on in some cases? The answer to these questions cannot be conclusive, but there is some evidence that at certain points in a text it is possible for skilled readers familiar with the genre to make extensive and accurate predictions about what the text as a whole will contain. In the case of the text just mentioned, I gave sentences 8 and 9 to two informants who had not read the article and asked them to list the questions they would expect the rest of the article to answer.

The first informant was a student of ecology, and her expectations reflect her general knowledge of the field and possibly the genre. Below I list the questions that she wrote down and in the adjacent brackets I have noted the sentences in the text that in my judgement supply the answers.

- What ecological requirements does the dormouse have? [Answer: s. 29–34; 37–46; 50–51]
- Why do they make it vulnerable to habitat change? [Answer: s. 34–36; 52; 54–55; 57–58; 61; 64–65]
- Why else is it vulnerable apart from the two reasons given? [Answer: s. 41; 59–62]
- Specifically, what forms of habitat change and climatic variation are particularly stressful to the dormouse? [Answer: s. 35–36?; 52?; 61; 67–68]
- What species of dormouse is being discussed? [No answer in the text]
- Where does it live? [Answer: s. 20–22; 24–27]
- What physiological, biological, behavioural adaptations does it possess, which enable it to survive its supposed 'vulnerable' life? [Answer: s. 47?; 63; 66]
- Is human interference involved as nature doesn't 'ready make' victims? – it evolves its species to adapt unless we come along and mess things up. [Answer: s. 35–36; 52; 55; 57]

You will see that the first informant's questions are provided with answers from the text in all but one case and that these answers account for 67% of the sentences that follow sentences 8 and 9; in other words, she has successfully predicted two-thirds of the text on the basis of just two early sentences.

One might imagine that it was the first informant's special expertise that enabled her to so effectively predict what the text would contain. But examination of the other informant's expectations shows that specialist knowledge appears to have played a relatively minor role. The other informant was in her forties; she had no special interest in ecology (or dormice), her first degree being in classics. Her questions, though, are equally comprehensive. The wording of the questions is again the informant's own:

- Where are dormice found – what kind of habitat? [Answer: s. 21–27?; 29–34; 37–40; 42–46; 56]
- What effect has habitat change had on the dormouse? [Answer: s. 20–27; 52–58]
- What are the optimum climatic conditions? [Answer: s. 66–68]
- How does habitat and climate relate to its diet/propensity to disease/ability to reproduce/predators, etc.? [Answers: s. 29–34; 37–41; 44–45; 46; 50–52; 55–56; 59–62; 64–65; 66–68]

- What are its other ecological requirements? [Answer: s. 41; 50–51]
- What was the nature of the studies that produced the above statements? [Answer: s. 12–13; 14–18?]
- How wide a coverage do the findings have – in different countries? [Answer: s. 18–19]
- What impact will the Greenhouse effect have? [Answer: s. 67–68]

With the exception of the sub-question concerning propensity to disease, all the second informant's questions were answered, accounting for 78% of the sentences that follow. In other words, the second informant predicted over three-quarters of the text on the basis of the same two sentences. Of course, the successful predictions of the two informants are a measure of the writer's own success at predicting what his readers will want to know. Either way it would seem that the whole development of the article is already enshrined in embryo in its beginning.

Signals as messages from writer to reader: previews and intertextuality

Reader and writer are like dancers following each other's steps, and the reader's chances of guessing correctly what is going to happen next in a text are greatly enhanced if the writer takes the trouble to anticipate what the reader might be expecting; that is one of the reasons for regularity of patterning in genres. The writer knows that readers will expect certain things on the basis of previous texts of the same kind that they have read and so takes the trouble to conform to those expectations; the act of conforming to those expectations confirms readers in the rightness of their original expectation and makes it still more likely that they will expect the same thing the next time they encounter a text of this type.

Had I chosen a typical narrative for the experiment reported in the previous section, however, it is unlikely whether my readers would have had the same success in predicting the course of the text. It is certainly not true that the whole development of a narrative is enshrined in its beginning. A majority of twentieth-century narratives begin *in media res* and it is usually difficult to predict the development of a story on the basis of such beginnings. Some narratives, though, do behave like non-narrative texts in beginning in such a way that the reader is able to generate reasonably accurate expectations. They do this in two ways. First they contain preview statements that function as signals to the reader about the nature of the text to come. Second, they make use of intertextuality, the relationship a text forms with previous texts such that production of the later text is in some respects affected – and the understanding a reader makes of it is likewise affected – by those earlier texts.

To illustrate both points, we turn to the beginning of Jorge Luis Borges' story *Death and the Compass*, as translated by Donald A. Yates. This story will be returned to in many of the chapters of this book, and while I shall on every occasion endeavour to make my discussion entirely intelligible without any knowledge of the story other than that provided in this book, the reader might like to take time out to read it, not least because it is a fine piece of writing better encountered in its original glory than in fragments and summary.

The beginning of *Death and the Compass* reads as follows; sentences are as always numbered for ease of reference

3.3   (1) Of the many problems which exercised the reckless discernment of Lönnrot, none was so strange – so rigorously strange, shall we say – as the periodic series of bloody events which culminated at the villa of Triste-le Roy, amid the ceaseless aroma of the eucalypti. (2) It is true that Lönnrot failed to prevent the last murder, but that he foresaw it is indisputable. (3) Neither did he guess the identity of Yarmolinsky's luckless assassin, but he did succeed in divining the secret morphology behind the fiendish series as well as the participation of Red Scharlach, whose other nickname is Scharlach the Dandy. (4) That criminal (as countless others) had sworn on his honour to kill Lönnrot, but the latter could never be intimidated. (5) Lönnrot believed himself a pure reasoner, an Auguste Dupin, but there was something of the adventurer in him, and even a little of the gambler.

(6) The first murder occurred in the Hôtel du Nord – that tall prism which dominates the estuary whose waters are the colour of the desert. (7) To that tower (which quite glaringly unites the hateful whiteness of a hospital, the numbered divisibility of a jail, and the general appearance of a bordello) there came on the third day of December the delegate from Podolsk to the Third Talmudic Congress, Doctor Marcel Yarmolinsky, a grey-bearded man with grey eyes.

This preview of the story to be told contains a number of signalling preview statements that tell the reader quite precisely what to expect. We are told that the story will contain a series of *bloody events* (s.1); given that there is mention of an *assassin* (s.3), we take it that these will be murders. The fact that there is a *series* (s.1) – and indeed a *periodic series*, with its intimations of regularity (cf. the periodic table of the elements in chemistry) – invites us to assume that these murders are part of a single picture and probably the work of a single person with a single motive, though importantly this is an assumption that goes beyond what Borges tells us. We know that one of the victims is called Yarmolinsky and that a character called Red Scharlach will be associated with the solving of the crimes. We infer that Lönnrot fulfils the role of detective; the references to *discernment* (s.1), *reasoner* and *Auguste Dupin*, the hero of Edgar Allan Poe's archetypal and genre-creating detective stories (s.5), all point in this direction. We also know that Lönnrot has some success in his investigations – he *foresaw* the last murder (s.2) and *succeed[ed] in divining the secret morphology behind the fiendish series* (s.3). Thus the reader has a shape to the story – knows the kind of story it is going to be – in advance of reading it. More than that, the beginning functions as an advertisement: the story will be *strange* (s.1) and therefore, of course, worthy of the reader's attention.

All of this would be achieved if the reader had never encountered a first paragraph like this before. The signals Borges uses are clear enough to be self-standing. As it happens, though, readers are quite likely to have previously encountered paragraphs like this if they happen to be aficionados of detective short stories, particularly detective short stories from the early part of the twentieth century and the end of the nineteenth. Borges is, in fact, making use of the way a text inevitably relates to previous texts and the way a reader's inter-pretation of it is affected by his or her reading of previous texts of the same genre or text-type. One of the ways traditional detective stories may begin is with a paragraph such as this. As evidence, consider first the beginning from a story by the most famous of all detective short-story writers:

3.4   Of all the problems which have been submitted to my friend Mr Sherlock Holmes for solution during the period of our intimacy, there were only two which I was the means of introducing to his notice, that of Mr Hatherley's thumb and that of Colonel Warburton's madness. Of these the latter may have afforded a finer field for an acute and original observer, but the other was so strange in its inception and so dramatic in its details, that it may be the more worthy of being placed upon record, even if it gave my friend fewer openings for those deductive methods of reasoning by which he achieved such remarkable results.

It will be seen that Borges' wording closely parallels that of Conan Doyle's. Both start with a sentence of similar construction, 'Of all/the many problems which x, y'. Both describe the case as 'strange'; both refer to the reasoning of the central character.

Now consider the following beginning by another early master of the detective story genre, G. K. Chesterton:

3.5   This queer incident, in some ways perhaps the queerest of the many that came his way, happened to Father Brown at the time when his French friend Flambeau had retired from the profession of crime and had entered with great energy and success on the profession of crime investigator.

Again we have the emphasis on the strangeness – 'queer' – and, as with the Borges, a claim of superlativeness of strangeness: Chesterton refers to the incident as 'the queerest of the many that came [Father Brown's] way', which compares with Borges' 'none was so strange'.

Superlativeness can take other forms. Here is another beginning:

3.6   The episode of the nail and the requiem was one of the most characteristic of all those in which, over a relatively brief period, I was privileged to watch Trevis Tarrant at work. Characteristic, in that it brought out so well the unusual aptitude of the man to see clearly, to welcome *all* the facts, no matter

how apparently contradictory, and to think his way through to the only possible solution by sheer logic, while every one else boggled at impossibilities
and sought to forget them. From the gruesome beginning that November
morning, when he was confronted by the puzzle of the sealed studio, to the
equally gruesome denouement that occurred despite his own grave warning
twenty-four hours later, his brain clicked successively and infallibly along the
rails of reason to the inevitable, true goal. [Emphasis in the original] (from
The Episode of the Nail and the Requiem by C. Daly King)

I have quoted this beginning in full because it not only illustrates superlativeness
('the most characteristic of all those in which . . . I was privileged to watch Trevis
Tarrant at work'), but it describes in preview a series of gruesome events and notes
that the central character foresaw the gruesome denouement but was unable to
prevent it. It also uses the first paragraph to characterise the detective's
investigative methods, much as Borges' opening does.

What I am trying to demonstrate is that the reader encountering Borges'
opening to his story may bring to it experience of many similar openings and these
will colour the way the reader interprets the writer's previewing signals. Borges'
first paragraph was almost written for him by the tradition into which he chose to
place his story. I have illustrated the point by reference to a rather old-fashioned
type of detective story, but it could have been made about any genre, narrative or
non-narrative, though it is obviously easier to demonstrate with a genre of a
relatively hidebound kind. Of course, I write only of the English reader's
experience of Borges' text; I cannot say whether a Spanish-language reader would
bring the same cultural points of reference to bear on it.

Intertextuality of the kind I have been describing is operative in both narrative
and non-narrative text but it is only in narrative that a writer is likely to exploit it
creatively. And this leads to my second point. I have been talking as if all the
reader's expectations about *Death and the Compass*, based on Borges' opening
paragraph, are correct. But they are not. Borges is exploiting the genre conventions to make the reader believe s/he is reading an old-fashioned detective
story, but it is only a detective story in a rather indirect and unusual way. At this
point, I must spoil Borges' story by telling it briefly; the story will be repeatedly
referred to throughout this book, as I have already noted.

> The body of a rabbi, Yarmolinsky, is found stabbed in his hotel room in the
> north of an unnamed city on the evening of 3 December. The detective in
> charge, Treviranus, believes him to have been accidentally killed by someone
> intending to rob the Tetrarch of Galilee in the room opposite. Lönnrot notes a
> piece of paper in a typewriter in Yarmolinsky's room with the words 'The first
> letter of the Name has been uttered' on it and infers that the solution is a
> religious one. In an interview published in a Yiddish newspaper he states that
> he believes the Name to be the name of God.
>   On the night of 3 January the body of a minor bandit called Azevedo is
> found stabbed in the west of the city; on the yellow and red diamonds on the

wall behind him are chalked the words 'The second letter of the name has been uttered'.

On the night of 3 February in the east of the city, during carnival, Treviranus receives a call promising information about the 'sacrifices of Azevedo and Yarmolinsky'. By the time Treviranus and Lönnrot arrive, the caller has been abducted by harlequins dressed in yellow, red and green diamonds, leaving behind a blood mark and a scrawled message 'The last of the letters of the Name has been uttered'. Treviranus questions whether a murder has occurred; Lönnrot on the other hand is suddenly and mysteriously struck by the fact that the Hebrew day starts at sundown.

Nearly a month later Treviranus receives a map in the post with the three murders marked on it; they form a perfect equilateral triangle. Treviranus passes the map to Lönnrot, who notes that there will be a fourth murder. He thinks so because there are four letters to the name of God in Hebrew and four points to the compass; further, the murders occurred on the fourth of the month according to the Hebrew calendar because the Hebrew day starts at sundown. Accordingly he infers that a fourth murder will occur on 4 March at the point in the south which would complete a perfect diamond shape on the map. He goes to that point a day earlier and finds himself in a building with stained-glass diamonds in the window, yellow, red and green. Here he is confronted by an old enemy, Red Scharlach, who reveals that Yarmolinsky was indeed murdered by accident as Treviranus had suspected and that the accidental killer was Azevedo, one of Scharlach's men. The words in the typewriter were just part of something that Yarmolinsky had been writing and were irrelevant to the case. Learning from the newspaper that Lönnrot believed the words to be significant, Scharlach had seen an opportunity to trap Lönnrot with his own intelligence; he therefore had killed Azevedo and scrawled the message on the wall to make him believe that the killings had a mystical significance. He had then faked a third death with the same purpose and sent the map to the detectives. Lönnrot realises that he has walked into a perfect trap. The story ends with Scharlach shooting him dead.

You can now see that Borges' opening paragraph was seriously misleading. The first sentence, 'Of the many problems which exercised the reckless discernment of Lönnrot none were so strange as . . .' implies that the problem is one of a series, not the last of the series. The second sentence is in breach of the Gricean maxim of Quantity, 'Make your contribution as informative as is required for the current purposes of the exchange' (see the bibliographical end-notes to Chapter 2) in that *the last murder* would not normally be understood to refer to the death of the subject of the clause, *Lönnrot*; a more natural wording here would be 'Erik Lönnrot failed to prevent his own murder'.

Third and less obviously, we can see that Borges has made misleading use of the signalling value of parallelism described in Chapter 2. The parallelism is between sentences 2 and 3 of the Borges' opening, with parallels of failures (to prevent the last murder, to identify the killer of Yarmolinsky) being balanced against parallels of success (foreseeing the last murder, divining the secret morphology behind the series). At the time we assume that the successes outweigh the failures; it is only at the end of the story that we realise that the successes give rise to the failures.

Finally, we realise that the last sentence is telling us that Lönnrot was an adventurer and a gambler, not a reasoner!

The deception is reinforced by the use of the repetition devices I described earlier. The story is rich in Matched sentences, signalled by parallel repetition (Coulthard, 1990). Sentence 6 in Example 3.3 is directly echoed in the forty-ninth sentence of the story where the second murder is announced:

3.7   The second murder occurred on the evening of the third of January, in the most deserted and empty corner of the capital's western suburbs.

This sentence repeats the words 'murder' and 'occurred' from sentence 6. It also contains a suspect complex repetition ('desert – deserted') and two closed set repetitions: 'first – second'; 'du Nord – western', the latter relying on the linguistic sophistication of the reader.

It also repeats a number of elements of sentence 7. To begin with, we have the simple repetition of 'third' and 'day'; this is supported by two closed set members 'December' and 'January'. Finally, we have a complex paraphrase between 'day' and 'evening'. In the translation by Donald Yates this link is fairly weak; it is stronger in the Spanish original, where the words are *dia* [day] and *noche* [night]. The repetitions between sentence 49 and sentences 6 and 7 have the cumulative effect of inviting the reader to make the same mistake as Lönnrot and find symmetry where no symmetry exists. This is then supported by further symmetries as the third 'crime' is reported.

The repetition is there to underline an effect already achieved through the intertextuality. What we have here is a writer exploiting intertextuality to mislead us. Occasionally, however, writers go further than this. Not content with misleading us, they may set up expectations in the reader, either by signalling or intertextually, that they then thwart. Shepherd (1988) shows how John Fowles exploits a reader's expectations in his novella *The Enigma*; in this story a MP goes missing and a police officer is called in to investigate the disappearance. At one point in the story he lists the various possible solutions and the counter-arguments to them much in the way that detectives do in traditional mysteries before solving the case. The reader therefore expects an answer to the question 'What happened to the MP?' or, more generally, 'What explains the mystery?' When the detective meets a woman who may possibly have had a relationship with the MP, we not unreasonably expect this to be the beginning of the answer to these questions. Instead, though, we are told how the detective and the young woman become attracted to each other. The detective story becomes a love story, and we are never told how or why the MP disappeared.

The startling effect of the change of direction Fowles introduces into his story would not be startling at all if our expectations of texts were not normally met.

Writers anticipate our needs by presenting information in the order we need it and in which we have received it in the past and we in turn have expectations that are shaped by our confidence that the writer will anticipate our needs.

Implications for the language learner

There are three important implications for the language learner of the characteristics of text described in this chapter. The first is a corollary of an implication drawn at the end of the previous chapter: the language learner needs to have larger questions to ask when encountering a text in the target language. One of the most useful roles that pre-reading activities can serve is to supply the learner with questions that they might reasonably ask of the text. The fact that the answers may be found scattered about the text and may not necessarily be near the place where the question first arose can be seen as licensing selective readings of text whereby the learner searches for sentences that answer his or her questions and reads just these.

Secondly, as we have seen, cohesive devices of various kinds can be seen as clues as to where a reader's questions are being answered. This cohesion can be used by learners to make principled selections from a text. The steps they might take include the following:

1. They should read the title and subtitle of the chosen text (excluding authorship ascription). If they are long enough and/or do not seem gimmicky in wording, they should make a note of the lexis they contain. If necessary, they should consult a dictionary; preferably this should be monolingual so that potential synonyms or paraphrases may be identified. Good advanced learners' dictionaries usually provide information on related words. Otherwise they should read the first substantial sentence of the chosen text and make a note of the lexis it contains, again consulting a dictionary as necessary.

2. They should then scan the text looking for a sentence containing three of the items noted or their paraphrases, etc. If the title is short, two will do.

3. Having found a sentence with three repeated items, they should read the sentence and then either look for the next sentence containing the items from the title and subtitle or look for a sentence containing three items from the sentence just read. As we have seen, the sentences will normally make sense together.

How would these steps apply to Example 3.2? Beginning with step 1, the title is too brief to be usable but the sub-title is ideal. In that sub-title, there are the items 'two', 'new', 'studies', 'elusive', 'dormouse', 'revealed', 'disappeared', 'several', 'counties' and 'England' in sentence 1 and in sentence 2 the items 'its' [the dormouse's], 'geographical', 'range' and 'shrinking'.

Moving to stage 2, if the learner then scans the text for a sentence containing three of these items, s/he will find that sentences 7, 12, 13 (though this is one that most learners would probably overlook), 21, 23, 24 and 27 all fit the bill. If s/he is alert, s/he might also notice that sentence 71 connects three times (co-reference, closed set, and repetition of 'counties') but the chances are that this will be missed. You can check for yourself that stage 3, reading the pairs of sentences together, works. All I will add here is that grouped together they produce a meaningful sub-text:

3.8   (1) *Two new studies of the elusive dormouse have revealed that it has disappeared from several counties in England. (2) Malcolm Smith reports on why its geographical range is shrinking.* (7) Only two scientific studies appear to have been published about British dormice this century. (12) Nevertheless, two studies, one on the distribution of the dormouse, the other about its ecological needs, have been published recently. (13) Both are by Dr Paul Bright and Dr Pat Morris of Royal Holloway, University of London – with the collaboration of Dr Tony Mitchell-Jones of English Nature on the distribution survey – and manage finally to shed some light on why the dormouse is so rare. (21) A quarter of its known sites are in Devon and 12 per cent in Dorset, the two counties in which the dormouse is most abundant. (23) The survey clarifies the extent to which the dormouse's range has contracted. (24) According to the naturalist and illustrator, Archibald Thorburn, writing in 1920, the dormouse was 'fairly plentiful in the southern and western counties of England, though rare in the Midlands and Norfolk'. (27) It is seemingly extinct in several counties where it was found late last century. (71) The objectives are to maintain and enhance existing populations, improve woodland management to encourage them, and reintroduce them to suitable woods in at least five counties in which they have been lost.

If the learner got even a sub-set of this sub-set, s/he would still have succeeded in getting some sense from the text by means of this stratagem. It can easily be forgotten how satisfying it can be to get something from a text apparently far beyond one's reading ability, and of course since the task involves a search for repeated lexis it is vocabulary-building at the same time.

The final implication of this chapter is that a learner will find it easier to make sense of a text if the intertextual connections are recognised. These cannot be assumed if the cultural practices associated with the learner's first language have not brought him or her into contact with texts of a similar kind. In some circumstances, teaching the language will include teaching the intertextual expectations necessary to make sense of texts in that language.

Bibliographical end-notes

Example 3.2 is the article 'Quietly Vanishing' by Malcolm Smith, published in *The Independent on Sunday*, 23 March 1997, p. 50. Example 3.3 is the beginning of *Death and the Compass* by Jorge Luis Borges, translated by Donald A. Yates, from *Labyrinths: Selected Stories and Other Writings*, Harmondsworth: Penguin Books. Example 3.4 is by Sir Arthur Conan Doyle, being the beginning of 'The Adventure of the Engineer's Thumb' from *The Adventures of Sherlock Holmes*.

Example 3.5 is the beginning of 'The Insoluble Problem' from *The Scandal of Father Brown* by G. K. Chesterton. Example 3.6 is taken from 'The Episode of the Nail and the Requiem' by C. Daly King in *Tales of Detection*, edited by Dorothy Sayers (1936), London: Dent & Sons Ltd.

The analysis of text in terms of cohesive devices, touched upon in Section 3.2, was pioneered by Halliday and Hasan (1976) and has since been illuminatingly extended by Hasan (1984, 1989). The approach has come under attack on a number of occasions, most notably by Morgan and Sellner (1980), on the grounds that the patterns of repetition in a text are a epiphenomenon of the coherence of the text and do not in themselves contribute to that coherence. But it is not necessary to argue that cohesion creates coherence; it is sufficient to note that the coherence of a text is reflected in and signalled by the cohesion in the text. Tanskanen (2000) argues that cohesion is a strategy used by writers to help readers create coherence from the text: a type of signalling, in other words. The particular categories of repetition used in this chapter are drawn with slight modification from Hoey (1991a, b) where the connections between sentences at some distance from each other is also described in some detail. Later work making use of this model includes Wessels (1993), Berber Sardinha (1997), Peng (1998) and Arcay Hands (1996, 1998, with Cosse 1998)

The term 'intertextuality' appears to have been coined by Julia Kristeva (see Moi 1986), and has been used to describe a wide range of relationships that may hold between discourses. Genette (1982) talks of 'transtextuality', reserving the term 'intertextuality' for exact quotation of one text within another; 'archtextuality' is the term he uses to describe the more abstract relationships that I have been describing in this chapter. Although Genette's categories are subtle, they have not taken hold, and 'intertextuality' is usually used to describe the way that a text's production and reception are governed by – and go on to affect – the history of text production and reception in a culture and a particular writer's and reader's experience of that culture. Fairclough (1992b) argues for a closer relationship between textual analysis and intertextual analysis; the latter is not always closely grounded in the detail of the text. Abraham (1993) looks at the ways in which student essays are closely connected as a result of class workshops, using Hoey (1991a) as the basis for her analysis. Hoey (1995) and (1996a) applies the same technique to newspaper articles with and without common sources. Schema theory can also be seen as a theory of intertextuality; bibliographical references will be found at the end of Chapter 7.

Malcolm Coulthard and I once planned a book on literary linguistics centring on analyses of *Death and the Compass*. Although I take responsibility for the analyses in this book, my debt to him is great. The latter part of the analysis in this chapter draws in part on Coulthard (1990, 1992) and Hoey (1994b).

4   The hierarchical organisation of texts

An apology and an introduction

I have already begun one chapter unconventionally, so let me begin another likewise. I nearly left this chapter out, because the description it provides is in some respects overly mechanical and could give the wrong impression of text/ discourse analysis. The positions it presents have been adopted as central by some linguists to the detriment of their descriptions; for this reason, too, it might have been better to have excluded it from the book. On the other hand it serves as a useful bridge between what I was saying in Chapter 3 and what I will be talking about in later chapters, and while the hierarchical structuring of texts can be over-stated, such structuring is still a real characteristic of such texts and needs to be accounted for. On balance, then, I left the chapter in because the insights it offers just about outweigh the risks. What the chapter seeks to do – and at this point I revert to the normal practice of the genre by outlining in advance the aim of the chapter, as a kind of abstract – is to extend the account of the ways writers and readers interact given in the last two chapters by introducing a new element into the picture (or more accurately reintroducing an element that has twice been briefly alluded to) – the fact that texts are hierarchically organised.

A reader's larger questions

A reader's questions are not necessarily answered in a single sentence; indeed it is absolutely normal for them to be answered over quite long stretches of text. We saw this when we looked in the last chapter at the thwarting of expectations in John Fowles's *The Enigma*. Similarly, not only did the two informants predicting the information to come in Example 3.2 predict a large proportion of the questions that the text would answer but the sentences they predicted tended to bunch in groups. We must therefore further modify the diagram depicting the interaction between writer and reader, as shown in Figure 4.1. What this figure indicates is that the writer has to anticipate the reader's needs both locally and globally. It is much harder to keep one's eye on the latter needs than the former. The exigencies of the immediate context are always in front of one, and most writers will report losing their sense of the overall picture at some point in their drafting, either

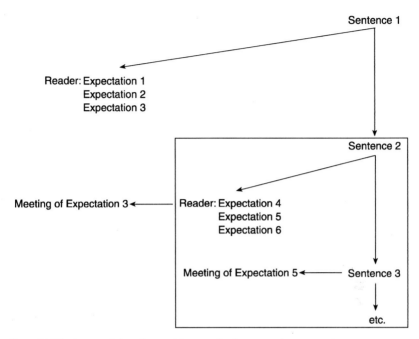

Figure 4.1 The interactivity of text with regard to larger-scale expectations.

because they get caught up in one particular point or simply because they forget what they have already written. If there is a problem for the native speaker writer, there is an even greater one for the non-native, who also has a different class of difficulties of sentence construction and lexical selection to engage with on top of all the native speaker's problems.

From the reader's perspective, what the figure reflects is that s/he may have an expectation that can only be met – or is better met – by a number of sentences. Obviously the reader will recognise when the process has started and will be satisfied that the expectation is indeed being met; at the same time s/he will continue to have local expectations that will be met on a sentence-by-sentence basis. Good native speaker readers do this without thinking, but the skill does not always transfer to the second language, where problems of moment-by-moment decoding have a similar impact on the ability to keep the whole picture in view as the equivalent problems of encoding have for the writer.

Texts with a simple hierarchical organisation

Sometimes the predictions a reader makes about what question(s) will be answered by a block of text become clearer only once the block is under way. Consider the following paragraph which begins a (very) short narrative involving Aesop; as previously, sentences are numbered for convenience of reference:

4.1   (1) Aesop, the Greek writer of fables, was sitting by the roadside one day when a traveller asked him, 'Tell me, my friend, what sort of people live in Athens?' (2) Aesop replied, 'Tell me where you come from and what sort of people live there, and I'll tell you what sort of people you'll find in Athens.' (3) Smiling, the man answered, 'I come from Argos, and there the people are all friendly, generous and warm-hearted. (3a) I love them.' (4) At this Aesop answered, 'I'm happy to tell you, my dear friend, that you'll find the people of Athens much the same.'

It is worth considering at this point what (if anything) you expect to happen in the narrative next. You would be entitled to feel that here the writer has left in the first paragraph too few clues as to the narrative's ultimate destination to enable you to make any confident suggestions.

The sentence that actually comes next begins a new paragraph and is as follows:

4.1a   (5) A few hours later another traveller came down the road, and he too stopped and asked Aesop, 'Tell me, what are the people of Athens like?'

Your predictions as to what will follow are likely now to be much more precise. Indeed some readers may feel able to predict successfully the whole of the remainder of the narrative, which runs as follows:

4.1b   (6) Again Aesop replied, 'Tell me where you come from and what the people are like there and I will tell you what the people are like in Athens.'
(7) Frowning, the man answered, 'I'm from Argos and there the people are unfriendly, mean, deceitful and vicious. (7a) They're thieves and murderers, all of them.' (8) 'I'm afraid you'll find the people of Athens much the same' was Aesop's reply.

Here the parallelism between sentences 1 and 5 triggers the precise expectation that there will be further parallelisms between the sentences in the first paragraph and the sentences to come in the second. Winter (1974, 1979) argued that it is possible to represent the parallelism as a mixture of repeated items and what he termed 'replacement', or, put another way, a mixture of constant items and variables. This mixture can be represented in tabular fashion, as shown in Table 4.1.

The run of constant elements shared by sentences 1 and 5 in the Aesop narrative tells the reader that these sentences are in a matching relation of similarity; the information each sentence offers is similar to that of the other. The effect of the pairing is to set up a larger comparison between the two halves of the narrative. Only the subtle absence of the greeting in sentence 5 hints that there will be a contrast between the two halves.

At the same time the time sequence aspect of the relationship between the two chunks of text must not be ignored. The temporal adjunct 'A few hours later' tells

Table 4.1 The parallelism between sentences 1 and 5 of *Aesop and the Travellers*

			asked	him	Tell me	my friend	what sort of	people you'll find in Athens
(1)	One day	a traveller	asked	him	Tell me	my friend	what sort of	people you'll find in Athens
(5)	A few hours later	another traveller	asked	Aesop	Tell me		what are ... like	the people of Athens
Constants	same day	a traveller	asked	Aesop	Tell me		what are like	the people of Athens
Variables	different time of day	different traveller			presence or absence of greeting			

the reader that the two chunks of text are in a sequence relationship. Whenever in a narrative there is one or more of the following:

(a) a clear change of time frame, typically marked by a temporal adjunct like the one just mentioned;

(b) a clear change of place, often marked by a clause reporting arrival in a new place;

(c) a change in characters referred to, either by the addition of a new person mentioned or by the removal of one of the present characters or, most strikingly, by a complete change of cast;

(d) clear structural transition, e.g. a new chapter;

(e) clear structural parallelism,

there is a *prima facie* case for identifying the chunk of text that is just under way as a new *episode* in the narrative. Episodes boundaries vary in their clarity but they do represent a decision by the writer to show a sequence relation between two chunks of text rather than simply between two sentences or clauses. They are therefore another way in which the global as well as the local needs of the reader are met. In the case of the boundary between the two chunks of the Aesop text we find three of these features present, (a), (c) and (e), so there are good grounds for seeing sentence 5 as beginning a new episode.

In light of the above discussion, we can see that the organisation of the complete narrative is as shown in Figure 4.2.

In the previous chapter we saw that text was constructed linearly as a result of the interaction taking place on a moment-by-moment basis between writer and reader. Now we see that text is also capable of being organised hierarchically

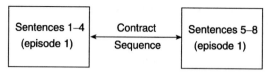

Figure 4.2 The organisation of *Aesop and the Travellers.*

and the relationships occurring between the 'chunks' of the text are similar to those found between sentences.

The units of the hierarchical organisation do not have to be of equal size. Consider, for example, Blake's poem *A Poison Tree*; line numbers have been added for convenience of reference.

4.2   I was angry with my friend:
       I told my wrath, my wrath did end.
       I was angry with my foe:
       I told it not, my wrath did grow.

       And I watered it in fears,   5
       Night and morning with my tears;
       And I sunned it with smiles,
       And with soft deceitful wiles.

       And it grew both day and night,
       Till it bore an apple bright;   10
       And my foe beheld it shine,
       And he knew that it was mine,

       And into my garden stole
       When the night had veiled the pole:
       In the morning glad I see   15
       My foe outstretched beneath the tree.

As before, there are grounds to suggest that there are (at least) two episodes. There is no marker of time sequence at line 3, but we do have a change of personnel and clear structural parallelism, marking a clear division between lines 1–2 and lines 3–16. Within the second episode, there are further markers of episode boundaries at lines 11 and 15, which mark a second level of 'chunking' within the text. (The way a text may have more than one level is handled in the next section.)

Table 4.2 also demonstrates a clear parallelism of the Matching kind between line 1 and line 3. This establishes a larger parallelism between the first episode and the second; what distinguishes this case from the previous one is the asymmetry between the two episodes. The whole point of the first episode is that the poet's wrath-telling brings the episode to an end, whereas not telling it in the second episode means that the chain of events goes on and on. Thus the organisation of this poem is very similar to that of the Aesop story (see Figure 4.3) except in

Table 4.2 Parallelism between lines 1 and 3 in *A Poison Tree*

(1)	I was angry with	my friend
(3)	I was angry with	my foe
Constants	I was angry with	a person
Variables		my attitude to the person

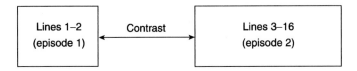

Figure 4.3 The hierarchical organisation of *A Poison Tree*.

respect of the asymmetry and the absence of any explicit marker that the second episode occurs in time after the first one.

The hierarchical organisation of a joke

Needless to say, not that many texts are organised in such a simple fashion as those illustrated in the previous section (and I have already indicated that even the Blake text is more complex than the above diagram implies). Many jokes are, however, organised in an only slightly more complicated fashion. Here is a joke told by my son and transcribed by me without alteration (though I interfered to the extent of asking him to give the characters names rather than identifying them by the regions of the UK they came from!).

4.3   (1) There were three men who were called Fred, Bill and Joe, and they were caught by a firing squad and they were all going to be shot. (2) So Fred was brought out and all the firing squad lined up ready to shoot him. (3) As they were about to press their triggers, he cried 'Tornado!' (4) And the firing squad all ran off thinking there was a tornado and he escaped. (5) Then Bill was brought out. (6) As the firing squad lined up he shouted 'Hurricane!' (7) And the firing squad all ran off thinking there was a hurricane, and *he* escaped. (8) Last of all Joe was brought on. (9) As the firing squad lined up he shouted 'Fire!' (10) And they shot him.

Episode boundaries can be found at sentences 5 and 8. We have (weak) time frame markers ('then', 'last of all'), change of character (in that a different character has been in focus in the previous stretch of text) and structural parallelism. As with the Aesop story and the Blake poem the larger parallelism is triggered by local parallelisms amongst the initial sentences of the chunks. The first parallelism

Table 4.3 Parallelism between parts of sentences 2 and 5 in a joke

(2)	(So)	Fred	was brought out . . .
(5)	(Then)	Bill	was brought out.
Constants		man	was brought out
Variables		name	

occurs between sentences 2 and 5 (see Table 4.3); interestingly the parallelism makes use of only part of one of the paralleled sentences. This sets up the first relationship between the episode relating to Fred's escape and that relating to Bill's. At the point of encountering sentence 5, of course, the reader cannot be certain whether the episodes being matched are being matched for similarity or contrast (though experience of a certain kind of joke structure, combined with the mention of three protagonists in the first sentence, would be likely to predispose him/her strongly to expect similarity at this point).

Identifying episode boundaries and local parallelisms is not enough, however, to account properly for the text. The three episodes are not given equal weight in the story. The first two establish a norm of escape strategies from which the third deviates. We can therefore see the first two episodes as forming a larger chunk which functions as a single entity in its relationship with the third. This relationship in the hierarchical organisation of the text is triggered in a very similar way (see Table 4.4).

The finality of the sequence and the subtle change in verb particle ('out' to 'on') are the only clues the reader/listener has at this point that the third episode will contrast with the other two, a state of affairs that is finally confirmed in the last sentence. The analysis therefore shows a double organisation, that might be represented as in Figure 4.4.

Setting

Figure 4.4 does not yet account for the story as we have it. In my account of the episode boundaries above I glossed over the fact that sentence 1 falls outside all three episodes. It does not, for example, participate in the parallelism and the first

Table 4.4 Parallelism among sentences 2, 5 and 8 in a joke

(2/5)	(So) (Then)	Fred/Bill	was brought out . . .
(8)	Last of all	Joe	was brought on.
Constants	place in sequence	man	was brought out
Variables	which place	name	

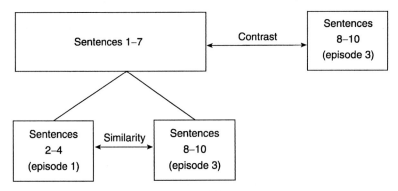

Figure 4.4 Partial hierarchical organisation of a joke.

part of it does not report an event. Whereas sentences 2–10 all involve action or verbal processes (Halliday 1994), i.e. they describe acts of doing or saying, the first half of sentence 1 is what Halliday would term an existential process, i.e. it asserts the existence of something or someone (a trio of characters in this case). At the beginning of narratives it is common for there to be material that either establishes the existence of some necessary entities in the fictional world about to be created or provides a description of some character or characters or place. Preliminary information about events may also be supplied. Variously labelled Orientation (Labov 1972), Stage (Longacre 1976, 1983) and Setting (Rumelhart 1975), the function of this pre-narrative material is to orient the reader and set the stage for what follows.

As a way of illustrating the kinds of information that may be supplied in a Setting, consider the following passage, which is the opening of Raymond Chandler's *The Big Sleep*:

4.4 It was about eleven o'clock in the morning, mid October, with the sun not shining and a look of hard wet rain in the clearness of the foothills. I was wearing my powder-blue suit, with dark blue shirt, tie and display handkerchief, black brogues, black wool socks with dark blue clocks on them. I was neat, clean, shaved and sober, and I didn't care who knew it. I was everything the well-dressed private detective ought to be. I was calling on four million dollars.

The main hallway of the Sternwood place was two stories high. Over the entrance doors, which would have let in a troop of Indian elephants, there was a broad stained-glass panel showing a knight in dark armour rescuing a lady who was tied to a tree and didn't have any clothes on but some very long and convenient hair. The knight had pushed the vizor of his helmet back to be sociable, and he was fiddling with the knots on the ropes that tied the lady to the tree and not getting anywhere. I stood there and thought that if I lived in the house, I would sooner or later have to climb up there and help him. He didn't seem to be really trying.

There were French doors at the back of the hall, beyond them a wide sweep of emerald grass to a white garage, in front of which a slim dark young chauffeur in shiny black leggings was dusting a maroon Packard convertible. Beyond the garage were some decorative trees trimmed as carefully as poodle dogs. Beyond them a large greenhouse with a domed roof. Then more trees and beyond everything the solid, uneven, comfortable line of the foothills.

On the east side of the hall a free staircase, tile-paved, rose to a gallery with a wrought-iron railing and another piece of stained-glass romance. Large hard chairs with rounded red plush seats were backed into the vacant spaces of the wall round about. They didn't look as if anybody had ever sat in them. In the middle of the west wall there was a big empty fireplace with a brass screen in four hinged panels, and over the fireplace a marble mantel with cupids at the corners. Above the mantel there was a large oil portrait, and above the portrait two bullet-torn or moth-eaten cavalry pennants crossed in a glass frame. The portrait was a stiffly posed job of an officer in full regimentals of about the time of the Mexican War. The officer had a neat black imperial, black mustachios, hot hard coal-black eyes, and the general air of a man it would pay to get along with. I thought this might be General Sternwood's grandfather. It could hardly be the General himself, even though I had heard he was pretty far gone in years to have a couple of daughters still in the dangerous twenties.

I was still staring at the hot black eyes when a door opened far back under the stairs . . .

The passage contains

(a)	identification of time frame	*It was about eleven o'clock in the morning, mid October*
(b)	identification of participants	*I was everything the well-dressed private detective ought to be . . . General Sternwood*
(c)	identification of place	*The main hallway of the Sternwood place*
(d)	preliminary events	*I was calling on four million dollars . . . I stood there and thought*

It also contains hints as to the kind of story it is going to be – a private eye story of course, but also a story about a knight in shining armour. This goes beyond a linguist's concerns, though, and is certainly not generalisable.

It is worth noting the kinds of sentences that are used to encode the Setting. Eight are existential clauses of the kind briefly mentioned above in connection with the joke, or are nominal groups with existential components omitted but readily suppliable:

4.5a   It was about eleven o'clock in the morning, mid October..

4.5b   Over the entrance doors . . . there was a broad stained-glass panel showing a knight in dark armour . . .

4.5c   There were French doors at the back of the hall . . .

4.5d   Beyond the garage Ø [there] were some decorative trees trimmed as carefully as poodle dogs.

4.5e   Beyond them Ø Ø [there was] a large greenhouse with a domed roof.

Many of the others are what Halliday terms Carrier-Attribute structures (Halliday 1994), which are structures in which (as Halliday's label implies) characteristics are attributed to someone, something or some concept.

4.5f   I was neat, clean, shaved and sober

4.5g   I was everything the well-dressed private detective ought to be

4.5h   The main hallway of the Sternwood place was two stories high

4.5i   Large hard chairs with rounded red plush seats were backed into the vacant spaces of the wall . . .

4.5j   The portrait was a stiffly posed job of an officer in full regimentals . . .

The point here is that discourse decisions have grammatical implications, and of course conversely every grammatical decision has potential discourse implications. Here and elsewhere in the book we will repeatedly find that patterns of text organisation are grounded in the detail of the text. Discourse description that does not engage with this detail is not truly linguistics – it may be literary, semiotic or rhetorical and have a value in such terms, but the linguistic description of text/discourse, as well as developing its own categories, must also engage with the categories of other levels of linguistic description. This is of course one reason why text is an important subject for the language teacher. To take just one rather mundane illustration, if the kinds of grammatical structures associated with description need to be practised, Settings may serve as a natural context in which to get the learner to encounter or practise writing them.

Returning now to the 'firing squad' joke, we can see that there is indeed a Setting, though its extent might be a matter of dispute. Certainly the first clause conforms entirely to what we expect. As noted earlier, it is an existential process and it provides us with identification of the three major participants. The next clause provides us with event information that we need to understand the joke.

There are two available analyses of this sentence. The first would be to say that the Setting comprises the existential clause only; this would make the second clause the first brief episode. The second would be to treat the event clause as part of the Setting, in that it provides preliminary and summarised events rather than full events. Emmott (1997) takes care to distinguish events that are described in some detail from events that have a summary status only, and associates the latter with the Setting function. Both analyses capture a truth about the story, but the latter is neater and accounts for the lack of obvious episode markers at the beginning of what was earlier labelled episode 1. If we follow the second analytical path, the organisation of the joke can be represented as in Figure 4.5.

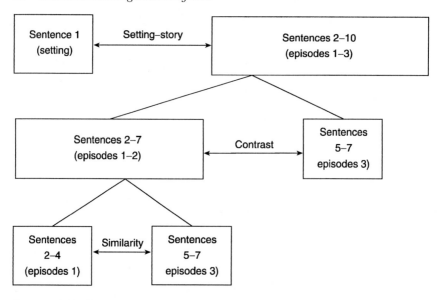

Figure 4.5 Fuller hierarchical description of a joke.

A more complicated example: a first visit to *Goldilocks and the Three Bears*

Thus far, we have been considering very short texts, the hierarchical organisations of which have been quite simple. It is time to look at a slightly more complex narrative, namely *Goldilocks and the Three Bears*. There are very many tellings of this traditional folk-tale and, unlike some folk-tales (*Red Riding Hood*, for example), they do not differ much. The telling I have chosen is that by Vera Southgate and is found below as 4.6; I shall repeatedly return to it in the course of the book.

4.6 (1) Once upon a time there were three bears who lived in a little house in a wood. (2) Father Bear was a very big bear. (3) Mother Bear was a medium-sized bear. (4) Baby Bear was just a tiny, little bear.

(5) One morning, Mother Bear cooked some porridge for breakfast. (6) She put it into three bowls. (7) There was a very big bowl for Father Bear, a medium-sized bowl for Mother Bear and a tiny, little bowl for Baby Bear.

(8) The porridge was rather hot, so the three bears went for a walk in the wood, while it cooled.

(9) Now at the edge of the wood, in another little house, there lived a little girl. (10) Her golden hair was so long that she could sit on it. (11) She was called Goldilocks.

(12) On that very same morning, before breakfast, Goldilocks went for a walk in the wood.

(13) Soon Goldilocks came to the little house where the three bears lived.

(14) The door was open and she peeped inside. (15) No-one was there so she walked in.

(16) Goldilocks saw the three bowls of porridge and the three spoons on the table. (17) The porridge smelt good, and Goldilocks was hungry because she had not had her breakfast.

(18) Goldilocks picked up the very big spoon and tasted the porridge in the very big bowl. (19) It was too hot!

(20) Then she picked up the medium-sized spoon and tasted the porridge in the medium-sized bowl. (21) It was lumpy!

(22) Then she picked up the tiny, little spoon and tasted the porridge in the tiny, little bowl. (23) It was just right!

(24) Soon she had eaten it all up!

(25) Then Goldilocks saw three chairs: a very big chair, a medium-sized chair and a tiny, little chair.

(26) She sat in the very big chair. (27) It was too high!

(28) She sat in the medium-sized chair. (29) It was too hard!

(30) Then she sat in the tiny, little chair. (31) It was just right!

(32) But was the tiny, little chair just right? (33) No! (34) Goldilocks was rather too heavy for it. (35) The seat began to crack and then it broke.

(36) Oh dear! (37) Goldilocks had broken the tiny, little chair and she was so sorry.

(38) Next Goldilocks went into the bedroom. (39) There she saw three beds; a very big bed, a medium-sized bed and a tiny, little bed.

(40) She felt tired and thought she would like to sleep.

(41) So Goldilocks climbed up onto the very big bed. (42) It was too hard!

(43) Then she climbed up onto the medium-sized bed. (44) It was too soft!

(45) Then Goldilocks lay down on the tiny, little bed. (46) It was just right!

(47) Soon she was fast asleep.

(48) Soon the three bears came home for breakfast.

(49) Father Bear looked at his very big porridge bowl and said in a very loud voice, 'Who has been eating *my* porridge?'

(50) Mother Bear looked at her medium-sized porridge bowl and said in a medium-sized voice, 'Who has been eating *my* porridge?'

(51) Baby Bear looked at his tiny, little porridge bowl and said in a tiny, little voice, 'Who has been eating *my* porridge and eaten it all up?'

(52) Next Father Bear looked at his very big chair. (53) 'Who has been sitting in *my* chair?' he asked in a very loud voice.

(54) Then Mother Bear looked at her medium-sized chair. (55) 'Who has been sitting in *my* chair?' she asked in a medium-sized voice.

(56) Then Baby Bear looked at his tiny, little chair. (57) 'Who has been sitting in *my* chair and broken it?' he asked in a tiny, little voice.

(58) Next the three bears went into the bedroom. (59) Father Bear looked at his very big bed. (60) 'Who has been lying on *my* bed?' he asked in a very loud voice.

(61) Mother Bear looked at her medium-sized bed. (62) 'Who has been lying on *my* bed?' she asked in a medium-sized voice.

(63) Baby Bear looked at his tiny, little bed.

(64) 'Here she is!' he cried, making his tiny, little voice as loud as he could.

(65) 'Here is the naughty girl who has eaten *my* porridge and broken *my* chair! (65a) Here she is!'

(66) At the sounds of their voices, Goldilocks woke up. (67) When she saw the three bears she jumped off the bed in a fright. (68) She rushed to the window, jumped outside and ran quickly into the wood.

(69) By the time the three bears reached the window, Goldilocks was out of sight. (70) The three bears never saw her again.

We begin by considering one of the episodes within this story, namely that in which Goldilocks steals Baby Bear's porridge. The organisation of this episode is more or less identical to that of the 'firing squad' joke, despite there being no punch-line. Perhaps the most difficult question is where the episode starts. There are two places where the episode might be thought to begin. The first of these occurs at sentence 13, where we have change of time frame ('soon') and change of place ('came to the little house where the three bears lived'). The second occurs at sentence 16. There is a change of place, marked at the end of the previous sentence ('walked in'), and subsequent episodes make use of the same sentence structure (sentences 25 and 39), retrospectively giving it some of the status of clear structural transition. There is also a move from pronoun 'she' in sentence 15 to full name 'Goldilocks' in sentence 16. Although the latter set of signals is less clear than the first, the better analysis is probably to treat the episode as starting at sentence 16, for reasons that will shortly become apparent.

In any case, you will notice that sentences 16–17 have some of the qualities of Setting, despite not being at the beginning of the narrative. We are given details of place as well as an important temporary characteristic of the main protagonist ('Goldilocks was hungry'). This is in fact quite normal. You may have noticed that the signals for episode boundaries and those for Setting largely match:

Setting	**Episode**
(a) identification of time frame	(a) a clear change of time frame
(b) identification of participants	(b) a change in characters referred to
(c) identification of place	(c) a clear change of place

Episodes can be seen as resetting the narrative, adjusting the original settings in accordance with the narrative's needs.

Within the episode there are obvious trigger sentences (sentences 20 and 22), indicating a close match amongst the three sub-episodes 18–19, 20–21 and 22–23. In the first case the match is a match for similarity in that in both cases the porridge is adjudged to be unacceptable (hunger losing out to refinement of palate) and in the second case the match is for contrast. All this can be represented diagrammatically as in Figure 4.6.

This, though, only represents the organisation of a small proportion of the narrative. To begin with, there are two other episodes in which Goldilocks wrecks Baby Bear's chair and sleeps in his bed, each following a very similar pattern to

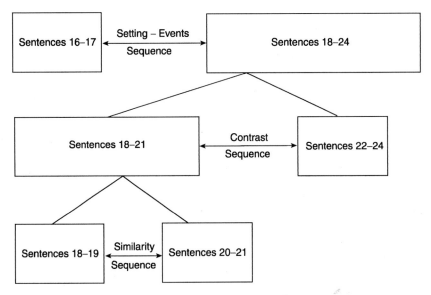

Figure 4.6 Partial hierarchical analysis of *Goldlilocks and the Three Bears*.

that of the porridge theft. The text therefore has an additional layer of organisation as shown in Fig. 4.7. This then is the reason why it seems better to recognise
a break at sentence 16. Sentences 13–15 provide a context for all three episodes
(and indeed beyond), rather than just the first.

Sentences 16–17 have a more local function on the other hand in that they
prepare us for the comparison of the porridges. A similar function is served by
sentence 25 in the 'chair' episode and by sentences 38–40 in the 'bed' episode. The
exact nature of the functions served by these pieces of text will be handled in
Chapters 7 and 8. Sentences 25 and 39 also serve as triggers of the matching
between the episodes. So we now have a structure that can be represented as in
Figure 4.8.

Such a diagram looks truly forbidding, but what it represents is in fact a simple
enough notion. It simply says that sentences 18–19 are very like sentences 20–21 in
structure, meaning and function, and that together these four sentences contrast
with another pair of sentences (s.22–23). The incident that all six sentences
together record occurs in response to a felt need recorded in sentences 16–17. All
eight sentences together describe an incident that turns out to be very like two
other incidents in the narrative (sentences 25–47). The three incidents occur

Figure 4.7 Additional layer of organisation for *Goldilocks and the Three Bears*.

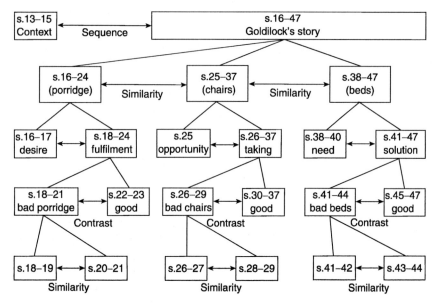

Fig. 4.8 A fuller hierarchical analysis of *Goldilocks and the Three Bears*.

because Goldilocks has put herself in a context where they can happen (sentences 13–15). Put in such terms, the hierarchical organisation of the text is straight-forward enough.

Even all this, though, only represents half the story. We still have sentences 1–11 to account for as well as sentences 48–69. Significantly the great majority of the latter and half of the former tell the bear's side of the tale. There are effectively two stories running in parallel that might be represented as shown in Figure 4.9.

It will be seen from Figure 4.9 that there are relationships across blocks of sentences that no neat hierarchical diagram can do justice to. It *is* an important fact about texts that sentences cluster together to form larger chunks, but it is not the case, as some linguists have argued, that texts can always be comprehensively analysed in terms of their hierarchical organisation.

A return to *Death and the Compass*

We saw in Chapter 3 that Borges exploited the interactivity of text to mislead his readers into believing that they are reading a detective story of a rather con-ventional kind, when the story is in fact the account of an elaborate trap designed to catch a detective who trusts too much in his own ingenuity. At the heart of this trap is a succession of murders or apparent murders which appear to have a great deal in common. It is Lönnrot's folly in detecting the symmetries among these incidents that leads to his downfall. This folly would not be interesting – or at least less interesting – if we did not share in it as readers. Like Lönnrot we see symmetries among the episodes and therefore go along with the inferences he

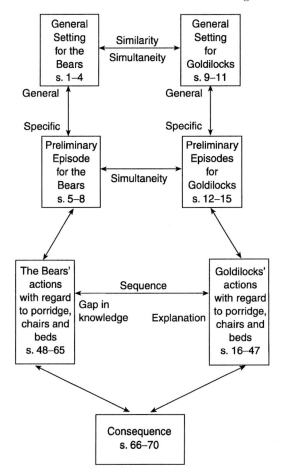

Figure 4.9 Another way of representing the hierarchical analysis of *Goldilocks and the Three Bears*.

draws about the possible explanations. We attempt to interpret what we are reading as having a hierarchical organisation including four 'chunks' of equal status (Figure 4.10).

The recognition of symmetries is encouraged by the kind of parallelism noted in Chapter 2. There are other parallels drawn out by Borges, e.g.

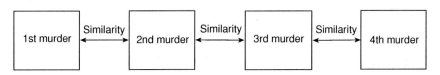

Figure 4.10 The reader's perception of the organisation of *Death and the Compass*.

4.7   (1st murder) One of the agents had found in the small typewriter a piece of paper on which was written the following unfinished sentence: '*The first letter of the Name has been uttered*'

4.8   (2nd murder) The words in chalk were the following: '*The second letter of the Name has been uttered*'

4.9   (3rd 'murder') Treviranus saw the sentence. It was virtually predictable. It said: '*The last of the letters of the Name has been uttered*'

(italics in every case in the original)

Another, slightly more subtle, symmetry is the following:

4.10   (2nd murder) On the wall, across the yellow and red diamonds, were some words written in chalk.

4.11   (3rd 'murder') He walked – tall and dizzy – in the middle, between the masked harlequins. (One of the women at the bar remembered the yellow, red and green diamonds.)

4.12   (4th murder) The early evening moon shone through the diamonds of the window; they were yellow, red and green.

There are other symmetries too: Treviranus is present at three of the murder locations; three of the murders involve stabbing (either real or fabricated); three of the victims (imaginary or real) are Jewish. But notice that the symmetries always involve three, not four, of the murders. In fact Borges has constructed a textual 'impossible object' in which a different set of contrasts come to view, depending on which points of similarity and difference one chooses to focus on.

First we note that, once we have read the story, the first chunk is different from the others in that it is the only unplanned murder and there are in consequence no diamond shapes of red, yellow and green. According to this perspective, then, the story has the organisation shown in Figure 4.11.

In some respects, though, it is the second murder 'chunk' that stands out from the others. It is a briefly told murder, taking up only one paragraph, compared with approximately ten for the first, eight for the second, and twenty-one for the last. I say 'approximately' because there are no conventions for counting dialogue paragraphs, and this points to a second difference between the second murder and the other three: there is no speech reported in connection with the second murder. Finally, the setting of the second murder is outdoors; the other three all take place indoors. So perhaps the organisation should be represented as in Figure 4.12.

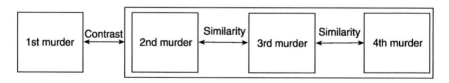

Figure 4.11 Another view of the organisation of *Death and the Compass*.

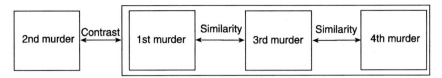

Figure 4.12 A third view of the organisation of *Death and the Compass.*

In many respects the fourth murder is most markedly different from its predecessors. Indeed there are so many differences that one has to remind ourselves that there was any symmetry to pick up on in the first place (the point of the compass and the diamond shapes are the most obvious points of similarity). The murder takes place on the 3rd of the month instead of the fourth, the victim is a gentile not a Jew, Treviranus is not involved, there are no signs referring to the letters of the Name and the murder is a shooting, not a stabbing. So, obviously, it would be appropriate to represent the organisation as in Figure 4.13.

But in some senses the most obvious difference is the one least signalled. The third murder is the most obviously different in that it is no murder at all, and for that reason, of course, there is no body. So, naturally, we can also represent the text's organisation as in Figure 4.14.

What Borges has in effect done is force readers to question the pattern-making skills they use in making sense of narrative. What looks as if it is neat and symmetrical is so only because we wilfully choose to overlook as irrelevant the points of difference between the 'chunks'. In other words, Borges is making us doubt the validity of the hierarchies we find in texts; he is saying that the reader who constructs such a hierarchy is, like Lönnrot, in part creating the pattern and not simply observing it. Which is where I came in – with an apology for spending a chapter on a feature of text that represents a partial truth about text (as our analysis of Goldilocks finally showed, as well as that of the Borges' text) and can be over-stressed. For all that, we cannot get far without some notion of hierarchy

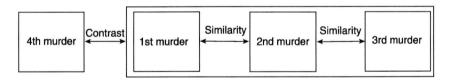

Figure 4.13 A fourth view of the organisation of *Death and the Compass.*

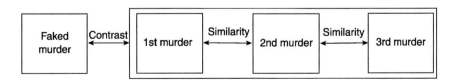

Figure 4.14 A fifth view of the organisation of *Death and the Compass.*

in text, and there are a neglected set of texts for which it is a fundamental feature –
the colony texts; these deserve a chapter of their own, and for *that* chapter I will be
making no apologies.

Bibliographical end-notes

The provenance of the Aesop tale (4.1) has unfortunately been lost. The text was
originally brought to my attention by a B.Phil. student at the University of
Birmingham. I am grateful to her not just because the text suits my argument well
but because it expresses a sentiment close to my heart. The poem (4.3) is 'A Poison
Tree' by William Blake. The joke (4.4) was transcribed by me from a telling by my
son. Passage 4.5 is from the beginning of *The Big Sleep* by Raymond Chandler,
published by Penguin Books. The telling of *Goldilocks and the Three Bears* used here
and given in Example 4.6 is that by Vera Southgate and was published in the
Ladybird series.

Linguists who have placed the hierarchical principle at the heart of their text-
linguistic theories include Graustein and Thiele (1987) and Mann and Thompson
(1986, 1988). Both of these teams of linguists adopt a clause relational approach to
text on the lines described at the end of Chapter 2 and their work is full of insight.
Both, however, at times force the data to fit with the requirements of a strict hierarchical organisation. The story grammarians also adopt a strictly hierarchical
perspective, though their work only claims to describe narratives (consult the
end-notes for Chapter 7 for a fuller bibliography). In Hoey (1983), I analyse a
Detail Tree structured text that challenges a strict hierarchical analysis.

It was Winter (1974, 1979) who first attended to the detail of the way repetition may
create a framework for the presentation of new information. Hoey (1983, 1987) uses
Winter's insights and presents them in the fashion presented here, i.e. in table
form, marking constants and variables, drawing on Fowler (1965). Hoey (1991a)
extends the notions of repetition and replacement by applying the categories to
pairs of sentences where parallelism is not apparent. Shepherd (1988) shows that
one of the less obvious characteristics of narrative is that they make extensive use
of repetition-signalled matching; this claim is supported in part by the narrative
analyses in this chapter.

Episode marking is described in Longacre (1976, 1983, 1989). Marley (1995) and
Darnton (1987a,b, 1998) both use Longacre's categories to valuable effect. Darnton
extends the criteria for identification of episode boundaries further and her work
is drawn on in this chapter. Emmott (1997) approaches narrative from a
psychological perspective; she is in particular concerned with the mental
frameworks a reader builds up and makes use of in the course of reading. She notes
that at what are often termed episode boundaries the narrative is re-set with
regard to characters, place, etc. such that the mental frameworks of the reader
are either de-activated or re-activated.

The grammatical terminology and categories used in this and subsequent chapters is drawn from Halliday (1994). In his introduction to that book (already used as data in Chapter 2!), he notes the importance of linking discourse analysis with grammatical description and warns against the dissociation of the two.

The way narratives begin is discussed in the widely-referenced works of Labov (1972) (with Waletzky 1967) (with Fanshel 1977), in Rumelhart's original story grammar (1975) (in both senses of the word 'original') and, yet again, in Longacre (1976, 1983, 1989) and Darnton (1987a, b, 1998).

My analysis of *Death and the Compass* in this chapter again makes use of Coulthard (1990, 1992). Coulthard's analysis is of the Spanish original; Fairclough (1992b) argues that all such analyses should be of the original language. My excuse here is that I am interested in how English language readers process the text and that Borges made use of a tradition that included English language texts. As will occasionally be apparent, I am familiar with the Spanish text.

5   The organisation of some 'Cinderella' texts

Introduction

One of the side-effects of the use of introspective data in the 1960s and early 1970s was that the invented sentences characteristically reflected not only the linguists' theoretical expectations but also their predilection for fictional narrative. We were frequently regaled with news about the activities of John and Mary but most grammarians neglected to introspect about the language they would use in a shopping list or would encounter in a TV listing magazine, even though it is indisputable that some people make more frequent use of these than they do of fictional texts. The preference of grammarians for fictional narrative as a model for introspected data was no more than a natural consequence of their confident literacy, a literacy that would have been encouraged in early years by fictions written in a style faintly reminiscent of the archetypal John and Mary citation.

Text analysts, by contrast, have for the most part rarely resorted to introspected data for other than passing illustrative purposes, and have also been careful to draw their data from a variety of sources, spoken and written. Thus, although narrative has certainly not been neglected, it has not been the only, or even the dominant, type of text to be subjected to scrutiny. Yet it is still the case that text analysts, like the grammarians they succeeded, have allowed their advanced literacy to affect their choice of data and illustration. The shopping list and the TV listing magazine are no more represented in the pages of text analysis than they were in grammars, and yet, as we saw in Chapter 2, they are as much a product and site of interaction between author and reader as any of the 'archetypal' texts typically used for illustration. Text analysts have developed descriptions designed to account for the interconnectedness of argumentative and narrative prose, without acknowledging the fact that not all texts take the form of continuous prose composed of complete sentences semantically related in respect of their lexis and the propositions they articulate. To take just one example, there is no cohesion (unless collocation is allowed) in a shopping list, yet the shopping list undoubtedly 'functions as a unity with respect to its environment', which Halliday and Hasan (1976) describe as the property from which a text derives texture.

This chapter is concerned with describing the Cinderella texts that get neglected in most text theories. These texts form a relatively homogeneous class and can be described in terms that allow integration with conventional descriptions of 'mainstream' texts; for example, the hierarchical organisation noted for 'mainstream' texts in the last chapter applies with equal force to such Cinderella texts. They are homogeneous in respect of their discourse characteristics but highly heterogeneous in respect of their appearance and use – the class covers a wide range of types of text from shopping lists to statutes, bibliographies to Bibles. To begin with, I shall use the criminal statute to introduce the major features of the class of texts in question, mainly because this genre has received slightly more attention than others within the class.

The criminal statute

The function of the criminal statute is to inform (though there is an implied directive in some cases) and it is composed of complete sentences. But there ends its resemblance to the kind of text that analysts have typically described. For the sentences differ markedly from those one encounters in other types of text (Crystal and Davy 1969), and the sections they combine to form are orthographically distinct from paragraphs; indeed, a statute sentence may itself be divided into paragraphs!

More crucially, from the point of view of this chapter, the sections of a statute are not necessarily coherent with each other. In Chapter 2 we noted that it is part of the sense we make of 'mainstream' texts that we infer relations between adjacent sentences. But there is no necessary connection between the adjacent sections of a statute. Consider sections 5 and 6 of the Badgers Act:

5.1   5. If any person is found committing an offence under section 1 of this Act on any land, it shall be lawful for the owner or occupier of the land, or any servant of the owner or occupier, or any constable, to require that person forthwith to quit such land and also to give his name and address; and if that person on being so required wilfully remains upon the land or refuses to give his full name or address, he shall be guilty of an offence.

6(1) Where after consultation with the Natural Environment Research Council it appears to the Secretary of State necessary for the proper conservation of badgers he may by order declare any area specified in the order to be an area of special protection for badgers.
(2) Any order made under this section shall be made by statutory instrument which shall be subject to annulment in pursuance of a resolution of either House of Parliament and may be varied or revoked by a subsequent order made in like manner.   (Badgers Act 1973)

It is hard to imagine any relation that could be said to hold between these two sections, or any question that might connect them. Furthermore, as it happens in this instance, there are no connections of the kind described in Chapter 3 between the sections such as lexical repetitions or pronouns; they are truly unconnected. This need not be the case of course. Sections are frequently connected by heavy lexical repetition, but it is interesting to note that no other cohesive devices are ever used, unless one counts cross-referencing (Bhatia 1983). Where relations between sections *can* be inferred, there is no tendency for them to occur more frequently between adjacent sentences than between non-adjacent, and sequence relations appear never to occur.

Perhaps more strikingly, whereas jumbling the paragraphs of a 'mainstream' text will result in certain unintelligibility, the effect of jumbling the sections of a criminal statute is surprisingly mild: the text means the same and has approximately the same utility.

The text as 'colony'

The last difference we noted between the criminal statute and the 'mainstream' text provokes an analogy with the natural world. When we try to understand creatures in the world around us, we tend to start from what we know best – ourselves. This anthropocentricity means that we incline towards taking the human as a model for all life-forms. At its most naïve this results in our treating animals as if they were people, but more subtly it affects our perception of what counts as a single creature. We are made up of interconnecting nerves, tissue, bones and so on, and we have a single identity. The nerves, tissue, and so on form recognisable units within the body – organs and limbs, and while most people in the Western world can afford to lose a little fat, the random cut of a limb or an organ has drastic and sometimes fatal consequences. If we are jumbled up, we die.

That these things are true of the human being leads us to suppose that the presence of such features helps define a single living creature. If we consider however the beehive or the ant hill, we may be challenged in such an assumption. In beehives and ant hills, all the individual creatures serve a superior end; it is not the survival of the individual that matters, it is the survival of the colony. (Indeed a bee or ant isolated from its colony has limited powers of survival.) A biologist who seeks to understand a human may choose to do so without extensive reference to other humans, but a biologist who seeks to understand the bee will need to show how the bee behaves and functions in its community. The beehive and ant hill are made up of many independent units, which are not interconnected in a physical sense, and the loss of one or more of them will not affect the viability of the colony. Yet, although we cannot be confident that a hive has a single consciousness, there is a sense in which it functions, and survives, as a single creature with a complex organisation that is, however, social rather than physical.

I have probably been sufficiently unsubtle in my spelling out of the contrast between the two types of 'creature' for the analogy I wish to make to be already transparent. 'Mainstream' texts are like people. They are made up of interconnecting parts and typically have a single author. The interconnecting parts combine to form conventional units (like paragraphs, sections or chapters) and the random excision of one of these will frequently impair and sometimes render unintelligible the text. Like people, if such texts are jumbled up, they die (though, unlike Humpty, they can in some circumstances be put together again).

On the other hand, taking the beehive or ant hill as an alternative metaphor from natural science (and no more), the criminal statute and other such texts might be characterised as *colonies*. Most of the remainder of this chapter will be devoted to exploring the analogy between the hive and the discourse colony.

The definition of a colony

The first step is to determine what will count provisionally as a colony; otherwise the analogy will evaporate as it is explored. What distinguishes the beehive from the human being is the fact that the former's organisation does not depend on its parts being connected in one and only one way: the bees enter the hive in no order. This property of the hive is sufficiently distinctive for it to serve as a working definition of the discourse colony: let us say that *a colony is a discourse whose component parts do not derive their meaning from the sequence in which they are placed.* If the parts are jumbled, the utility may be affected but the meaning remains the same. Thus the criminal statute, as yet our only example of a colony, is composed of sections the legal force of which is not affected by the sequence in which they are placed. Reordering the sections may make crucial points more difficult to find but it will not change the nature of the legislation in any respect, still less will it render the statute meaningless.

What other discourse types conform to the working characterisation just given? The list is on the face alarmingly diverse. It includes shopping lists, letter pages, dictionaries, hymn books, exam papers, concordances, small ads, lonely hearts columns, class lists, bibliographies (to papers), abstracts (in volume form), constitutions, address books, newspapers, encyclopaedias, cookery books, seminar programmes, journals, certain kinds of reference books (e.g. *Films on TV*), footnotes to literary works, telephone directories, the *Book of Proverbs*, TV listings (such as the misleadingly named *Radio Times* in the UK), gardening columns (sometimes), horoscopes (in newspapers), menus, and conference proceedings. A couple of more outlandish examples will be discussed near the end of the chapter.

Three objections might be made to some of the inclusions in the above list. First, it may be pointed out that some of the text types just listed have a very rigid sequence and that if the component parts are shuffled the texts become useless. For example, if one shuffles the entries in a telephone directory, no required number can be located; the same is true of dictionaries, encyclopaedias, and so on. This is of course true, but the working definition of a 'colony' distinguishes *utility* from *meaning*. Jumbling the component parts of a colony may affect the utility of the text – this is even true of the criminal statute to a small degree – but it does not affect the meaning of the text: it still says the same things. The crucial factor is that no component part is dependent on its neighbours for its meaning; the function and meaning of an entry in a telephone directory is obtained from its place in the whole, not its place in a sequence.

The second objection relates to the last point. Several of the putative colonies listed contain groupings the integrity of which needs to be maintained although their components are not strictly sequenced. Examples are hymn books, where the hymns are typically gathered under general headings related to the needs of worship, and newspapers, which boast sports pages, arts pages, foreign news pages, etc. It could be said that the meaning of a sports report is affected by its placement on the sports page rather than the front page. If a report on Parliament were found on the entertainments page, a satirical intention might be suspected.

The answer to this objection is important both as a modification to the somewhat simple sketch of a colony given so far and because it brings colonies in line with 'mainstream' texts. Just as sub-texts may be embedded within larger texts (Chapters 1 and 2) and just as hierarchical organisation is a normal feature of 'mainstream' text (Chapter 4), so embedding occurs in colonies as well and colonies have hierarchical organisation. Whereas, however, a distinction can be made between embedding and hierarchical organisation with regard to mainstream text, the former being a complete text embedded within and extractable from the outer text, and the latter being a matter of the relationship of chunks of text to each other without those chunks being separate, self-standing or extractable, in colony texts the distinction often disappears. A colony may be embedded inside another colony and in so doing a hierarchical organisation is normally created. Thus a newspaper is a colony whose component parts are themselves colonies (sports page, arts page, etc.); these colonies may in turn contain colonies, e.g. the sports page contains football results, and so on. Likewise the hymn book is a colony made up of component colonies relating to Easter, Christmas, and the like.

Embedding can, however, occur in the sense used in Chapters 1 and 2. It will be apparent, for example, that a 'mainstream' text can also be embedded within a colony. A letter to the editor is continuous prose and may be described using normal text analytical systems (Williames 1984), but it functions as a component within a colony. A sports report is similarly amenable to traditional analysis while functioning as a component of a sports page. Statute sections, articles, and encyclopaedia entries are all further clear examples of this kind of embedding.

Less obviously, but in fact nearly as frequently, a colony may be embedded within a 'mainstream' text. The following is a particularly simple instance:

5.2   The numbers sold were given as follows:

Great Britain (in round figs.)	135,150,000
Tangier	81,873
Bahrain	93,689
Kuwait	90,781
Muscat	70,462

As usually happens the printers appear to have started the printing with the serial number '00001' or '000001' and continued up to somewhere between 500,000 and 600,000, but using the three different cylinders more or less at random.
                                                                 (*Gibbons Stamp Monthly*)

The embedded list is a short and uncomplicated colony, the lines of which could be in any order (and seem to be).

The third objection that may be made is that if one re-sequences the stories on a news page, one does more than affect the utility – indeed the utility in this case will not be substantially impaired – rather one affects the emphasis given to certain stories, and it could reasonably be argued that a change in emphasis is in fact a change in what is being said. To the extent that emphasis is part of the meaning, the component parts of a colony do derive their meaning from the sequence in which they are placed, and so the working definition falters. Matters of emphasis are, however, marginal to the meaning of a text; each story in a news page, whatever emphasis it is given, is independent of its neighbours as regards its interpretation. Genuine exceptions are when a series of related stories are placed on the same page, e.g. at a Royal wedding; less obvious cases are when readers are apparently invited to make connections between unrelated items, e.g. tabloid placement of sex stories in juxtaposition with pin-up pictures. It is sufficient to note that this is not the dominant practice in a newspaper and that insofar as it is the case, the newspaper is not behaving like a colony, as it is here being defined.

The properties of a colony

I have devoted some space to dealing with possible objections to the treatment of certain types of texts as colonies but I have not yet described the properties of a colony (apart from that used to set up the category in the first place). Interestingly there appear to be quite a few; I have identified nine. Though all colonies do not manifest all properties, there is a sufficient similarity between types of colony to suggest that the category is not a valueless fiction.

If the first, and defining, property is that bees enter the hive in no order, the second, and corollary, property is that bees normally do not mate. In other words the adjacent units of a colony do not form continuous prose, or at least have no greater tendency to do so than non-adjacent units. This is true even where the components are themselves continuous prose. Thus an encyclopaedia entry for 'aardvark' will not be semantically related to a preceding entry on the town of 'Aarau' in any way.

There are exceptions to this, as has already been noted. Some adjacent sections of a statute are cohesive and can be read as continuous prose, for example:

5.3　1. If, save as permitted by or under this Act, any person wilfully kills, injures or takes, or attempts to kill, injure or take, any badger, he shall be guilty of an offence.

(2) If, save as permitted by or under this Act, any person has in his possession or under his control –

(a) a recently killed badger, or (b) a pelt from a freshly killed badger, he shall, subject to subsection (3) below, be guilty of an offence.

(3) A person shall not be guilty of an offence under subsection (2) above if the killing of the badger concerned was permitted by or under this Act.

2. If any person shall –

(a) cruelly ill-treat any badger, (b) use in the course of killing or taking, or attempting to kill or take any badger, any badger tongs, (c) subject to section 7(3) of this Act, dig for any badger, or (d) use for the purpose of killing or taking any badger any firearm other than a smooth bore weapon of not less than 20 bore or a rifle using ammunition having a muzzle energy of not less than 160 foot-pounds and a bullet weighing not less than 28 grains, he shall be guilty of an offence.   (Badgers Act 1973)

But the important point here is that such juxtaposition is not invariable and equally strong connections exist between non-adjacent sections, for example:

5.4   1. If, save as permitted by or under this Act, any person wilfully kills, injures or takes, or attempts to kill, injure or take any badger, he shall be guilty of an offence.

(2) If, save as permitted by or under this Act, any person has in his possession or under his control –

(a) a recently killed badger, or (b) a pelt from a freshly skinned badger, he shall, subject to subsection (3) below, be guilty of an offence.

(3) A person shall not be guilty of an offence under subsection (2) above if the killing of the badger concerned was permitted by or under this Act.

8. A person shall not be guilty of an offence under this Act by reason only of –

(a) the taking or attempted taking of any badger which had been disabled otherwise than by his act and was taken or to be taken solely for the purpose of tending it;

(b) the killing or attempted killing of any badger which appeared to be so seriously injured or in such a condition that to kill it would be an act of mercy;

(c) the unavoidable killing or injuring of any badger as an incidental result of a lawful action.

Sometimes adjacent components are linked in such a way that it is desirable or necessary to read them together, e.g. Psalms 42 and 43, where the chorus of the latter is only recognisable as being a chorus in conjunction with the former. This is true also of dictionaries. An example is the following entry from *Chambers Universal Learner's Dictionary*.

5.5   **eccentric** (ik'sentrik) *adj.* (of a person, his behaviour *etc.*) odd; unusual: *He is growing more eccentric every day; an eccentric old man; He had an eccentric habit of collecting stray cats* – nc an eccentric person: *Children often laugh at eccentrics* **eccentrically** *adj.*: *She was dressed very eccentrically.*

In this example, the entry for 'eccentrically' omits the definition, which is meant to be derived from the previous entry. To the extent that the entries require to be read together, they are exceptions to the property of colonies that the components do not form continuous prose. As with the statute, however, there are as many relations between non-adjacent components as between adjacent. This is exemplified by the following pair of entries (for 'easy' and 'difficult') from the same dictionary:

5.6   **easy** *adj.* 1 not difficult: *This is an easy job (to do); Those sums were easy.*

> **difficult** *adj.* 1 hard to do or understand; not easy: *He can't do difficult sums; it is a difficult task; It is difficult to know what is the best thing to do.*

Here not only is there the direct parallel of 'not difficult' and 'not easy' but there is even a parallelism between 'easy job' and 'difficult task' and between 'sum . . . easy' and 'difficult sums'. The relations so set up are, I would argue, as strong as any between 'eccentric' and 'eccentrically'.

Sometimes the identification of a relationship between entries may highlight an ideologically striking feature. Compare, for example, the following pair of sub-entries, again for 'man' and 'woman', from the *Collins COBUILD English Dictionary*:

5.7   People sometimes address a man as '**man**' when they are angry or impatient with him (sub-entry 11)

> People sometimes address a woman as '**woman**' when they are ordering her to do something or when they are angry or impatient with her; an offensive use. (sub-entry 8)

There is near identity here – but the small difference is revealing. The clause 'when they are ordering her to do something' reveals that the language is predisposed to allow men to behave towards women in a way that has no exact linguistic parallel for women wishing to behave the same way towards men.

You will recognise that the relationships being identified here between dictionary entries hundreds of pages apart are identical to those described in Chapters 2 and 3 as occurring between adjacent or near-adjacent sentences in mainstream texts.

A third property of colonies is that bees need a hive. In other words, there needs to be a framing context that will provide conditions for the interpretation of the colony or alternatively provide a characterisation of the colony. At first sight it might appear that this is true of all texts, whether colonies or not. The difference is that the framing context of a colony is usually essential for its interpretation in a way that is not normally the case for 'mainstream' texts. A few examples may help to make the point clearer. The prefatory material for a statute is typically as follows:

5.8

Badgers Act 1973
1973 Chapter 57

An Act to prohibit, save as permitted under this Act, the taking, injuring or killing of badgers. *25 July 1973*

> Be it enacted by the Queen's most Excellent Majesty, by and with the advice and consent of the Lords Spiritual and Temporal, and Commons, in this present Parliament assembled, and by the authority of the same, as follows:

Apart from the splendid speech act ('Be it enacted . . .'), the title and prefatory material serve two main functions. Firstly they label the colony as an *Act*, and secondly in the statement of enactment, they provide a crucial context for interpretation of the sections that follow. Without them, one would be forced to interpret the sections as recommendations or predictions rather than as statements of law.

To take another example, the entries in *Collins Dictionary of the English Language* are preceded by a number of pieces of prefatory material necessary to the interpretation of the entries. *Dictionary* labels the colony type: the prefatory material, which includes a list of abbreviations and a pronunciation key, allows one to 'decode' the colony's components correctly. Both sets of prefatory material are metalingual in that they are concerned with the form and purpose of the component parts not with their contents.

We have seen that *Act* and *Dictionary* characterise the text type; we could add 'pronunciation *key*' and '*list* of abbreviations'. In each case the title characterises the form of the text, not the content only. Other examples are '*Encyclopaedia* Britannica', 'Stanley Gibbons Simplified *Catalogue*', 'Thomson Local *Directory*' and '*Journal* of Linguistics'. A dictionary that did not label itself as such is hard to imagine; an Act that did not do so would be impossible under the UK's current legal system, and I would imagine the same is true of most other legal systems. By contrast 'mainstream' texts do not normally have titles that characterise the form of the text in this manner. We do not have 'Macbeth *Play*' or 'Nostromo *Novel*'; the Tudor play by John Heywood, *The Play Called the Four PP*, betrays its early date of composition, while conversely Beckett's *Play* and *Film* betray a later sophistication. The literary essay alone appears exempt from this generalisation, and even here *On Life* is more common than *Essay on Life*; indeed, insofar as the genre still exists, the *On* has gone the way of *Essay*. This need only be compared with the inconceivability of *Badgers* or *Of the English Language* as titles for a statute and dictionary respectively for it to be apparent that the exceptions are more apparent than real.

While some colonies have titles and prefatory material that are designed to aid the interpretation of the colony, others have titles that do not characterise the text type but its provenance and contents:

5.9   **APPLIED ENGLISH LANGUAGE STUDIES UNIT**
POSTGRADUATE STUDENTS 1996/97

5.10   **MERSEYRAIL**
TRAIN TIMES
FROM 27 SEPTEMBER 1998 UNTIL 29 MAY 1999
[map omitted]
NORTHERN LINE

The difference between these content headings and the content description found in the title of, say, a typical scientific paper is that the paper's content may be understood without the title – the title is for purposes of reference (and attraction). The colony's title, however, is necessary for the correct interpretation of the contents. Thus an arbitrary list of names becomes meaningful when we know that they are all registered postgraduate thesis students in a particular discipline. Timetables become useful when one knows where the trains are going. In such cases the component parts relate to one another only via the framing title. In marked contrast the parts of a scientific paper relate to each other independently of the influence of the title.

The framing context will in many instances include not only a label of the text type and/or a basis for its interpretation but also a date of operation or applicability. Thus the Badgers Act is dated 1973, the postgraduate student list, 1996–7, and the Merseyrail timetable, 'from 27 September 1998 until 29 May 1999'. Dictionaries are not dated as a rule but catalogues almost invariably are. For some colonies, the date is the most important part of the framing context. A news item acquires its newsworthiness from appearing on a page that is headed and dated; much the same is true of programme details in TV listings. Examination papers only function as such if prefaced with a title, a date and a rubric, and only if the date in the prefatory material matches the date of reading is the paper operative; and while journal articles themselves may not be dated and numbered, journals always are. This feature of the 'hive' is however not ubiquitous. Indeed the presence of a 'hive' itself is not a universal feature. Some sets of exercises are labelled by the topic they teach, e.g. *Percentages,* rather than by the text form. Shopping lists never have prefatory material unless on a pre-printed pad. Hymn books may have metalingual titles (e.g. *Hymns* Ancient & Modern, *Songs* of Praise) but increasingly often do not (e.g. One Voice); I do not know whether this is also true of the worship songs of other faiths. Bibliographies likewise need neither title nor prefatory material, and the same is true of computer-generated concordances. Classified ads may be labelled but again need not be. But these colonies are in the minority: most have hives.

The fourth property of colonies is in some ways one of the most basic. Human beings and other such organisms have a single consciousness (if not a single author on earth); hives are assumed not to have. In the same way, a 'mainstream' text normally has one or more named authors who take responsibility for the whole text; a colony, on the other hand, either usually has no named writer, the author being some organisation such as British Telecom or Merseyrail, or else has multiple authors who are responsible for components of the text but not for the whole. Editors, like queen bees, control the whole text, but they are never the writers/authors of every component. This feature of colonies is a reflection of the way they are used. It is not important who is responsible for an entry in a telephone directory nor is it significant who drew up a class list, because since we do not need to read the whole of a colony to use a part, each component is in some sense a separate communication. In some cases, as for example with a statute or a constitution, it is important that the document is not seen as emanating from a named individual; in regulatory documents such as these, individual authorship would diminish the text's authority.

The anonymity of many colonies affects the way they are regarded. It has just been noted that statutes and constitutions are given an authority that would not normally be given to a document emanating from a known source. Likewise, people consult dictionaries or encyclopaedias as arbiters of fact and often regard them as offering a final court of appeal. More trivially, it might be argued that 'It says in the newspaper' betokens greater credence than 'so-and-so says'.

Not all colonies share the property of having no named (or multiple) authors. Many cookery books are presented as having a single author, even though the recipes may not be unique to those books. Bibliographies are often named; the writer(s) can, however, only pass on information in such cases. Although major dictionaries are these days inevitably the work of a largely anonymous team, smaller dictionaries are still presented as by named authors, as were the pioneering dictionaries of Dr Johnson and others. Collections of papers may be by a single author, although it is likely that they previously appeared individually in multi-author colonies. Shopping lists are never attributed to an author, but the user knows who he or she is!

The fifth property of colonies is an important one, and has been alluded to briefly in my discussion of the previous point. An individual bee may be separated from the hive. In other words, a component of a colony may be made use of without it being necessary for the user to refer to other components. This is clearly the case with dictionaries, encyclopaedias, cookery books, hymn books, journals, telephone directories and address books, though there may be cross-referencing between components on occasion. At first sight the criminal statute may seem to be an exception to this generalisation, but attention to the way statutes are used in the courtroom confirms that their component sections may be used in isolation.

A number of the colonies are normally scanned prior to close attention being given to an isolated component. If you are looking for your name on a seminar list, you scan until you find it and then note the details. If you wish to purchase a second-hand car, you scan the classified ads until the required model is found; then a rather different reading strategy is adopted. It is normally advised that examination papers should be read *in toto* before any attempt is made at answering, but only selected questions will be answered and those questions will be intelligible independently of the others.

The only marginal exception to the generalisation, which otherwise seems to hold in all cases, is, once again, the shopping list. There is a sense in which one is unlikely to identify just one item on a shopping list to respond to and no other. However, it is also true that one responds to each item on the list as if it were independent of the others and there is no requirement that they be responded to in order – indeed there may be several shops to visit before all items are covered.

The sixth property follows on from the fifth. A bee may join a new hive. Thus an arts report in a newspaper or a paper in a journal may be reprinted in a collection. Addresses may be copied from one address book to another, and bibliographical references taken and re-used. A high proportion of telephone numbers are transferred from one edition of a directory to the next, and a news item or letter to the editor may appear in several editions of a paper and in a weekly review (like the *Guardian Weekly*). Small ads may be re-used in more than one context, and items on one shopping list may be transferred to a new one. However, though this is a common property of colonies, it is not universal. Exam questions do not as a rule reappear in subsequent papers, nor does a class list reappear in a new context.

The seventh property is a corollary of the sixth, though it also characterises colonies for which the sixth does not apply. The population of a hive changes through time. In other words, colonies may have components added, removed, or altered after first publication. Of course many 'mainstream' texts undergo revision too, but in each such case the author has to ensure that the new material is integrated with what surrounds it. In the case of a colony, revision is a mechanical matter and, as long as there is no cross-referencing, new components can be inserted, or old ones removed, without any changes to the surrounding text. This is true of statutes which are subject to amendment or repeal. It is also true of newspapers which go through several editions, encyclopaedias, constitutions (which may be revised piecemeal at every AGM), dictionaries and shopping lists. Some colonies, though, are beyond such revision, e.g. The Book of Proverbs or the Psalms; others have no opportunity for second editions e.g. TV listings, journals, collections of abstracts.

Until now, what has been in focus has been what distinguishes the colony from the 'mainstream' text. It is time to integrate the above description of this new class of texts with that for 'mainstream' texts. In Chapters 2 and 3 the latter kind of text was seen to be typically composed of continuous prose made up of complete sentences. It was also noted there that the way these sentences combine into a single coherent text is by means of semantic relations perceived by readers to be holding among the sentences and among the lexical items of which they are composed. As was discussed in Chapter 2, such relations divide into two broad classes – Matching relations, where statements are considered in respect of what they share or where they differ, and Sequence relations, where statements are seen as following one from the other temporally or logically. 'Mainstream' texts are made up of statements so related.

We now need to look at how these relations apply to colonies. Initially I noted that it is often impossible to infer clause relations between adjacent sections of a statute. This position needs now to be modified slightly. For the eighth property of a colony is that many of the bees serve the same function in the hive. In other words, many of a colony's components serve the same function in the colony. The majority of sections in a criminal statute serve the function of creating offences, the majority of entries in a dictionary serve the function of defining words, and so on. Insofar as they serve the same function, such components can be said to be in a weak Matching relation with each other. This, however, does not contradict the earlier claim that the components of colonies stand independent of each other. In the first place, *all* similarly functioning components are in a Matching relation with each other; in other words, it is in no way important whether they are adjacent or not. In the second place, the relations are weak.

Consider the following two sections from the Badgers Act:

5.11   4. If, save as may be authorised by licence granted under section 9 of this Act, any person marks, or attaches any ring, tag or other marking device to any badger (other than one which is lawfully in his possession by virtue of section 8(2)(a) of this Act or of such a licence) he shall be guilty of an offence.

5. If any person shall be found committing an offence under section 1 of this Act on any land, it shall be lawful for the owner or occupier of the land, or any servant of the owner or occupier, or any constable, to require that person forthwith to quit such land and also to give his name and address; and if that person on being so required wilfully remains upon the land or refuses to give his full name or address, he shall be guilty of an offence.

One might note that something more closely approximating to 'mainstream' text would have been achieved had section 5 immediately followed section 1 (quoted earlier on in Example 5.4). Nevertheless the two sections are indisputably in a Matching similarity relation which might be represented diagrammatically as in Table 5.1.

But this relation is weak; any behaviour could have been inserted in the second column. Urquhart (1978) notes that 'readers seem to operate sometimes on the principle of imposing maximum relevance' (p. 216). He gives as an example the following pair of sentences:

5.12   Children with mongolism are known to have an increased risk of developing leukaemia, a type of cancerous proliferation of white blood cells. The general relationship of chromosomal abnormalities and a tendency to develop cancer is also interesting.

He notes that a reader seeking maximum relevance would identify the first sentence as being in a particular-general relationship with the second, and would

Table 5.1 The matching parallelism of sections 1 and 5 of the Badgers Act, 1973

(1)	If any person	marks etc. any badger	he shall be guilty of an offence
(5)	If any person ...	remains upon land	he shall be guilty of an offence
Constant	If any person	behaves in some way	he shall be guilty of an offence
Variable		nature of behaviour	

therefore 'deduce that children with mongolism suffer from chromosomal deficiencies'. However, another connection might be: 'Sentence 1 is interesting. The general relationship of chromosomal abnormalities is also interesting'. In other words, the two sentences are matched in respect of their offering interesting facts. Urquhart notes that 'it seems likely that many readers, at least, will not be content with such a level of relevance'.

Urquhart's point applies forcefully to colonies. If a colony has a particular purpose and the majority of its components fulfil that purpose, then to say that the components are matched because they fulfil that purpose is to say very little and to be content with minimum rather than maximum relevance. Thus, while it is an important property of the colony that many of the bees serve the same function in the hive, and one which allows us to relate colonies to 'mainstream' texts, it should not lull us into assuming that colonies are really 'mainstream' texts after all or that there is nothing more to be said about them.

A final point needs to be made about the matching of the components of a colony, namely that 'mainstream' text is rarely made up of matching relations only, still less of nothing but matching similarity relations. In this respect also, therefore, colonies are different. They offer the purest and simplest form of 'matching' text, one that would indeed be intolerable for linear reading purposes. Their nearest equivalent among 'mainstream' texts would seem to be the simplest of children's narratives which are built out of nothing but time sequence relations. Colonies and simple narratives might be seen as two extremes, all texts in between being more complex in their combination of Matching and Sequence relations.

The characteristic relations between their propositions is not the only point of contrast between colonies and narratives. Another characteristic of 'mainstream' texts, of course including narratives, is that they are connected by repetition devices – or cohesive links – as discussed in Chapter 3. It is possible to regard such links as partaking of many of the semantic relations that operate between sentences. Thus complex paraphrases in the form of antonyms (e.g. *hot – cold*) are equivalent to Matching contrast relations between clauses, unspecific nouns (e.g. *dormouse – mammal*) are equivalent to Matching particular-general relations, and simple paraphrases (or synonyms) (e.g. *leave – depart*) are equivalent to Matching compatibility relations, while simple repetition and the use of a pronoun mark the ultimate in Matching relations – that of identity. It will be noted though that the equivalence in each case is between a link and a Matching relation; there are no links that could be considered analogous to Sequence relations in the clause relational system. So narratives, a text type characterised by the dominance of Sequence relations, are bound together at the word/phrase level by links that are Matching in kind. A passion for symmetry might therefore lead one to expect that colonies, a text type characterised by the dominance of Matching relations, might be bound together by links that are sequential in kind. But what would a sequential link look like?

When I was defining the colony, I dismissed as irrelevant the fact that jumbling a colony's components might affect its utility though not its meaning. For the purposes of the definition, that was reasonable, but it remains the case that if utility is affected by jumbling, some property of the colony is being lost. That property is what we are now interested in. Most colonies, for the sake of utility, make use of some form of arbitrary or non-arbitrary sequence to make selection, reference, and cross-reference possible.

The two arbitrary systems are alphabetic ordering and numerical ordering; the non-arbitrary system is ordering by time or date. Alphabetic ordering is a feature of dictionaries, concordances, class lists (sometimes), bibliographies, address books, encyclopaedias, and telephone directories, amongst others. It is worth noting that there is nothing natural about the sequence of letters in the alphabet; it is an entirely conventional and arbitrary system and exists almost exclusively for the purpose of making colonies useful. Nor is there any reason why any of the above could not be ordered in some other way than alphabetically by head-word. Rhyming dictionaries are organised by reverse-alphabetical order, crossword dictionaries (in part) by word length, thesauri by a combination of alphabetical and numerical systems. Chinese dictionaries are ordered in terms of the number of strokes involved in writing the characters (a subtle form of numerical sequencing). I have no doubt that the Post Office has telephone directories organised numerically and/or by address (i.e. by a combination of numeric and alphabetic ordering). In any case the holding of such texts in computer files makes multiple access routine.

Numerical ordering is even more arbitrary than the alphabet, for there is at least an orthographic property of the component that is made use of in an alphabetic ordering; numbering on the other hand is attached to components without regard for any formal or content features that they might have. Of course this does not apply to cases where numbering is explicitly linked to priority; such instances are not true colonies. Colonies that use a numerical ordering system include examination papers, exercises, abstracts (in collections), constitutions, hymn books, most shop catalogues, and statutes. Similar to numerical ordering (and often used in combination with it) is what might be termed superimposed alphabetic ordering, i.e. where components are labelled (a), (b), (c) etc. or 1(a), 1(b), 2(a), 2(b), and so on.

Ordering by time or date is less common, and those texts that make use of it are sometimes more marginal as examples of colony than those that make use of alphabetic and numerical ordering. Whereas numerically-ordered colonies may be jumbled and renumbered without change of meaning, temporally-ordered colonies only mean the same thing if the temporal markers are retained along with the component. Examples are seminar programmes, repertory theatre brochures and TV listings (of which more anon). Stamp catalogues combine all three kinds of ordering. Countries are alphabetically ordered, issues are temporally ordered, and stamps within issues are numerically ordered by face value.

A few colonies make use of none of these systems, e.g. shopping lists, newspapers, classified ads, and cookery books. The reasons for this differ from colony to colony. Newspapers and cookery books are both made up of sub-colonies, and these are referred to by page number in an index or list of contents; the index will be returned to below. Classified ads are likewise made up of sub-colonies, which are themselves usually numbered; it is therefore strictly the sub-colonies that make no use of an ordering system rather than the colony as a whole. Shopping lists are normally used at a single go, and the reader is more often than not the author; utility is not therefore affected by a lack of ordering or reference system.

I began my discussion of this property by asking whether there might be a polarity between colonies and narratives, in respect of their use of cohesion, analogous to that in respect of their clause relations. The answer would appear to be 'yes'. It seems reasonable to argue that those colonies that make use of one of the ordering systems just described are using Sequence links. Numerical and temporal ordering can in many cases be regarded as functioning somewhat like conjunctions, some of which are used to signal sequence. But alphabetic ordering cannot be so regarded since it is not added to the components to connect them but makes use of a formal feature of some key words contained within the components. Just as links of the traditional kind encourage readers to make connections within a text and thereby to find it cohesive, so also alphabetic sequence links encourage readers to see units as following one from the other. But they are only cohesive because writer and reader connive in making them so. We do not notice alphabetic sequencing in words unless we are encouraged by other features of the text; there is no intrinsic cohesive relation between alphabetically-ordered words, only a relation created and supported by the context. The same is, in fact, true for the Matching links.

Texts classified according to the properties of a colony

If a representative selection of types of colony is put into tabular form showing which properties they share, we can see which colonies are most central and which less so (see Table 5.2). Some colonies, such as the dictionary and the directory, appear to display all the properties characteristic of colonies. Others, like the shopping list and the letter page, display somewhat fewer; a partial explanation for this may be that they are more likely to be read in their entirety than, say, a dictionary. Some of the properties are more pervasive than others. Thus, in addition to the first, defining, property, all colonies share the corollary property that adjacent units do not form continuous prose. This could therefore function as the defining property as readily as property 1. Indeed if it were to do so, it would eliminate at least one troublesome case. TV listing magazines are colonies made up of colonies which are themselves made out of colonies. At the innermost level, however, i.e. the programme listings for a TV or radio channel for a particular day, the first criterial property is not applicable. It is not possible to jumble the units of a programme listing, because they are still presented (in the UK) in terms of a twelve-hour clock. If a twenty-four hour clock were used, the programme listing would be a typical colony. As it is, we must assume ellipsis of a.m. and p.m. for each half-day. The temporal labelling also gives rise to the possibility of describing the listing in terms of simple Sequence relations. So, for example, the following listing:

5.13   **11.10 Prairie Album**
A woman recalls life on a farm, with the help
of sixties watercolours by Blake James.
Repeat   Subtitled   30133996

11.30 Powerhouse
Political news. With Imran Khan, solicitor
for the family of murder victim Stephen
Lawrence. *Subtitled*   7170

12.0 Sesame Street
Pre-school fun and education   23847
(Channel 4 listings for 9 December in *Radio Times*, 5–11 December 1998)

Table 5.2 Features of different types of colony

Colony feature	1	2	3	4	5	6	7	8	9	Total
Dictionary	+	+	+	+	+	+	+	+	+	9
Encyclopaedia	+	+	+	+	+	+	+	+	+	9
Telephone book	+	+	+	+	+	+	+	+	+	9
Hymn book	+	+	?	+	+	+	+	+	+	8/9
Address book	+	+	+	?	+	+	+	+	+	8/9
Criminal statute	+	+	+	+	+	?	+	+	+	8/9
Abstracts (e.g. LLBA)	+	+	+	+	+	+	−	+	+	8
Newspaper	+	+	+	+	+	+	+	+	−	8
Seminar programme	+	+	+	+	+	−	+	+	+	8
Academic journal	+	+	+	+	+	+	−	+	+	8
Classified adverts	+	+	?	+	+	+	+	+	?	7/9
Class list	+	+	+	+	+	?	+	+	?	7/9
Examination paper	+	+	+	+	+	?	−	+	+	7/8
TV listings	+	+	+	+	+	?	−	+	+	7/8
Bibliography	+	+	−	−	+	+	+	+	+	7
Constitution	+	+	+	+	+	−	+	−	+	7
Concordance	+	+	−	+	+	+	?	?	+	6/8
Cookery book	+	+	+	−	+	+	?	+	−	6/7
Shopping list	+	+	−	?	?	+	+	+	−	5/7
Letters page	+	+	+	+	+	?	−	?	−	5/7

Key to Column Labels and Indicators
1   Meaning not derived from sequence
2   Adjacent units do not form continuous prose
3   There is a framing context
4   No single named writer and/or anon
5   One component may be used without referring to the others
6   Components can be reprinted or reused in subsequent works
7   Components may be added, removed or altered
8   Many of the components serve the same function
9   Alphabetic, numeric or temporal sequencing.
+/−   indicates whether a colony has this property
?   indicates that it is arguable whether a colony has this property or that a colony may not always have
     the property.

could be clumsily converted into prose, thus:

5.13a   At 11.10 we have Prairie Album, in which a woman recalls life on a farm, with the help of sixties watercolours by Blake James. This is a repeat and is subtitled; the computer code for video recorders is 30133996. After Prairie Album, at 11.30 we have Power House, a programme of political news, featuring Imran Khan, solicitor for the family of murder victim Stephen Lawrence. This is also subtitled and the computer code this time is 7170. Following these programmes is Sesame Street at midday, offering pre-school fun and education; the computer code for this is 23847.

The point is that the marginality of the TV listing is not therefore solely a matter of fixed ordering of components. Nevertheless it should be apparent that it is not necessary to work through the sequence from the beginning to find the programme for a particular time. In use, therefore, a listing programme functions like a colony, and apart from the defining property, it shows all the signs of being a colony, sharing six of the characteristic properties of colonies.

The way colonies are read

Interestingly, all colonies except the shopping list share the property that their individual components may be utilised without regard to the other components; and, as we have already noted, this is true even of the shopping list at any one moment of its use. It is this property that perhaps explains why colonies exist and why also they are of practical interest. Reading can take several forms, and texts have developed in response to these forms. We may read in a quick, even skimming, fashion, noting everything but not taking the trouble to relate what we read back to earlier material, and perceiving only general connections between sentences, and some texts have clearly been written with this in mind, manifesting as they do simple linear organisation; the simplest narratives are of this type. Alternatively we may read with great care relating what we read to all that we have been reading, making careful and precise connections between sentences. This kind of reading, which is necessarily slower and in a sense more specialised, is appropriate to academic writing and literature, both of which assume and have been written to make use of it. A third possible reading strategy, however, is to scan a text with a view to finding the answer to a particular question. For this kind of reading it is not necessary to assimilate surrounding material; the reader seeks to match the lexis of his/her question to the lexis of the text and only attempts to comprehend if a sufficient match is achieved to give rise to the hope that the question may be answered. Colonies, I suggest, have largely arisen in response to this reading strategy: they are organised so as to allow the reader to select what he or she needs. Interestingly the colony organisation of statutes would appear also to be a way of inhibiting uncooperative readings (Hoey 1985a).

It should not be assumed, however, that there is a one-to-one relationship of reading strategy and text type. It is possible to read literature linearly and seek complex connections in simple narratives. More pertinently, from the point of view of this chapter, we may read a colony linearly or interconnectedly. This is, for example, my normal practice with a collection of short stories, even though they can be read in any order and were in all probability not originally written or published in the sequence in which they appear. In an early episode of the British comedy series *Till Death Us Do Part*, Mrs Garnett is seen reading (and enjoying) a telephone directory – an extreme instance of lack of correlation between reading strategy and text type.

'Mainstream' texts may likewise be read as if they were colonies. We do not have to process and comprehend the whole of a text to find the answer to a question. To facilitate this colony-like use, almost all serious discursive works of book length, including this one, are followed by a short alphabetically ordered colony designed to enable the reader to select from the main text and read handfuls of sentences in isolation as if they were colony components. This colony, known as the index, is an invitation to treat the 'mainstream' text as a colony. To work, however, it requires that the text has the property of numeric ordering in the form of chapter and page numbering, and figure and diagram labelling. It is quite possible that you are reading this mainstream text as if it were a colony. If, for example, you have no interest in teaching or learning English as a foreign language you will probably skip the next section (and might be recommended so to do). The final section you may choose to return to, just in case it is of interest, though its title – 'A footnote' – might, on the other hand, persuade you to leave it as not particularly important to the argument as a whole. (Of course you could be mistaken in this.)

Implications for the language learner

The colony-like exploitation of 'mainstream' texts has certain implications for the testing of reading and writing. It certainly suggests that to test reading as if it were a single skill is to overlook crucial 'colony' skills that need to be acquired along with those associated with linear processing of 'mainstream' text. Paradoxically, though, it is probable that we are over-testing the 'colony' skill, not under-testing it. Whenever we set a comprehension question that can be answered by reference only to the wording of an isolated sentence within a passage without regard for the other sentences, we are in fact testing a 'colony' skill, whether we realise it or not. For the simplest and quickest way of answering such questions is to scan them looking for a match of lexis. There is no harm in this, but it seems desirable that we should know which skill we are testing and not, in reality, test one skill when we believe we are testing another.

For writing, too, there seem to be implications. Some essay markers appear to treat student texts as if they were colonies, checking off the points as they are made without concern for whether they are part of a coherent, developing discussion. In response to this, student texts can be found that seem to be written as colonies: the sentences can be jumbled without great violence to the meaning, since they are largely written as a series of separate points. Whether the texts are produced to meet examiner expectations or the examiners have adjusted their expectations to correspond more closely to the reality is not clear. What is clear is that this phenomenon is not an isolated one. Sutherland (1985) cites student descriptive texts which could be jumbled without loss of meaning; the sentences of these texts are even numbered like colonies! I suspect that parallel examples could be found anywhere in the world where the acquisition of facts, or the production of factual texts, is being tested. Again, there is not necessarily any harm in this as long as colonies do not become the model for all text writing. Also, if we are going to encourage colony production, it would be helpful if this were conscious and wholehearted; what we do not want to elicit are colonies masquerading as 'mainstream' texts.

From the point of view of teaching academic reading, perhaps the most important implication of the 'colony' analysis is that academic textbooks have many of the features of a colony. The sections are often self-standing and are characteristically numbered and they often contain numbered and lettered points; key items are often in bold face or otherwise orthographically singled out. Learner readers may need to be taught to transfer (or develop for the first time) the referencing skills of their first language if they are to make best use of such texts. In particular, they have to break the habit of feeling that they have not read something if their eyes have not passed over every word. The language teacher needs to set tasks that force the student to select, making use of the colony features of the textbook. My own experience has been that there will be resistance in some quarters to this, so deeply ingrained is the belief that only complete reading counts as reading! One task that is worthwhile with those studying English for academic purposes is to give them (part of) a chapter of an appropriate textbook, e.g. a Chemistry secondary school text, and ask them to create a specialist dictionary from it *without* using a pre-existing dictionary. They will normally find that the words in bold are directly or indirectly defined in the course of the chapter – again showing that academic textbooks (apparently mainstream texts) and dictionaries (archetypal colonies) have much in common.

A footnote

One final thought, intriguing or worrying, depending on one's point of view: everything said about colonies applies to two types of entity that one would not normally regard as texts – libraries and computer folders such as *My Documents* on Windows 95. The contents of both may be jumbled with no loss of meaning (though of course there would be massive loss of utility in the case of the library); the components of neither combine to make continuous prose. Both have a hive and both make use of a numerical and/or alphabetical system of ordering. Their components may be transferred to new hives, and are always used independently of all the other components; the majority of components in each hive serve the same function. The hives change through time – new books or files are added, old ones removed. Their authorship is in both cases multiple (though it need not be so for computer files). In other words, the library and the computer folder are almost perfect colonies.

Perhaps, though, this thought should not disturb. The recent history of linguistics suggests that the boundaries of our units should not be protected like barricades. Brazil (1985) has drawn attention to the importance of the 'here and now' in accounting for choices made in conversation. That 'here and now' is not inhibited by formal discourse boundaries; a later conversation may presuppose the whole of an earlier conversation. For some purposes it may be helpful to regard such conversations as two separate discourses; for others it may be productive to see them as one. Likewise, for most purposes, the library is best seen as many discourses, but if it illuminates the nature of an encyclopaedia to regard the library as a single discourse then we should not feel nervous of doing so. Alternatively, we may regard the encyclopaedia as library-like and composed of a multitude of miniature discourses – in other words we may regard the bees as single creatures and the hive as no more than their clubhouse; if then that in turn illuminates the 'mainstream' text such as the university physics textbook, which may never be read in its entirety, may be accessed invariably either through the index or through the contents page, and will hardly ever be read in the order in which it is presented (cf. Roe 1977), then we should be happy to accept the insight. Our discourse boundaries are the product of our theories, not the raw data to be accounted for. Colonies are discourses that bring to the forefront such issues.

Bibliographical end-notes

The basic notion of the colony and its properties was proposed in Hoey (1986c), some of the text of which has been incorporated into this chapter. The application of the notion to statutes can be found in Hoey (1985a, 1988). Shalom (1997) and Marley (2000) have both discussed the properties of lonely hearts columns. Georgakopoulou and Goutsos (1997) discuss colony texts as non-patterned texts.

Shepherd (1993, 1997) shows that certain non-conventional narratives – which she terms 'fringe' narratives – can be successfully analysed using the notion of the colony. The narratives she selects for analysis are the novel *Flaubert's Parrot* and the film *Distant Voices, Still Lives*. In both cases, not only do the elements conform to many of the properties I have assigned to colonies, but there is also the non-adjacent matching I have identified in this chapter as occurring in statutes and dictionaries.

White (1999) proposes a 'solar system' model for news stories that has some of the properties of a colony but crucially has a central, initial statement around which the other elements revolve. This most interesting addition to our ways of discussing text organisation points to the probability that colonies are but the tip of an iceberg.

6 A matrix perspective on text

The structure of a happening and its possible tellings

In the previous four chapters we have seen that texts are interactive and hierarchically organised. In this chapter I will attempt to demonstrate another way of describing the organisation of texts, that continues to emphasise both the interactivity of text and the chunking of text, but views these features in a slightly different way.

In a paper published in 1981, 'Grammar versus Reference in the Analysis of Discourse', Kenneth Pike seeks to distinguish between the structure of a happening and the structure of a telling of that happening. He argues that if we could find a way of describing the structure of a happening separately from its telling, then we might have a way of comparing the kinds of telling that people could use to report the happening. His position can be represented diagrammatically in Figure 6.1. I shall argue against this view of the relationship between happening and telling a little later in the chapter, but for the moment let us notice that Pike's position allows him to develop a fruitful strategy for the description of happenings, one which proves of value in the description of narratives.

Pike suggests that a happening can be represented by means of a matrix, with participants forming one parameter and time bands forming the other. This is best illustrated using Pike's own example. He imagines a world in which three participants, Abe, Bill and Clara, go about their business in the same town on the same day and cross paths. The cumulative happening of their day (or part of it) can be represented in matrix form as in Table 6.1. I have modified Pike's method of representation slightly but the example remains his in every other way (including the unfortunate gender stereotyping). The horizontal parameter

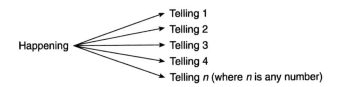

Figure 6.1 The relationship of happening and possible tellings according to Pike (1981).

Table 6.1 The structure of a 'happening' concerning Abe, Bill and Clara

	A	B	C
1	Abe went downtown to work	Bill left his office on an errand in the city	Clara went downtown to shop
2	He met Bill	He met Abe	She shopped
3	He had lunch with Bill	He had lunch with Abe	She shopped
4	Seeing Clara go past, he invited her to join them but she declined, saying that she felt ill.	He watched as Clara walked past, Abe invited her to join them and she refused.	She glanced up as she walked past and saw her good friend Abe with that horrible man Bill. She pretended to be ill and left hurriedly.

represents the participants A, B and C; the vertical parameter represents the time stream arbitrarily broken up into time bands. What we have then is a matrix with twelve cells, with labels for the cells derived from the participants and time bands (Figure 6.2).

It should be obvious that a similar matrix could be constructed for any other set of events as long as we are prepared to accept the premise that happenings exist prior to tellings. Pike makes the point that any telling of this happening can be seen as tracing a path through the matrix. Consider, for instance, the following possible telling; cell labels have been added for reasons that will become immediately apparent:

6.1   (A1) When Abe set out to work that morning he little knew how eventful it would prove. (B1) Unbeknown to him his old friend Bill whom he had not seen for years had just left his office on an errand in the city and was as a consequence in the neighbourhood. (A2/B2) Within a short time they bumped into each other. Their meeting like that was an amazing coincidence (A3/B3) and they both agreed it had to be celebrated in style – with a good lunch. (A4) Abe thought it was his lucky day because while they were eating another good friend, Clara, passed near their table. Of course Abe immediately called over to her and invited her to join them but she just looked disconcerted, made some excuse about feeling unwell and left. (B4) Bill had watched in dumb embarrassment as all this happened, guessing only too accurately her real reason for declining. (C1, C2, C3) Poor Clara had gone out shopping about the time that Abe and Bill had set out on their respective journeys. (C4) She had been looking at the window displays when suddenly she had seen her good friend Abe sitting alongside Bill, one of her least favourite people in the world. His presence had meant that when Abe had invited her to join them she had made an excuse about feeling unwell and had left in a hurry. So it all ended in a mess with (A4) Abe puzzled at his friend's apparent rudeness, (B4) Bill deeply embarrassed at the encounter with his old girlfriend Clara and (C4) Clara mortified at having apparently snubbed Abe.

This telling is unlikely to win me a Nobel prize for literature, but it will be seen that the path I have taken through the matrix is that represented in Figure 6.3, where the arrows represent the order in which events are reported in the story. It will be noticed that certain cells are passed through twice. All the bottom row cells occur twice in my telling, first as event and then as summary.

The diagrammatic representation given above is too messy to be transferable to the matrices of more complex happenings or, as we shall see, to more complex tellings of this happening. A more elegant representation of the path shown in Fig. 6.3 is that given in Fig. 6.4. Such a diagram takes a moment or two to get used to, but once the principle underpinning it is understood it becomes easier to read than the earlier web-like one.

This and subsequent diagrams seek to preserve some of the features of the matrix of which they are derivations. They should be read, like normal texts, horizontally and then downwards. So in this case the path that the telling takes is one that moves horizontally across and down the first two vertical columns and then down the third column separately. How this works can be seen by

	Abe	Bill	Clara
Time band 1	A1	B1	C1
Time band 2	A2	B2	C2
Time band 3	A3	B3	C3
Time band 4	A4	B4	C4

Figure 6.2 An abstract representation of Table 6.1.

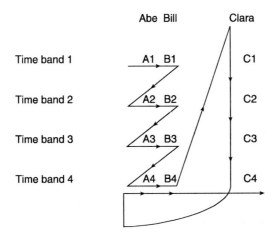

Figure 6.3 The route through the matrix taken by Example 6.1.

Abe	Bill	Clara
AI	B1	
A2/B2		
A3/B3		
A4	B4	
		C1
		C2
		C3
		C4

Figure 6.4 An alternative representation of the path taken by Example 6.1.

matching the diagram with Example 6.1. The symbol '/' indicates that it is impossible to separate the telling of two cells of the matrix.

Clearly, the telling I have just given is far from the only possibility. Another, as Pike points out, is to tell the story in flashback fashion. This might produce the following version:

6.2   Abe couldn't understand it. There he had been at lunch with his good friend Bill when Clara had gone past. Normally Clara seemed to welcome his company but today for some reason she had rejected his invitation, rather churlishly as it seemed to him, making some transparent excuse about a headache. Goodness knows what Bill had thought of it all. Poor Clara! She had not meant to upset Abe but she couldn't have stood a whole lunchtime with that detestable man Bill. All in all it was a terrible mess. And yet the day had started well enough. Around about the same time Abe had set out for work, Bill had gone out on an office errand and Clara had set out on a shopping trip. Within a short time Abe and Bill met and at that stage of course the day seemed destined to be a good one. Little did they know as they greeted each other that embarrassment in the form of Clara lurked nearby, blissfully unaware as she window-shopped of the difficult situation she was soon to face. Abe and Bill went off to have lunch together in the very shopping precinct where Clara was shopping. Once that happened, there was no avoiding the confrontation. It's funny – you can never predict these things!

Figure 6.5 is a matrix analysis showing how this might look. The path for this telling moves horizontally across the bottom row of the matrix and then passes across and down the first three rows.

Clearly there are a large number of possible tellings for this happening. First, and fairly obviously, one could choose to omit some of the cells of the matrix. It

A4	(B4)	C4
A1	B1	C1
A2/B2		C2
A3/B3		C3

Figure 6.5 A matrix analysis of Example 6.2.

B2/A2
B1 A1

Figure 6.6 A representation of the path taken by Example 6.3.

would be possible, for example, to tell the happening by passing down just one of the columns. This would give one of the characters privileged status but would deny the narrator omniscience in the telling. Alternatively, one could start, as so many narratives do these days, *in media res*, as in the (partial) telling below:

6.3   'Bill, my old mate! How are you?' Abe's hand shot out to shake the hand of his startled friend.
      'What are you doing here?'
      'Well, I'd just popped out of the office on an errand for my boss.'
      'What a coincidence! I was just off to work'. . .

This telling takes the path shown in Figure 6.6 through the matrix. Presumably a full telling would have then continued A3/B3 A4 B4 (C4).

Pike (1981) gives tellings of his own and demonstrates other possible paths through the matrix. He also attempts to associate certain of these paths with the rhetorical preferences of particular cultures. This would seem a productive line of enquiry, though it is not one that will be pursued in this chapter. Clearly, though, learners of English coming from cultures whose characteristic paths through the matrix would be different from those most normal for English speaking cultures may on occasion find narratives hard to follow. More seriously, they may provide tellings that seem awkward to their readers/listeners.

Perhaps the most striking claim Pike makes is that any path through the matrix is possible. In support, he offers a telling that appears to follow a random path but still ends up as an acceptable text. It is hard to put that claim to the test convincingly in writing, because I could have carefully selected any 'random' sequence to illustrate the point I wish to make. Nevertheless, if you will take me on good faith, the following is a random sequence of matrix labels.

C4 C1 B4 A3 A4 B2 B1 B3 C2 A2 C3 A1.

In order to create a narrative out of such a sequence one needs to use a combination of evaluation and character introspection to achieve a measure of coherence. Here is my attempt to produce a narrative from this sequence. (I have added cell labels to the narrative so that you can test the adequacy of my telling.)

6.4   (C4) Poor Clara! She was mortified by what had just happened. She had been walking past a restaurant in the main shopping precinct of Liverpool when her good friend Abe had called to her from one of the tables and invited her to join him for lunch. She normally would have accepted with alacrity but unfortunately on this occasion Abe was not alone – he had his old school-friend Bill with him, and Bill was just about her least favourite person on Earth. She had hurriedly made an excuse about having a headache and left, but she feared that she had hurt and puzzled Abe. She cursed inwardly. (C1) If only she hadn't set out for the shops that morning, none of this would have happened. (B4) Bill of course had known only too well what her real motive had been and had sat there looking very embarrassed as Abe's invitation had been turned down.

I said poor Clara! but perhaps I should have said poor Abe! Abe, (A3) who up to that point had been having a delightful lunch with Bill, (A4) had absolutely no idea why Clara had refused. When he'd seen her passing the table where they were eating, it had seemed the natural thing to do to invite her to join him and Bill. (B2) Bill had bumped into Abe (B1) shortly after setting out on an errand in the city and (B3) had agreed readily to his proposal that they have lunch together. Perhaps if Abe had known about Clara's aversion for Bill and (C2) that Clara was out shopping, he would have felt less delighted at the coincidence of (A2) his having met Bill like that in the middle of the street. But he didn't know about Clara's aversion and in any case how could he have guessed (C3) that Clara would shop in the very precinct where the restaurant was? (A1) Perhaps he would never have left for work in the morning if he had known what would befall.

To sum up, then, there would appear in principle no impossible path through the matrix, as long as the route chosen is motivated by evaluation and internal meditation on events. It should be added, though, that the size of the matrix and the corresponding number of cells to be connected place practical limitations upon the truth of this claim. A detailed matrix derived from *War and Peace* with its dozens of participant columns and thousands of time bands would certainly not permit a random path through the matrix, though a cruder and simpler matrix of the same novel, with fewer and broader time bands and only the major participants represented, might. However for such a possibility to be considered possible, we must re-examine the nature of the matrix.

The matrix as a kind of telling

We have seen how Pike has attempted to account for the potential 'tellings' of a happening by representing the happening as a matrix and representing tellings as paths taken through the matrix. As was noted, however, this relies on the assumption that it is possible to capture the structure of a happening through a matrix, an assumption that is open to serious question. The first problem is that many narratives have no happening behind them; they are fictitious. Yet the way a fictitious narrative is told need not be different from the way a factual narrative is told; Truman Capote's *In Cold Blood*, a factual account of a murder and its aftermath, reads like fiction, while Defoe's fictional *Moll Flanders* has some of the properties of autobiography.

The second problem is more fundamental. This is that there is no reason to believe that happenings have any kind of structure or indeed even that there are objectively defined phenomena that can be called 'happenings' at all. When in 1990 Mrs Thatcher resigned as Prime Minister of the United Kingdom, British papers were full of the story. Whole pages were devoted to relaying the minutiae of the events of the day. Her resignation was the happening. By the end of the decade, however, as historians looked back on British politics in the twentieth century, her resignation had become just a single chapter in a larger story; her period in power as Prime Minister had become the 'happening' and her resignation an event within that 'happening'. By the end of the next millennium, however, Britain will itself perhaps be no more than a single 'happening' in a world story and Mrs Thatcher will have done well if her period of power constitutes even a single event within that story. In other words, a 'happening' may be general or particular, large or small. It only exists because someone thinks it is tellable and the particularity of the events are likewise dependent upon this tellability; its structure is the product of selections made by a potential teller.

All this does not mean, though, that Pike's matrix has to be dismissed as unusable. Both the problems we have mentioned disappear if we see the matrix as itself a type of telling – or, more precisely, as the analysis of a telling. We can therefore rescue Pike's idea and indeed make it more useful if we recast Figure 6.1 as Figure 6.7. What this figure is intended to represent is a rather different relationship between alternative tellings. It assumes that a telling always precedes and produces our sense of something being a happening. The telling may be non-linguistic, e.g. film, cartoon strip, or it may exist only inside a potential narrator's mind in the form of evaluations about recent occurrences as potentially tellable. From the telling we may derive a matrix that represents the assumed happening that the telling reports, and this matrix can then be used to generate other tellings that take different routes through the matrix from that taken in the original telling.

Notice that this allows us to compare alternative tellings and to compare the telling we have with the tellings we might have had. If we have alternative tellings, they are presumably mappable onto the same matrix. The two versions can then be compared in terms of different paths taken through the same matrix. If, on the other hand, we have just one version and wish to compare what we have with the other options the author had but chose not to call upon, we can create a matrix from the telling and then investigate what other paths were possible.

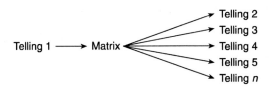

Figure 6.7 A revised representation of the relationships among possible tellings.

The variable precision of matrices

Matrices can vary in the amount of detail they display, as I was hinting in my reference to *War and Peace* above. To illustrate this, let us look again at the Goldilocks story, which (in case you are reading this text non-linearly) is to be found in Example 4.6 (pp. 62–64). It would be possible to create a matrix for *Goldilocks and the Three Bears* with just two participant columns – Goldilocks as one participant and the Bears as a group participant, as the title of the story encourages us to do – and with only a few time frames, as shown in Table 6.2. This is a simple matrix which treats the different vandalistic/thieving actions of Goldilocks as composite events, rather than treating each act of eating, sitting, and lying down as a separate event. A more complex matrix is shown in Table 6.3. Both matrices are correct and accurate, though they are not equally precise. The reason that both are possible is that the 'time spans' in the matrix can be seen as answering the question 'What happened next?' Since this question reflects a relationship between reader and text, the answer can be variably precise and this explains the flexibility of time frames. Likewise the three bears largely function as a unit but Baby Bear has moments that differentiate him from the others; the columns

Table 6.2 A broad matrix analysis of *Goldilocks and the Three Bears*

	Goldilocks	The Three Bears
1	??Goldilocks goes for walk	Mother makes porridge, which is too hot so they all go for walk
2	She comes to the bears' house and enters	They walk
3	She finds and tastes the porridge and eats Baby Bear's porridge	They walk
4	She sees and sits on the bears' chairs, breaking Baby Bear's chair	They walk
5	She sees and lies on the bears' beds, going to sleep in Baby Bear's bed	They walk
6	She sleeps	They return from their walk and discover the porridge eaten
7	She sleeps	They discover that the chairs have been sat upon (!) and that Baby Bear's is broken
8	She wakes up	They discover that the beds have been slept in and that Baby Bear's is still occupied
9	She makes her getaway	They watch her escape

Table 6.3 A fuller matrix analysis of *Goldilocks and the Three Bears*

	Goldilocks	Father Bear	Mother Bea	Baby Bear
1	??Goldilocks goes for walk	Father goes for a walk with Mother and Baby while the porridge cools	Mother makes porridge, which is too hot so they all go for walk	Baby goes for a walk with Mother and Father while the porridge cools
2	She comes to the bears' house and enters	He walks	She walks	He walks
3	She finds and tastes Father Bear's porridge, rejecting it	He walks	She walks	He walks
4	She tastes Mother Bear's porridge, rejecting it	He walks	She walks	He walks
5	She eats Baby Bear's porridge	He walks	She walks	He walks
6	She sees and sits on Father Bear's chair, rejecting it	He walks	She walks	He walks
7	She sits on Mother Bear's chair, rejecting it	He walks	She walks	He walks
8	She sits on and breaks Baby Bear's chair	He walks	She walks	He walks
9	She sees and lies on Father Bear's bed, rejecting it	He walks	She walks	He walks
10	She sees and lies on Mother Bear's bed, rejecting it	He walks	She walks	He walks
11	She goes to sleep in Baby Bear's bed	He walks	She walks	He walks
12	She sleeps	He returns from his walk with his family and discovers his porridge has been tasted	She returns from her walk with her family and discovers her porridge has been tasted	He returns from his walk with his parents and discovers his porridge has been eaten
13	She sleeps	He discovers that his chair has been sat upon (!)	She discovers that her chair has been sat upon (!)	He discovers that his chair has been broken
14	She wakes up	He discovers that his bed has been lain in	She discovers that her bed has been lain in	He discovers that Goldilocks is in his bed
15	She makes her getaway	He watches her escape	She watches her escape	He watches her escape

can therefore number either two or four (though of course the flexibility is very much less great here).

One thing one might notice from Table 6.2 is that there is only one participant present at a time until the very last time frame. Like a one-handed puppeteer, the narrator puts down one participant before picking up the other. So Goldilocks is either walking elsewhere or sleeping while the bears are on stage; the bears are always walking elsewhere when Goldilocks is in focus. This explains, of course, why it is suitable for young children.

From the larger matrix (Table 6.3), one might notice that Father and Mother Bear have identical columns and therefore do not really function separately in the story, and that Baby Bear's column is very similar but has significant differences; in short, it reveals another hierarchical relationship similar to those discussed in Chapter 4, in connection with Fred, Bill and Joe.

The matrix analysis of a newspaper story

So far we have looked at either a fabricated happening (Abe, Bill and Clara) or a folk tale. Now we look at a kind of narrative that usually has a happening behind it, the news story. In the example below I have removed surnames to avoid potential distress to relatives of the victim:

6.5   A market trader was shot dead outside his home yesterday after two men blew up his car and van.

Mr Alex S., aged 34, raced from his home in Hamilton, near Glasgow, Lanarkshire, as the vehicles went up in flames. He chased two men who had placed incendiary devices in the vehicles, causing an explosion which ripped the roof from the van.

One of the men turned and fired a loaded shotgun into his stomach. Mr S., a father of two girls aged 11 and six, staggered towards his home but collapsed before he could reach his door.

A neighbour, Mrs Martha R., said: 'I came out when I heard his wife, Marion, screaming. Alex chased the men, then I heard a shot and he came staggering up the lane clutching his stomach.'

A relative said: 'He was a quiet man who hardly spoke to anyone. We can't understand why this has happened.'

Police are investigating a theory that Mr S. was the victim of a market traders' war.

As before, there are various levels of detail that a matrix might be constructed to reflect. The matrix that I provide in Table 6.4 is reasonably detailed; alternative matrices might well have left out Mrs S. and the police, for example. On the other hand one might have chosen to give a separate column to each of the two men, whereas the matrix below treats them as a single entity. Of course, no matrix can pretend to be an accurate reflection of what happened; matrices are analyses of the narrative, not the reality behind it.

Table 6.4 A matrix analysis of 'market trader' news story

	A (Alex S.)	B (2 men)	C (Mrs Martha R.)	D (Police)	E (Mrs S.)
1		The men placed bombs in Alex S.'s vehicles			
2	Alex S. raced from his home	The cars went up in flames	Mrs Martha R. came out		Mrs S. screamed
3	He chased the men	The men ran off	She watched		
4	He was shot in the stomach	One of the men turned and shot Alex S. with a shotgun	She heard the shot		
5	He staggered towards his home clutching his stomach	They ran off (implied)	She watched Alex S. staggering up the lane		
6	He collapsed and died				
7			She told her story to reporters (implied)	The police began investigating	

Certain features of this new kind of matrix are different from the 'Abe, Bill and Clara' matrix considered above. To begin with, there are empty cells. If the narrator neglects to tell us what a character was doing, either through ignorance or because s/he does not know, then the analyst can only follow suit. Second, some cells contain actions that have to be inferred. Third, the final cell in Alex S.'s column is blocked out to indicate that, for him, the time stream stops.

We have demonstrated that it is possible to create a matrix for a newspaper text like this, but do we learn anything from it? I think the answer will vary from text to text, but with regard to this text we learn something about the redundancy it contains, its character as newspaper writing, and its relation as narrative to possible fictional tellings.

The text displays several kinds of redundancy. The first becomes visible if we consider the path the text takes through its own matrix (Figure 6.8). It will be seen that several cells appear more than once in the path taken by the news story. In the

Alex S.	2 men	Mrs Martha R	Police	Mrs S
A4/A6				
	B1/B2			
A2	B2			
A3				
	B1			
	B2			
	B4			
A5				
A6				
		C2		E2
A3				
		C4		
A5				
			D7	

Figure 6.8 The path through the matrix taken by the 'market trader' news story.

A column A3, A5 and A6 all appear twice. The same redundancy is apparent in the B column: Bl appears twice and B2 three times. Since A4 is readily derivable from B4, this means that in convoluted fashion the story of Alex S.'s murder has been told twice. This corresponds to one's intuition that newspapers often stretch a story by repeating it with variation. It would be possible to investigate the patterns of repetition more fully with the help of the matrix. It would also be possible to compare different newspapers' matrices from the point of view both of which cells they chose to repeat and of which cells they chose to keep empty. Neither of these possibilities is, however, taken up here.

A second kind of redundancy concerns column C. It is informative to construct a telling that arises from reading the columns horizontally, omitting no information available in the cells. The following represents my attempt at providing such a telling. As with earlier examples, I have left the cell labels in so that it is possible to see on what basis I constructed my telling.

6.6   (Al) Unbeknown to Alex S., (Bl) two men placed incendiary devices in his vehicles, causing an explosion which ripped the roof from the van. (A2) Mr S. raced from his home (B2) as the vehicles went up in flames. (C2) Mrs Martha R. came out when she heard (D2) his wife, Marion, screaming. (A3) Mr S. chased the two men (B3) who were running off; (C3) Mrs R. watched all this happening. (B4/A4) One of the men turned and fired a loaded shotgun into Alex's stomach. (C4) Mrs R. heard the shot. (A5) Mr S. staggered towards his home (B5) while the men made their getaway. (C5) Mrs R. watched him come staggering up the lane clutching his stomach. (A6) He collapsed and died (?) before he could reach his door. (C7) Mrs R. told her story to the reporters. (D7) Police are investigating a theory that Mr S. was the victim of a market traders' war.

In this telling, which uses a simple path through the matrix, it will presumably be apparent that Mrs R. stands out as an unnecessary character in the story. Were it a fiction, one would be entitled to start inferring that she is a busybody, poking her nose into other people's business, but unwilling to lend a hand when it is most needed. Such inferences would be reasonable on the evidence because in the above telling her 'cells' are not needed. She is superfluous to the story. But this is not a fictional text and such inferences would in fact be strikingly unjust. If we look again at the path taken by the original news report we see that the sequence that includes Mrs R.'s actions is as follows

C2 E2 A3 C4 A5

It will be noticed that the repetition of cells A3 and A5 occurs in the environment of the C cells. The reason is, of course, that the story is being told a second time in Mrs R.'s own words. And that suggests why it would be unjust to draw unkind inferences about her character from her presence in the story: she is in fact a major source of the story. Once one recognises that, one can see that it is the first half of the story that is redundant, not the second. Furthermore, one realises that one has been ascribing to the narrator the same omniscience that one is used to ascribing to fictional narrators. We are inclined to assume that the narrator is in control in the same way that a fictional narrator is. But the reporter is, in reality, not entitled to have transferred to him or her the same authorial status as we readily ascribe to Dickens or Homer. Examining the matrix of a news report can therefore allow one to discover, through the redundancy, where the news came from.

A fictional telling of this 'happening' might have taken a number of routes through the matrix. It is likely that the repetitions so characteristic of news reporting would have disappeared and that the time sequence would have been straightened out. (I am not here considering some of the more adventurous kinds of telling; clearly writers like Nabokov and Julian Barnes take exceedingly unusual routes through matrices on occasion.) Perhaps more significantly the cell A1 would almost certainly have been filled just as Mrs R.'s whole column of cells would in all likelihood have been emptied. In other words a fictional telling would not only take a characteristically different route but it would characteristically utilise a different selection of material from the matrix. The point being made here is that genre is in part a reflection of choices of ordering, though without the implication that something existed prior to the telling that was waiting to be ordered.

A matrix perspective on *Death and the Compass*

The relationship between genre and path through the matrix exists for literary genres as well as non-literary ones. As an illustration of the way this can on occasion be illuminating, let us consider once again Borges' story *Death and the Compass*, a summary of which will be found on pages 46–47, for those readers who are taking a non-linear route through the text (or have short memories). An analysis of this story is given as Table 6.5.

The matrix in Table 6.5 is simplified in some respects. There are no columns for the murder victims or the newspaper editor, and the time bands are crude in

Table 6.5 A matrix analysis of *Death and the Compass*

	L (Lönnrot)	RS (Red Scharlach)	T (Treviranus)
1	Lönnrot wounds Scharlach	Red Scharlach is wounded but escapes	
2		RS plots revenge	
3		One of his men kills Yarmolinsky by accident	
4	L investigates the murder and finds words in a typewriter; he therefore looks for a solution involving the name of God		Treviranus investigates the murder and guesses the true cause of death
5	L is interviewed by a newspaper editor		
6		RS reads the interview	
7		RS kills the man who killed Yarmolinsky so as to create the illusion of a symbolic pattern	
8	L investigates the second murder and sees a pattern		T investigates the second murder
9		RS fakes a third death so as to continue the illusion of a symbolic pattern	
10	L investigates the apparent murder and sees a pattern		T investigates the apparent murder and guesses that the death is a fake
11	L is sent a map by T	RS sends a map to T	T receives the map which he forwards to L
12	L goes to a place where he has inferred from the map that a fourth murder will take place		
13	L discovers the truth of RS's plot and is killed	RS reveals the truth to L and then kills him	

places. (We will be re-looking at the time bands in the next section where some justification for the simplifications introduced here will be offered.) I hope, though, that the analysis does no serious violence to the underlying structure of the 'happening' that Borges purports to report.

A chapter might fruitfully have been devoted to considering the possible tellings that Table 6.5 could generate. The path actually taken by Borges is roughly as shown in Figure 6.9. As before, the slash between T4/L4 and T10/L10 indicates that there is no useful sense in which the telling of these cells of the matrix can be separated. What Figure 6.9 tells us is that the telling begins by passing down columns T and L, omitting only L1 of column L but ignoring column RS entirely, until almost the end of the 'happening' that Borges' story purports to tell; the story is then told a second time from the very beginning this time passing down column RS. This is the classic detective story structure. A murder is detected, and the story is then told through the eyes of the detective and/or through those of an assistant (such as Dr Watson). At the climax the detective proceeds to tell the story again, recounting the events that led up to the crime and the clues discovered after the crime that led him or her to the criminal. In *Death and the Compass* the only novelty in the path chosen through the matrix by Borges is that the second telling is performed by the villain rather than the detective.

Borges' telling, then, is one that passes down the columns rather than crossing the rows. It is instructive to consider what the story would have looked like if Borges had taken a path that passed across the rows instead of the one he chose (i.e. L1/RS1, RS2, RS3, L4/T4, L5, RS6, etc.). Such a path through the matrix would produce a quite different kind of narrative. Instead of a detective story in which the reader seeks to unravel the mystery along with the sleuth, we would have a cat-and-mouse thriller, in which the main interest for the reader would be one of wondering whether the hero will discover the villain's plot against him in time. Possessed of a full knowledge of Red Scharlach's plan, we would, with such a telling, be hoping that Lönnrot would see beyond the obvious clues and detect the true state of affairs. The 1970's American detective series *Colombo*, starring Peter

Treviranus	Lönnrot	Red Scharlach
	T4/L4	
	L5	
	L8	
	T10/L10	
T11	L11	
	L12	
	L1	RS1
		RS2
		RS3
		RS6
		RS7
		RS9
		RS11
	L13	RS13

Figure 6.9 The path through the matrix taken by Borges in *Death and the Compass*.

Falk, was invariably told following this kind of path through the matrix; the viewer witnessed a crime being committed at the very outset of each episode, usually with the criminal meticulously erasing the traces of the crime, and then watched as Colombo used a variety of strategies to break down the perfect alibi of the villain. What we certainly did not get from such a telling was the puzzle-solving pleasure of the traditional detective story, and in fact it is a property of such stories that they depend upon the path through the matrix, either starting part of the way down the columns or leaving crucial cells empty.

A second possible path through the *Death and the Compass* matrix would be one that started at the top of the matrix but only utilised columns T and L after row 2, omitting RS3 until near the end. This would restore the detective element but would alert us to the likely connection between the crime and Red Scharlach. Interestingly, Borges comes close to adopting this option in the original story. The first paragraph of the story, discussed from a rather different perspective in Chapter 3, reads:

6.7   It is true that Erik Lönnrot failed to prevent the last murder, but that he foresaw it is indisputable. Neither did he guess the identity of Yarmolinsky's luckless assassin, but he did succeed in divining the secret morphology behind the fiendish series as well as the participation of Red Scharlach, whose other nickname is Scharlach the Dandy. *That criminal (as countless others) had sworn on his honour to kill Lönnrot,* but the latter could never be intimidated. Lönnrot believed himself a pure reasoner, an Auguste Dupin, but there was something of the adventurer in him, and even a little of the gambler. (my italics)

It will be noticed that the crucial information about Scharlach's vow of revenge is tucked away in pre-narrative exposition where it is not part of the path taken by Borges through the matrix and is less likely to be noticed by the reader.

Another path through the matrix might start at row 3 and work steadily across the rows in a downward direction thereafter. Once the bottom row was reached, the first two rows would be provided. This telling would remove any detection element but would turn the story into a mystery; in this mystery the curiosity of the reader would be focused on what Scharlach's motives were in setting up the 'periodic series' that captures Lönnrot's attention, and the climax would be the revelation of the revenge motive.

Perhaps the most interesting alternative telling would the one provided by starting at the top of the matrix and passing down the RS column, making only occasional forays into column A. Such a telling would present the story from Red Scharlach's point of view. The effect would be to change the story from being a tale of detection to one of studied revenge comparable with the tales of Edgar Allan Poe. In such a telling our interest as readers would be in the elaborate calculations of the plotter as we saw him weave his intricate web with which to ensnare the intended victim. Borges is known to have admired the work of Poe and also that of G. K. Chesterton, whose Father Brown stories are among the most elegant of detective short stories and whose writing style Borges appears to emulate in more than one place in this particular story; we have already seen in Chapter 3 how the beginning of *Death and the Compass* exploits intertextually the strategy for beginning detective stories sometimes adopted by Chesterton and others. What we seem to have therefore in *Death and the Compass* is a story with the content of an Edgar Allan Poe revenge story told in the sequence and the style of a G. K. Chesterton detective story. We also have a challenge to a view of story as an underlying constant and of narratives as variables, held by narratologists such as Genette (1972) and Chatman (1978) and implicit in Pike's matrix theory, since the various possible tellings/narratives would be received and understood in such different ways that we would have to doubt whether they were, in any useful sense of the term, telling the same story. Once again, then, we find that *Death and the Compass* is posing important questions for written discourse analysts.

An extension of the notion of the matrix

Up to now I have treated the matrix as if it were unproblematic, even though I indicated clearly at the outset that there were certain unsatisfactory features to the descriptive approach as outlined by Pike. It is time to reconsider the properties of the matrix.

Consider again the Aesop story we examined in Chapter 4 (see Examples 4.1a and 4.1b on page 54). The matrix for this, on the lines laid down so far, is the incredibly uninteresting one shown in Table 6.6. While it would be perfectly possible to discuss this matrix in the same manner as before, it should be obvious that in some sense it would not be worthwhile to do so. Put bluntly, this matrix misses the point. The story is about the parallels and differences between two travellers and the matrix does not reflect this at all adequately. However, the observation that the rows of our matrices are in fact answers to the repeated question 'What happened next?' offers us a way forward. For once we recognise that the rows are answers to questions, we allow ourselves the possibility of using other questions. In other words, there is no reason why a matrix should not be produced in which the rows answer questions that are altogether more precise. Consider the alternative matrix for the Aesop story shown in Table 6.7. It will be noticed that this matrix makes explicit something that was implicit in earlier matrices, namely that the vertical columns permit and, indeed, represent a potential comparison between characters. Sometimes the comparison has been fairly overt; for example, in the Goldilocks matrix, the cells completed for the three bears were directly comparable. More often the comparison has been less apparent; nevertheless, in every case where more than one cell in a row has been completed, the 'What happened next?' question has been paraphrasable (somewhat clumsily) as 'How did A, B and C compare in respect of how what happened next affected them?'

In the matrix for the Aesop tale, as noted, the comparison has become explicit and this means that we no longer need a separate column for each character. The effect is that the alternative tellings we might consider all centre around the

Table 6.6 A first matrix analysis of the 'Aesop' story

	A (Aesop)	B (1st traveller)	C (2nd traveller)
1: What happened first?	Aesop was asked about the people of Athens by a passing traveller	The traveller asked Aesop about the people of Athens	
2: What happened next?	He responded by asking the traveller about the people of Argos	He was asked about the people of Argos	
3: What happened next?		He praised the people of Argos	
4: What happened next?	He told the traveller that Athens is much the same	He got an answer to his question	
5: What happened next?	He was asked about the people of Athens by a second traveller		The 2nd traveller asked Aesop about the people of Athens
6: What happened next?	He responded by asking the traveller about the people of Argos		He was asked about the people of Argos
7: What happened next?			He criticised the people of Argos
8: What happened next?	He told the traveller that Athens is much the same		He got an answer to his question

travellers. Figure 6.10 shows the sequence actually chosen. But other paths could have been selected. Consider the following telling:

6.8   Aesop, the Greek writer, was sitting by the roadside one day when two travellers in short succession came up to him and asked what sort of people lived in Athens, the city to which they were travelling. To both he replied 'Tell me where you come from and what sort of people live there, and I'll tell you what sort of people you'll find in Athens.' Both travellers turned out to be from Argos but they had very different views of the sort of people that lived there. The first traveller answered with a smile, 'In Argos the people are all friendly, generous and warm-hearted', while the second answered, 'Argos

Table 6.7 An alternative matrix analysis of the 'Aesop' story

	A (1st traveller)	B (2nd traveller)
1: What question was Aesop asked?	The first traveller asked Aesop what the people of Athens were like	The second traveller asked Aesop what the people of Athens were like
2: What response did he make?	Aesop asked him what the people of Argos were like	Aesop asked him what the people of Argos were like
3: What was the traveller's reaction?	He praised the people of Argos	He criticised the people of Argos
4: What answer did Aesop give to the original question?	Aesop told him he would find the people of Athens much the same	Aesop told him he would find the people of Athens much the same

```
A1      A2      A3      A4
B1      B2      B3      B4
```

Figure 6.10 The path through Table 6.7 taken by the original teller of the 'Aesop' tale.

people are unfriendly, mean and vicious. They're thieves and murderers, all of them.' Aesop's reply to the second traveller was, however, identical to the reply he gave to the first traveller. 'You'll find the people of Athens much the same,' he said.

This version achieves greater compression by passing across the rows, though at the expense of the pointedness of the first version. Although other versions are also possible, it is of some importance that a telling constructed out of a random sequence of the cells would be hard to render intelligible. It is also hard to imagine a telling with empty cells. I will return to these points at the end of this chapter.

We have seen that all narrative matrices could be interpreted as comparing the actions, reactions, behaviour, etc. of characters in any particular time span. Furthermore, it will be noticed that the questions asked as the vertical dimension of the revised Aesop matrix were not random but reflected the expected sequence associated with conversational structure. This means that the matrices we have considered can be seen as the product of the interaction of two kinds of relation. Thus Abe, Bill and Clara and the other narratives we have analysed can be represented diagrammatically as in Figure 6.11. In similar fashion, the Aesop story can be represented diagrammatically as in Figure 6.12.

Once we see matrices as the product of such parameters, it is a small step to recognising that a matrix could be constructed that did not include time sequence as one of its parameters. Consider, to begin with, the following extract from an advertisement for Denclen, a liquid cleaner for dentures:

	Comparison
Time sequence	Abe, Bill and Clara

Figure 6.11 Pike's matrix seen as the product of interaction of two relations.

	Comparison
Time sequence and exchange structure	Travellers and Aesop

Figure 6.12 The 'Aesop' story seen as a product of two relations.

6.9   (1) Many denture wearers are worried about their dentures. (2) Some find they just can't get rid of the stains; others complain that invisible tartar causes denture odour – so embarrassing! (3) Many of these people just aren't cleaning their dentures correctly – brushing them with toothpaste or soaking them in ordinary water just isn't good enough. (4) None of these methods will remove stubborn stains and hardened tartar, but liquid DENCLEN will. (5) The special brush really delves into all the cracks and crevices, rooting out decaying food matter and removing the most established stains and tartar.

This can be represented in matrix form as shown in Table 6.8. It will be seen that the matrix operates in non-narrative text in much the same way as it did in narrative text. We have as our horizontal parameter two topics that are compared and in place of time sequence as our vertical parameter we have a quasi-logical sequence of the problem-solution type (Winter, 1976; Hoey, 1979, 1983), a kind of sequence that we shall look at in some detail in the next chapter. The compressed matrix is shown in Figure 6.13.

Notice that various alternative 'retellings' present themselves. It would be easy to rewrite the text so that the DENCLEN column is passed down first and the toothpaste column passed down second. The effect of this would be quite a subtle one. The advertisement as we have it offers its product as a relief to people who have not apparently heard of DENCLEN. If the order of passing down the columns is reversed, the advertisement would insinuate that the people who ignored DENCLEN were in some respects stupid or morally suspect, given the self-evident and known virtues of DENCLEN, as the following version shows:

6.10   (1) Many denture wearers are worried about their dentures. (2) Some find they just can't get rid of the stains; others complain that invisible tartar causes denture odour – so embarrassing! (4) Liquid DENCLEN will remove stubborn stains and hardened tartar. (5) The special brush really delves into all the cracks and crevices, rooting out decaying food matter

Table 6.8 A matrix analysis of an advertisement for DENCLEN

	A (toothpaste or soaking)	B (DENCLEN liquid)
(1) What is the problem?	Some [denture wearers] find they just can't get rid of the stains [on their dentures]; others complain that invisible tartar causes denture odour – so embarrassing!	Some [denture wearers] find they just can't get rid of the stains [on their dentures]; others complain that invisible tartar causes denture odour – so embarrassing!
(2) What can be done about it?	brushing them with toothpaste or soaking them in ordinary water	liquid DENCLEN
(3) How effective is this?	just isn't good enough	really delves into all the cracks and crevices, rooting out decaying food matter and removing the most established stains and tartar

and removing the most established stains and tartar. (3) Many people just aren't cleaning their dentures correctly – brushing them with toothpaste or soaking them in ordinary water just isn't good enough.

In the circumstances it is not surprising that the manufacturers of DENCLEN chose the altogether less threatening alternative 'telling'.

The text we have just been considering still has a form of sequence as one of its parameters. It is, however, possible to create a matrix for which both parameters are non-sequential. An example of a text which can be represented by a matrix with no sequential parameter is Example 2.11 (page 28) that we looked at in Chapter 2. This passage has, in fact, a compressed matrix with the same feature along both parameters – comparison (see Figure 6.14). It is at one and the same time a comparison of public and private values and a comparison of the various issues upon which ethical positions may be adopted. A matrix analysis of the passage is shown in Table 6.9.

Basically, then, the text is produced by passing successively across the rows of the matrix. Another 'telling' might have passed down the columns. The effect of this would, however, have been to treat the information given in the two columns

	Comparison
Problem-solution	toothpaste, water and DENCLEN

Figure 6.13 The DENCLEN advertisement seen as a product of two relations.

	Comparison
Comparison	public and private value judgements on ethical issues

Figure 6.14 The passage from *Good God* seen as a product of two relations.

Table 6.9 A matrix analysis of the passage from *Good God*

	Public values	**Private values**
(1) How do we feel about new roads?	we applaud the new motorway	we lament the new road widening
(2) Why?	it will save travelling time and help the economy	it will mean more pollution and noise and the neighbours' children will not be able to cross it on their own
(3) How do we feel about the effects of new technology?	we are pleased that the price of components is going down because of new technology	we feel sorry for our friend whose business is closing down because it cannot compete
(4) Why?	–	–
(5) How do we feel about money being spent?	we are pleased to hear that people are spending more money	we do not intend to waste our own money on things we do not need
(6) Why?	it helps get the country out of recession	–
(7) How do we feel about our civilization?	we are proud of our modern civilization	we have got our priorities very wrong
(8) Why?	it has been drummed into us, we have advanced much further than any previous age	(a) the crime rate, the suicide rate, drug addiction and alcoholism, homelessness and poverty (b) scientists now warn us that the world is finite and we cannot carry on demanding more and more from it

as of equal importance and novelty; it would also have resulted in a passage with the kind of construction we were looking at in Chapter 4. The writer's apparent intention is to focus on the individual discrepancies between our value systems, not to look at public values as a system and then at private values as a system. He therefore opts not to give public values and private values separate paragraphs of their own, even though such a strategy would have resulted in an equally coherent and intelligible text. In other words, 'tellings' are context-bound; the order chosen is dependent on the purpose of the writer. It is also, of course, dependent on the previous text. In this case the preceding sentence is:

6.11   Our values, like the values of the islanders, are full of contradictions

A telling that went down the columns rather than across them would tend to make the contradiction singular rather than plural.

The matrix brings certain features of the text to light that might otherwise be overlooked. These might be described as the exposure of false symmetry, on the one hand, and the highlighting of true symmetry on the other. Starting with exposure of false symmetry, I note that many of the statements about public and private virtues appear to be accompanied by a 'because' clause or prepositional phrase:

> because of new technology
> because it cannot compete
> because it helps get the country out of recession
> because we have advanced much further than any previous age.

These seem to match the two independent clauses 4a and 5a which could have been connected to independent clauses 4 and 5 by *because*. But on closer inspection there only *appears* to be symmetry. The first two *because* clauses do not in fact introduce a basis for the evaluation, but an explanation of the ethical problem being reacted to; this is shown up in the empty cells in row 4. On the other hand, the true symmetry that is pointed up by the matrix is, of course, that represented in rows 7 and 8, where the non-parallelism of the syntax might lead one to overlook the continuation of the underlying content parallels.

It will be gathered from the discussion of the last two passages that the alternative 'tellings' available for non-narrative texts are restricted by context, notions of givenness, and matters of focus but that, nevertheless, alternative 'tellings' do exist. The same is true for narrative texts in circumstances where neither parameter of the matrix is time sequence. Consider again *Goldilocks and the Three Bears*, for which an alternative matrix exists, not dependent on time sequence. An extract from this is shown in Table 6.10. Such a matrix largely spells out what we already knew from the hierarchical analysis, indeed what every young child knows, namely that Goldilocks behaves in a similar fashion with regard to the three kinds of creature comfort (forgive me!) that the bears' house offers. However, it does throw up the same false symmetries that we found with the *Good God* passage. In the first place we might be tempted by the 'beds' column into thinking that Goldilocks is looking for a happy mean; indeed until I analysed this text in this way for this book, that is how I assumed her searches to be structured. The beds are:

too hard   just right   too soft

with the antonymic relationship between 'hard' and 'soft' reinforcing the scale within which Baby Bear's bed represents the mean.

Table 6.10 An extract from a non-sequence-oriented matrix of *Goldilocks*

	Porridge	**Chairs**	**Beds**
What did Goldilocks see?	Goldilocks saw the three bowls of porridge and the three spoons on the table	Then Goldilocks saw three chairs: a very big chair, a medium-sized chair and a tiny little chair	There she saw three beds: a very big bed, a medium-sized bed and a tiny, little bed
What effect did these things have on her?	The porridge smelt good, and Goldilocks was hungry because she had not had her breakfast	–	She felt tired and thought she would like to sleep
What did she do with the things she saw?	Goldilocks picked up the very big spoon and tasted the porridge in the very big bowl	She sat in the very big chair	Goldilocks climbed up onto the very big bed
How did she react?	It was too hot!	It was too high!	It was too hard!
What did she do with the remaining things she saw?	Goldilocks picked up the medium-sized spoon and tasted the porridge in the medium-sized bowl	She sat in the medium-sized chair	Then she climbed up onto the medium-sized bed
How did she react?	It was lumpy!	It was too hard!	It was too soft!
What did she do with the remaining thing she saw?	Goldilocks picked up the tiny, little spoon and tasted the porridge in the tiny, little bowl	Then she sat in the tiny, little chair	Then she lay down on the tiny, little bed
How did she react?	It was just right!	It was just right!	It was just right!
What effect did she have on the thing?	Soon she had eaten it all up!	The seat began to crack and then it broke	–

However, the status of the middle way is not given to Baby Bear's other possessions. I have read tellings of the story where Mother Bear's porridge is too cold, but the writer of this version presumably recognised that this made little sense in the context of the porridge having all come from the same pot and the bears having gone for a walk to allow it to cool. So in place of 'too cold' we have 'lumpy'. Not only does this come from a different scale with 'smooth' at the other end, but it is not marked with 'too' to mark excess of the quality. The symmetry is doubly broken.

More subtly the same is true of the attributes given to the chairs. Both are marked by 'too' but they come from different scales – hardness (again) and height. Further, the hardness is assigned to Mother Bear's chair, not Father Bear's. Thus hardness and softness are variably the properties of her possessions; no consistent picture is built up of her through these attributes. Again, one supposes that an adult bear's chair could not plausibly be presented as too low.

In effect all the clauses 'N was (too) adj.' mean the same thing – 'It was not just right', making a basic contrast between this and Goldilocks' evaluation of Baby Bear's possessions 'It was just right'. Given that all the evaluations of Father and Mother Bears' possessions effectively mean the same thing, this supports the earlier observation that the parent bears' columns are identical and that for the purposes of the narrative they have no separate identity.

Some implications for language learning

There are several potential applications of the matrix principle to language teaching. The first of these relates to the possibility of some cells being empty. While in time-sequence-oriented narrative matrices empty cells are quite normal and unproblematic, in other kinds of matrix, such as those considered in the previous section, an empty cell is often more noticeable. If a student has produced an unbalanced text, (for example, a comparison of two points of view with the weight of arguments loaded to one side), one way of showing what is missing might be to draw a simple matrix based on his or her text and show that some of the cells are empty.

A second implication relates to the possibility of taking an unlikely path through a matrix. If a student has made all the relevant points but has done so in an order that is difficult to follow, in some cases the answer might be for the teacher to draw a matrix based on his or her text, and show how a simpler route might be taken through the same material and what the implications of such a route might be.

A third implication relates to what might be termed the problem of an inconsistent (or overconsistent) perspective. If a student tells a story in simple time sequence but jumps from one perspective to another or sticks unhelpfully to only one perspective, then he or she might be shown with the help of a matrix what other alternatives were available. It does not necessarily follow that the sequence chosen was unacceptable. Many narratives are written from only one perspective (*Robinson Crusoe* and *David Copperfield* to name but two) and many others control the change of perspective with great skill (e.g. *War and Peace*). However, if a telling seems not to work in the judgement of readers, the explanation may lie in an inconsistent perspective, which can be identified readily by means of a matrix.

The implications I have mentioned so far are negative in nature. A more positive implication of matrix analysis for language learning lies in the development of logical and critical thinking. If students are given a matrix with empty cells, they can be invited to consider what type of material/argument might need to be supplied to fill the cells. Alternatively, they might be invited to consider what implications leaving the cells empty might have for the soundness of the writer's argument.

Probably the most important, and perhaps the most obvious, implication for language learning lies in the development of writing skills. Students might be given a matrix with brief notes in each cell and invited to write a complete text. The effect would be not only to test and develop the normal syntactic and lexical skills, but also to give practice in the skill of organising a text. The advantage would be that this skill could be developed without any particular form of organisation being prescribed in advance.

Bibliographical end-notes

The Abe, Bill and Clara matrix is drawn with minor modifications from Pike (1981); the various (re)tellings of the 'happening' (Examples 6.1–6.4) are my own, though Pike supplies similar tellings in his own paper. The news story concerning the murdered market trader (6.5) was brought to my attention by Carmen Caldas-Coulthard and is discussed from the point of view of speech representation in Caldas-Coulthard (1988); my analysis has benefited from discussions with her about the text. As before, the quotation from Borges' *Death and the Compass* (6.7) is taken from the translation by Donald A. Yates, published as part of the volume *Labyrinths* (New Directions Publishing Corporation, 1964), reprinted in Penguin Books, 1981. The DENCLEN advertisement (6.9) was current in national newspapers in 1999. Example 6.11 is from *Good God: Green Theology and the Value of Creation* by Jonathan Clatworthy, Charlbury: Jon Carpenter Publishing.

The text of this chapter draws heavily upon two conference papers, themselves substantially overlapping, in which matrices are defined and described (Hoey 1991c, 2000). The notion of the matrix applied to narrative is taken from Pike (1981), though it should be noted that I have omitted much that Pike would regard as important from my discussion of his paper. The notion of the matrix applied to non-narrative is taken from Tim Johns (1980) who argues for the existence of a particular kind of non-sequential non-narrative structure that he terms a 'matrix' structure; while I deny that the matrix has structural status, preferring to view it as an analytical device, the second half of this chapter has been greatly influenced by his work. Hoey (1985b, 1997a) discusses the way that matrix may help explain paragraphing decisions; the later paper relates these also to collocational and colligational choices.

7 Culturally popular patterns of text organisation

Introduction

The defining characteristic of a colony, discussed in Chapter 5, was that its component parts do not derive their meaning from the sequence in which they are placed. Conversely, of course, the defining feature of what I have been loosely labelling 'mainstream text' is that its component parts *do* derive meaning from their place in the overall text. In Chapter 2, we saw that texts may be seen as an interaction between writer and reader in which the writer seeks to answer the questions that s/he thinks his or her reader will want answering, and the reader seeks to anticipate the questions that the writer is going to answer. To make the reader's task easier, writers normally adopt one or more of three strategies. First, they may attempt to anticipate accurately the questions that their readers want answered in the order that they want them answered. Second, they may spell out the questions that they are answering as they answer them. Both these strategies were discussed in Chapter 2 and were touched upon in Chapters 3 and 4. The third strategy that a writer can adopt, however, is to answer an agreed sequence of questions, to operate in effect with a template of questions that both writer and reader know about and can refer to. It is these sequences of questions, these text templates, that this and the next chapter are concerned with.

Schemata and scripts

One of the first linguists to consider what these 'templates' might look like was Rumelhart, who with Ortony in 1977, offered the following fragment of (fabricated) text for consideration:

7.1 Mary heard the ice cream man coming. She remembered her pocket money. She rushed into the house. (from Rumelhart and Ortony 1977)

Before reading on, try answering the following questions: What does Mary want to do? How old is she? What country does she live in? What kind of area does she live in? To the first, you will, I trust, have answered that she wants to buy an ice cream. To the second, you are quite likely to have answered 'between 8 and 12' on the grounds that girls between these ages tend to show enthusiasm for ice cream; girls older than that usually are too sophisticated to show their enthusiasm and girls younger than that are normally not permitted to be out of the house without parental accompaniment. You might have assumed the country to be an English-speaking country (because her name is Mary, not Maria, Marie or Marja) with a tradition of itinerant ice cream vendors with musical chimes, i.e. either the United States or the United Kingdom. You may feel less certainty about the kind of area she lives in, but I would expect some readers at least to speculate that Mary lives in a semi-detached or terraced house in the suburbs, since ice cream vans tend not to operate in the country or in the inner cities, and it is easier to 'rush into' a house with a small garden (or none) rather than one with a long drive.

The point here is that the reader does half the work for the writer. The writer's words activate knowledge in the mind of the reader which the reader brings into play in his or her interpretation of the text (unless there are counter-indications in the text that might prevent him or her from doing so). The seventeen words of Rumelhart and Ortony's mini-text above are therefore read as if they said something like the following:

7.2   *Mary*, probably a young girl because young girls tend to have pocket money and to get excited by the prospect of ice cream, *heard* the chimes of the van driven by *the ice cream man*, which signalled that he was *coming* and that he was willing to sell ice cream. Wanting an ice cream and knowing that she would have to pay for it, she needed a source of money as she had no, or insufficient, money on her. *She remembered* that she still had *her pocket money* which would be sufficient to pay for an ice cream. Because she knew that ice cream vans do not stay long in one place and that she would therefore lose her chance to buy an ice cream if she did not act quickly, *she rushed into the house* where she lived outside which she was standing, in order to get the money so that she could buy an ice cream.

It is important to note, though, that other interpretations of the text are possible; the words do not *have* to have the meaning that reader and writer co-operate in making. Placed into a context where the ice cream man is a heavy-footed bogeyman, famed for his slaughter of young women for trivial sums of money with an ice pick, the passage could be read very differently. Mary could be a young woman who, terrified at hearing the step of the psychopath and realising that her pocket money represents a dangerous temptation for the monster, rushes into the house to secure herself and her money. The point, of course, is that only someone with a warped mind (like me) is likely to read it in such a way.

Another such fragment of text (again fabricated) is supplied by Schank and Abelson (1977):

7.3   John knew his wife's operation would be expensive. There was always Uncle Harry. John reached for the telephone book.

The same points can be made here. We assume the country where the story takes place to be the United States since the names indicate an English-speaking country and operations are not charged for in most other English-speaking countries. This could be mistaken; cosmetic surgery, for example, is not free in the United Kingdom. But in the absence of contra-indications we assume the operation to be of the health-sustaining kind. Furthermore, we assume that Uncle Harry is a rich and probably generous relative and we take it for granted that John's reasons for reaching for the phone book are to get Uncle Harry's number so that he can be asked for a gift or loan of money to pay for the wife's operation. We are likely to assume they both live in the same big city, in that John would not have the phone books for all areas of the United States. We also are likely to assume that they are not close; otherwise John would know Uncle Harry's number already.

Again, other readings are possible. The same warped mind that imagined an ice-pick wielder in Mary's story could interpret the text as meaning that John does not want to pay for his wife's operation and therefore contacts the local Mafia man in order to arrange for her murder. Again, though, such an interpretation is unlikely to occur spontaneously unless the writer has already signalled its feasibility.

Rumelhart and Ortony and Schank and Abelson have similar ways of explaining the phenomenon we have been describing, though their terminology differs. They talk in terms of schemata and scripts in the reader's (and writer's) minds. For the purposes of this chapter, the difference between the terms is unimportant for reasons that will become quickly apparent. Crudely, a schema is a static representation of knowledge, whereas a script is a narrative representation of knowledge. A schema represents the (non-narrative) connections between facts; a script represents the sequence in which likely events will occur.

The view of these authors is that knowledge of the world, our remembered experience of the world, is not randomly distributed in the mind, but is carefully organised in terms of schemata or scripts. Consequently whenever one part of that knowledge is activated, the rest becomes available at the same time and is brought to bear on the task of interpreting the text that provided the activation. The illustration of a restaurant is often used. If we enter a restaurant, we are unsurprised if a stranger in smart clothes approaches our table with a menu in his or her hand. If we sit at a table in a library, on the other hand, we expect no such thing and would immediately suspect that we were the butt of someone's humour (or the victim of some survey of public opinion) were such a figure to approach us. If we read about a meal in a restaurant, the same knowledge is activated as if we were in the restaurant ourselves (so the argument goes) and so the writer does not feel obliged to explain the presence of an unnamed pro-active stranger in the way that s/he would in other contexts.

Culturally popular patterns of organisation

Revealing though concepts such as schema and script are for a general understanding of the writing and reading processes, they are of limited value in text analysis or in the teaching of reading or writing. This is because there appears to be no practical limit to the number of schemata or scripts we can hold and the exact content and boundaries of each schema or script are open to real question. It is no accident that the restaurant script is so often cited – it happens to be an unusually self-contained and bounded set of knowledge and expectations. Furthermore, even if these problems were solvable in principle, we would still never in practice be able to list, let alone describe, all the schemata/scripts that a reader develops in his or her life or that a writer is capable of making use of. In short schemata and scripts are not practicable analytical tools. What we need is something that allows us to generalise about these schemata/scripts without losing the insight that readers co-operate with writers in making a common meaning.

The answer in part lies in the fact that readers seem to bring two kinds of knowledge to bear on the texts they read – the specific knowledge described by schemata and scripts and a more generalised set of expectations that are shared across a range of texts. If we look again at Schank and Abelson's incomplete mini-text, we can see that the question that the reader is likely to ask on being told that *John knew his wife's operation would be expensive* is *What did he do about it?* In other words, the reader will recognise the situation described in the first sentence as a problematic one and will expect a response to the problem described. This would have been true even if no specific schema could be activated. Thus the sentence:

7.4   John knew the gill net would be expensive

is extremely unlikely to trigger any schema in your mind, unless you happen to be keen on fishing (a gill net being a net that is suspended in water as a way of trapping fish by their gills). Yet the more generalised expectation would be as strong here as it was when the expensive item was an operation. Just as the word *operation* triggers the schema of hospitals, welfare systems and so on, so the word *expensive* triggers a 'generalised script' of problem followed by attempt at solution.

I have just talked in terms of a 'generalised script' in order to show the relationship of this concept to schemata and scripts. Henceforward, however, I shall talk of 'culturally popular patterns of organisation', not least to make it clear that such patterns are in many respects closer to structures than to schemata and scripts as usually defined. Unpacked, my preferred label is intended to convey the following points. The word 'patterns' is chosen because they have a structuring effect similar to that of the hierarchical organisation described in Chapter 4 and to that of the matching matrices described in Chapter 6. The term 'organisation' is chosen in preference to 'structure' to indicate that, although there are preferred sequences and combinations of elements, there is no impossible sequence or combination (compare my beginning and ending to Chapter 1); John Sinclair, cited in Sinclair and Coulthard (1975), argues that linguistics should only refer to structures when there is at least one impossible sequence or combination of elements. They are referred to as 'culturally popular' in acknowledgement that they do not have a universal status but occur within particular cultures, as again illustrated in Chapter 1. The interactivity of text, the potential for hierarchicality in text and the availability of colony structures I claim as universals of text; no such claim is made, on the other hand, for the culturally popular patterns that this and the next two chapters will be describing. Finally, they are 'popular' in acknowledgement of the fact that all kinds of patterns of organisation are possible but some of the patterns will be very rare while others will recur with great frequency. There is no demarcation line between the two types of pattern, so the point at which one stops describing different types of pattern will be determined by utility rather than principle.

The Problem-Solution pattern

Having explained what is involved in the label 'culturally popular patterns of organisation', we can turn our attention back to what is arguably the most common pattern of all (or at least the most thoroughly described), the Problem-Solution pattern. The basic outline of the Problem-Solution pattern posited above can be illustrated in a short fabricated text (the only virtue of which is its skeletal nature). Sentence numbers have been added for convenience of reference:

7.5   (1) I was once a teacher of English Language. (2) One day some students came to me unable to write their names. (3) I taught them text analysis. (4) Now they all write novels.

This vainglorious text contains the minimum elements of the pattern under consideration and can be projected into a dialogue as follows:

7.6
Text:	I was once a language teacher.
Questioner:	What problem arose for you?
T:	My students came to me unable to write their names.
Q:	What did you do about this?
T:	I taught them text analysis.
Q:	What was the result?
T:	Now they all write novels.

The aim in projecting a text into dialogue in such a way is to ensure that the questions spell out the relationship between the sentences; the dialogue should make sense and there should be no distortion of the meaning of the text (except that necessarily occasioned by the change of emphasis that introducing questions cannot help but bring). In this case, the questions all support the initial identification of the text as organised by a Problem-Solution pattern, with sentence 1 being the Situation, sentence 2 the Problem, sentence 3 the Response and sentence 4 the Positive Result.

The function of the Situation element in our fabricated text, sentence 1, is to provide background information. In some senses the Situation only belongs to the pattern retrospectively. There is nothing about the first sentence that triggers any expectations of a pattern to be followed. Once sentence 2 has appeared, however, in answer to the second of the questions, answers to questions 3 and 4 are highly likely to appear as well. The length of the answers here is a function of the artificiality of the example, but in authentic text the answers may vary greatly in length, some texts devoting pages to answering the question 'What did x do about it?', others treating this question peremptorily but providing expansive answers to the question 'What problem arose?'. Answers may also be shorter as we shall see in later, authentic, examples. J. R. R. Tolkien's *Lord of the Rings* answers the same four questions as in Example 7.6 above, but takes well over a thousand pages to do it.

The trigger of the pattern is the word *unable*, which, like *expensive*, negatively evaluates a Situation and invites a description of some Response, and the pattern effectively begins at this point, with the identification of some Problem. Problem can be defined as 'an aspect of the Situation requiring a Response' (Hoey 1983) and gives rise to the expectation of a Response. This element of the pattern is often referred to in the literature as a Solution, though strictly the latter label is inappropriate since what is expected is the description of something done to deal with the Problem, not necessarily something that was *successful* in dealing with the Problem – a subtle distinction, but an important one.

Sentence 3 provides the required Response to the Problem, as is indicated by the question it was possible to insert between sentences 2 and 3: *What did you do about this?* This is, of course, not the only question that might be used to connect these two sentences; indeed a number might be used. Some of these would represent alternative formulations of the same request for information. Thus the question *What was your way of dealing with this problem?* represents another way of formulating the question *What did you do about this?* Other questions might be more general, e.g. *What did you do?*, which allows an unplanned reaction such as *I panicked* to serve as an answer as well as the intentional Response that the fuller form of the question demands. Still other questions might focus on different aspects of the organisation. So, for example, the question *What did you teach in the circumstances?* attends to the general-particular relationship that holds between sentences 1 and 3:

7.7   I was once a teacher of English Language

I taught [my students] text analysis.

To understand fully the place of sentence 3 (or any other sentence) in the text as a whole, the analyst needs to tease out all the possible questions that might be asked. However, when investigating a particular pattern, that is not necessary. For the purposes of identifying the Problem-Solution pattern, the question *What did you do about it?* suffices.

A Response does not bring the pattern to a close. If my fabricated text had finished with *I taught them text analysis* you would have felt it to be significantly incomplete. It is only when the Response can be shown to be in truth a solution that the pattern is felt to be complete, and this is done with either a Positive Result or a Positive Evaluation, or quite commonly both. This is, of course, provided by sentence 4.

The signals of a Problem-Solution pattern

We have seen in earlier chapters that writers may signal the questions they are answering or intend to answer. The same is true of the Problem-Solution pattern and the other patterns I shall be describing. So our fabricated text might have occurred thus:

7.8   I was once a teacher of English Language. One day my students came to me unable to write their names. My *way* of *dealing with* this *problem* was to teach them text analysis, with the *result* that they now all write novels.

The signal *do about* cannot be introduced into this particular text but it occurs quite naturally in all kinds of narratives and other kinds of text. Indeed the phrase *do something about x* is one of the most fundamental and common signals of the pattern and perhaps for this reason often occurs in stories written for very young children.

Here are just two examples, the first from *Mr Nosey* by Roger Hargreaves, the second from *Big Dog. . . Little Dog: A Bedtime Story* by P. D. Eastman:

7.9   The people of Tiddletown decided that Mr Nosey was becoming much too nosey, and so they held a meeting to discuss *what to do about him.*
       'We must find some way of stopping him being so nosey' said old Mr Chips the town carpenter.
       'That's right!' said Mrs Washer who ran the Tiddletown laundry, 'He needs to be taught a lesson.'
       'If only we could think of a way to stop him poking his nose' said Mr Brush the painter. And then, a small smile spread over his face. 'Listen' he said, now grinning. 'I have a plan!'

7.10   'Did you get any sleep last night, Ted?'
       'Not a wink, Fred!'
       'My bed is too little!'
       'My bed is too big!'
       '*What can we do about it*, Ted?'
       'I don't know, Fred.'
       'I know what to do!' said the bird. 'Just switch rooms. Ted should sleep upstairs and Fred should sleep downstairs!'

In both cases the phrase is introduced to mark the Problem and to point towards a Response. In both cases also, a suggested Response is shortly offered.

In addition to these specialised lexical items, the prime function of which seems to be to signal relations and patterns, writers (and speakers) have available to them other kinds of signalling vocabulary. Thus negative evaluation items, for example, can be used to signal Problem. Thus, in another version of my fabricated narrative we have:

7.11   I was once a teacher of English Language. *Unfortunately* my students did not know how to write their names. I taught them text analysis. Now they all write novels.

In this version the trigger *unable* has been removed and replaced with the writer's negative evaluation of his student's situation. Sometimes, though, negative evaluations or lexical signals of the kind described above are assigned to a participant within the text. Examples 7.9 and 7.10 contain examples of both. The evaluations (*too nosey, too big, too little*) and the lexical signal *do about* are in both passages assigned to characters rather than directly to the writer.

Strictly speaking, all the signals referred to so far can be seen as evaluative, whether this is their only function like *terrible* or they have a pattern-referring function like *solution*. But there are non-evaluative signals as well; some lexical items such as *poverty, disease,* and *burglary* refer to real world matters that are almost always regarded as problematic – almost always, because there are occasionally situations, for example, *a vow of poverty*, where these words would not be regarded as markers of Problem. Jim Martin distinguishes two kinds of evaluation or appraisal (to use his own terminology): inscribed and evoked. Inscribed appraisal is explicitly encoded evaluation. Evoked appraisal refers to lexical choices that evoke in the reader an evaluation. In some cases the evaluation that is evoked is very strong and quite unambiguous (e.g. *thrill-killing, genocide*); for such instances, Peter White, who has followed up Jim Martin's work, has coined the term 'provoked appraisal' (White 1999); the example of *thrill-killing* is his own.

An instance of evoked appraisal serving as a signal of Problem in our fabricated example would be:

7.12   I was a teacher of English Language. One year some of my students were *illiterate*. I taught them text analysis. Now they all write novels.

Illiteracy is strictly a factual description, but it evokes a negative evaluation and therefore a Problem. Indeed it does this so regularly that the word is sometimes bandied about as a term of abuse aimed at writing felt to be below standard; in such cases, of course, the evaluation is inscribed, not evoked. The adjectives 'inscribed' and 'evoked' have, however, different implied actors. The writer inscribes the evaluation; on the other hand, it is the word that evokes (or provokes) an evaluation in the reader. For this reason, when referring to lexical signalling of patterns, I shall refer to evoking signals rather evoked signals.

We can represent the simplest Problem-Solution possibilities diagrammatically as shown in Fig. 7.1. Working down the diagram, we note that Situation is optional and in certain kinds of text, e.g. advertisements, the exception rather than the rule. We note also that a more accurate label for Problem is Aspect of Situation Requiring a Response and that this label will help us distinguish the Problem-Solution pattern from other types of pattern in the next chapter. Each of the vertical stages represents a question being answered and, as is probably fairly

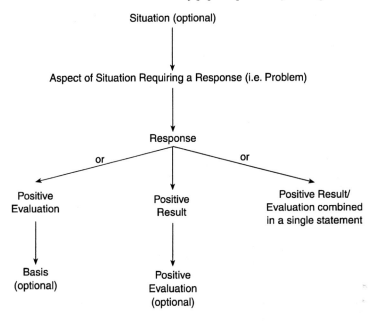

Figure 7.1 The Basic Problem-Solution patterns.
Source: Adapted from Hoey 1983.

obvious, the three branches represent alternative possible textual realisations. Example 7.5 illustrates the third option.

An intermediate stage between Problem and Response

Only so much can be learnt from fabricated texts, whether those of others or my own. One feature that is missing from my examples but which is visible in authentic Examples 7.9 and 7.10 is the presence of a stage half-way between Problem and Response, which the Story Grammarians (Stein and Glenn and others) have termed 'Plan'. The label is not entirely satisfactory as we immediately shall see, though it does account well for some half-way stages. A characteristic of this element of the pattern is that it either defines what might count as an adequate Response or makes a suggestion as to what Response to adopt. Thus in Example 7.9, Mrs Washer goes beyond simply stating that Mr Nosey's nosiness has to be stopped; she specifies that '*He needs to be taught a lesson*,' a particular kind of Response, quite different, for example, from just securing windows and doors or keeping well away from him whenever he is about. Then again Mr Brush signals the imminent shift from Response with the words '*I have a plan!*' The reader is not told what the plan is and has to infer it from subsequent events, but we recognise a shift of focus from Problem without having yet reached the point of Response. Quite often a sentence occurs which defines what will count as an appropriate Response without being followed by a statement of Plan.

Instead of a Plan statement, we often encounter a Recommended Response. An example occurs in Example 7.10. The bird announces that s/he has a solution (*'I know what to do!'*) and then recommends a course of action. This Recommended Response is not yet an actual Response, in that it does not answer the question *What did they do about it?*, but it shifts attention from Problem to Response. Recommended Responses account for more interim stages than do true Plans. Advertisements and editorials very frequently substitute Recommended Responses for actual Responses and in these contexts they are not felt to be interim and the actual Responses are likewise not felt to be missing. In narratives and much science writing, however, the need for actual Response is strong and in such contexts Plan/Recommended Response is felt to be a stage on the way.

I shall not represent these intermediate stages in subsequent diagrams since they are optional, but their presence should always be looked for.

Two advertisements displaying Problem-Solution patterning

The following extract from an advertisement for an Internet service, which will also serve to illustrate the main features of the pattern as so far described, allow us to look more closely at the way signalling works:

7.13   TRYING TO WORK WITH THE INTERNET?

IS THE INTERNET TURNING YOU INTO A MONSTER? LET MCIS HELP YOU CONTROL THE BEAST.

MCIS is a Total Internet Solutions Provider and can assist you in the following areas: [A list follows]

The first sentence invites readers to identify the Situation described with their own. (Presumably those who answer 'no' will turn their attention elsewhere.) The second sentence triggers recognition of the Problem-Solution pattern with the word *monster*, a recognition that is confirmed in the following sentence by the use of the near-synonym *beast*. It is important in any analysis to identify the signals that trigger recognition of the pattern and subsequently confirm its existence, since they are a direct linguistic reflection of the pattern. The frequency of the signals that will be found varies somewhat according to genre, with signals being rarer in academic scientific writing than in popular science reporting, for example. The reasons for this are to do with the knowledge a reader may be expected to bring to the text. The greater the knowledge that the reader shares with the writer, the less need there is for the writer to make explicit linguistic reference to the pattern being followed, since the significance of the information being provided will be quite obvious to the reader.

A Problem having being indicated in the advertisement, a Response is sure to follow, and the offer of one comes in the third sentence (in the terms used above, a

Recommended Response); this also contains a Positive Evaluation/Result within it (*help*). This Evaluation/Result is repeated in the final sentence (*can assist you*).

One signal in this extract perhaps deserves a little more attention in that it shows the subtlety and complexity of the lexical signalling system, namely the word *control*. Of 112 examples of *to control* drawn from a sub-set of the British National Corpus, 38 (34% of my examples) were used in conjunction with clearly problematic situations, i.e. *to control urinary incontinence, to control weeds, to control insect pests, to control his violent nature, to control fish frying odours, to control air pollution*, etc. Another 62 (55%) were used in conjunction with situations capable of being problematic, i.e. *to control the bladder* (cf. *urinary incontinence*), *to control personal behaviour* (cf. *his violent nature*), *to control the trade of fish frying* (cf. *fish frying odours*), *to control the air we breathe* (cf. *air pollution*), etc. This combination of meanings exactly matches with the apparent intentions of the advertiser. On the one hand, the text claims to be describing a clearly problematic situation (*the beast*) which needs to be prevented from doing damage to the reader; on the other hand, the reality it encodes is closer to the second use of *control*; the Internet is a situation capable of being problematic, rather than one that is necessarily problematic, so what is being offered is a service that will prevent the Internet becoming a problematic situation. Thus, a single item simultaneously functions to signal Response to Problem and an underlying, implicit situation where the need is to forestall a Problem before it happens. In 1983, I described the latter kind of situation as a special sub-class of Problem-Solution pattern where Problem equalled Delicate Situation and Response equalled Means of Avoiding Problem.

The above discussion might lead to a misunderstanding if not immediately corrected. It is not the case that Problem-Solution patterns merely mirror reality. We are not observing patterns in the world that the text merely reflects, though presumably the text does reflect some aspect of the author's perception of reality. As evidence of the complex relationship that holds between what a writer encodes as problem and what a reader is willing to recognise as problem, consider the opening sentences from an advertisement for cold wax treatments that appeared in the 1980s, masquerading as an advice column:

7.14   CAROL FRANCIS TALKS ABOUT UNWANTED HAIR REMOVAL
The other day my teenage daughter asked me about hair removal for the first time. Apparently, her new boyfriend had passed a comment about her legs being hairy, and she wanted to do something about it before a party on Friday night.

Fortunately, she was talking to the right person, because I've tried everything. So I explained all the different methods and told her to make up her own mind. Here's what I told her.

The advertisement triggers recognition of the Problem-Solution pattern with the words *wanted to do something about it*. A Problem is being unambiguously signalled. But what is the Problem? Again, the text is unambiguous: the Problem is *hairy legs*. I have to accept that because the text has linguistically encoded it thus, the pronoun *it* referring back to *her legs being hairy* which is what *she wanted to do something about*. But I do *not* accept that the writer's decision to encode *hairy legs* as a Problem reflects everybody's reality; I do not accept that the text is transparently reflecting something that would be universally recognised as a real-world problem. For me, the problem is the boyfriend. But I recognise the pattern that has been signalled by the copywriter, and I interpret the remainder of the text in the light of what the writer has chosen to signal, not in terms of my own real-world perceptions. (Which does not prevent me reflecting critically upon the value systems that the writer has chosen to encode; cf. Fairclough 1989.)

Recycling in Problem-Solution patterns

The pattern so far described will account for some texts but there are many that will prove not to fit despite having many features apparently in common. Consider the following variant of Example 7.5:

7.15   (1) I was once a teacher of English Language. (2) One day some students came to me unable to write their names. (3) I taught them text analysis. (4) This however had little effect.

On encountering this, the reader is likely to ask, *So what did you next do about it?* Whereas the earlier versions had a sense of completeness about them, however inadequate they might have been in other ways, this version is likely to feel incomplete. The same questions are being answered as were answered in Example 7.5, but because the answer to the question *What was the result?* is negative, the pattern has to recycle, as shown in Figure 7.2.

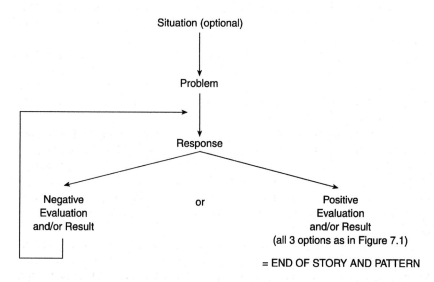

Figure 7.2 The recycling effect of Negative Evaluation in Problem-Solution patterns.

There are actually several types of recycling. One possibility is that each negative evaluation redefines the nature of the Problem. Another is that the Problem remains unaltered but the Response changes. An example of the latter type of recycling can be found in the following story by a seven-year-old girl (my daughter); as previously, sentence numbering has been added for convenience of referencing:

7.16   My Love Story
        (1) One wet day Mary was bored and decided to go up into the attic to see what she could find. (2) After a while she came down looking very excited, she had an idea she couldn't go in the attic, it's too dirty for she had her best dress on. (3) She went to the swimming baths and learnt how to swim. (4) She learnt how to do it very well indeed. (5) She learnt the backstroke and the front stroke. (6) She learnt the doggy paddle as well but she got bored soon and went to find something else. (7) She found a sports class and she won three races and lost one, but soon she got bored of that too. (8) Then she found a church and she thought, I haven't got a husband and she got married and you know what? (9) They did all those things which she thought she would enjoy with her husband, and she didn't get bored at all. (10) In fact she really really really liked it and her husband did really really really much. (11) They even went to the seaside and they enjoyed living together evermore.

This story is organised around repeated attempts to solve the same Problem, which is established in the very first clause, *Mary was bored*. The word *bored* is an inscribed Negative Evaluation of an unspecified Situation and therefore triggers an expectation in the reader of a Problem-Solution pattern. In sentence 2 a Plan for Response is mentioned: *she had an idea*. What follows is, however, a series of four Responses to the same Problem, the first three of which are negatively evaluated, in two cases after having been positively evaluated or shown to have had a Positive Result. The final Response is repeatedly positively evaluated both by the writer and by the characters within the story, of which more below. The pattern of the story, then, is shown in Figure 7.3; here and in subsequent diagrams, material in italics represents quotation from the text.

Although this analysis looks complicated, it is in fact extremely simple, consisting as it does of repeated patterns of Problem-Response-Negative Evaluation/ Result, where each instance of the last element reinstates the original Problem. Notice that the provision of a Positive Evaluation in such circumstances does not bring the pattern to an immediate close as we would predict on the basis of Figure 7.2; if a Positive Evaluation is followed by a Negative Evaluation, the latter overrides the former.

The structure of this child's rather charming story is very similar to that of the traditional British folk song, 'The Old Woman Who Swallowed a Fly' (see Figure 7.4). The song may be well known but in case it is not, let me quickly note that it is about an old woman who swallows a fly and then swallows a spider to catch it; this

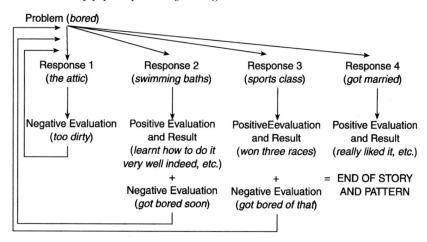

Figure 7.3 Analysis of *My Love Story.*

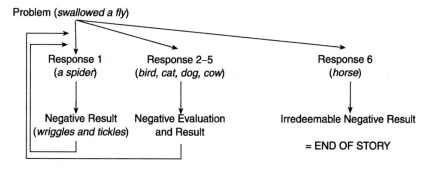

Figure 7.4 Simplified analysis of *There Was An Old Woman Who Swallowed a Fly.*

only makes the Problem worse, so she then in quick succession swallows a bird to catch the spider ('How absurd to swallow a bird'), a cat to swallow the bird ('Now fancy that, to swallow a cat'), a dog to swallow the cat ('What a hog, to swallow a dog'), and a cow to swallow the dog ('I don't know how she swallowed a cow'), each of which worsens the Problem. Finally she swallows a horse and the song comes to an abrupt end with the words 'She's dead of course'. The pattern is, as already noted, the same as that for *My Love Story*, except that, importantly, it is a Negative Evaluation that brings the story to a close, despite what I was saying earlier about the recycling effects of Negative Evaluation.

As the labelling of the Figure 7.4 reveals, what distinguishes the two kinds of Negative Evaluation/Result is the irretrievability or otherwise of the Result. If the Negative Result is beyond retrieval, it functions exactly like a Positive Evaluation for the purposes of pattern completion.

Evidence for this can be found in the child's joke (Example 4.3), analysed in Chapter 4 in terms of its hierarchical organisation, to be found on p. 57: each of the

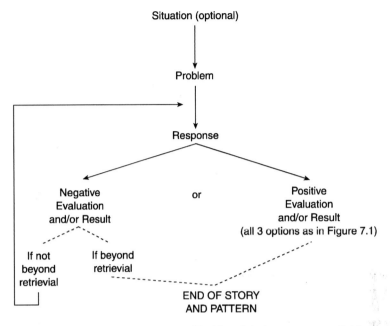

Figure 7.5 Modified representation of range of Problem-Solution patterns available.

episodes in this joke is complete in its own terms, the incompleteness of the first two episodes coming from their lack of a humorous pay-off that would justify their being told in the first place, and not from any need to learn more about the escapes of Fred or Bill. The third episode is likewise complete, the only difference lying in the irretrievably negative result of Joe's Response, which in its contrast with the previous two stories gives the joke its point. The point here is that the reader will not ask, *So what did Joe do about this?* despite the Negative Evaluation. We must therefore modify our earlier diagram to take account of this possibility (see Figure 7.5).

Participant-linking in Problem-Solution patterns

In two respects, *My Love Story* and *The Old Woman Who Swallowed a Fly* represent fairly simply structured texts. In the first place, like most narratives, they tell their stories in strictly linear fashion, with the order of the reportage of events matching exactly the supposed 'events' they purport to report. In the second place, the stories as told only offer one point of view. In *My Love Story* we momentarily hear the husband's position on the marriage – *her husband did [like it] really really really much* – but otherwise all the events are told from Mary's perspective, and the old woman's is the only perspective we consider in the song; we do not hear the complaints of any of the animals, swallowed whole in order to catch some previously unlucky creature. Another way of making the same point is that if we were to apply the matrix analysis discussed in the last chapter to either of the stories, we would get a matrix with one full column and one virtually empty one and the sequence of the telling would be a straight reading off the matrix with no variations in the order of telling. With this in mind, consider the following very brief *New Scientist* text:

7.17   **No smell garlic**
A Tokyo rice grower, Toshia Nakagawa, reckons he has won the battle to produce a type of garlic which retains its seasoning qualities without the smell. (2) In the past, chemists have succeeded in removing the smell to reduce antagonism between lovers and non-lovers of the root; critics how- ever have argued that the processing destroys the flavour. (3) Nakagawa started his experiments in 1958, planting heads which appeared to have less smell than others and using different types of fertilisers. (4) Now he claims the breakthrough has been made – the final tests with his new product were with a herd of cows fed with the garlic whose milk showed no odour at all.

The pattern we find in this text is one of the options indicated in Figure 7.5 above, now shown in Figure 7.6. The first difference between this and the previous analysis (of *My Love Story*) is that this diagram represents the *pattern* not the *order of occurrence* of the elements. Since patterns are in the last analysis (excuse the pun) a sequence of answers to regularly co-occurring and predictable questions, we would have been able to infer from the discussion of matrices in the last chapter that the Problem-Solution questions might be answered in different orders. In popular science writing and in advertisements, in fact, the sequence often begins with a statement of Response. The relationships among the elements remain the same however.

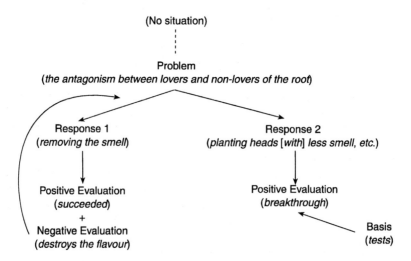

Figure 7.6 Slightly simplified representation of the Problem-Solution pattern in *No smell garlic*.

Sentence 1 encapsulates the pattern. There is a positive Evaluation (*won*) of a Response (*battle*) to what we have, reading linearly, to identify tentatively as Problem, in the absence of any better categories. (In the next chapter, I will offer a more satisfactory way of accounting for this part of the first sentence.) Sentence 1 having provided a kind of abstract for the story, sentence 2 then begins the pattern in more detail. It confirms the tentative categorisation of Problem in sentence 1; *antagonism between lovers and non-lovers of the root* is clearly signalled as Problem by the word *antagonism*. In the same sentence we are told of a Response to this Problem: *removing the smell to reduce antagonism*, and the Response is initially given a Positive Evaluation and Result (*succeeded*). However, the second half of the sentence offers a parallel Negative Result (*the processing destroys the flavour*) and this signals a return to Problem for the scientists (and explains Nakagawa's battle in sentence 1). Sentence 3 meets the expectation of another Response to the Problem, without implying a positive result; the sentence answers the question *What did Nakagawa do about it?* In sentence 4, Nakagawa's Response is positively evaluated (*breakthrough*) and a basis is given (*tests . . . showed*) for the Evaluation.

It may seem redundant to talk through the analysis in this way when most of what I have just said duplicates what is available in visual form in Figure 7.6. And so it is – but I have added one important set of details. I have spelt out *whose* Problem, *whose* Response and (important, this, as we shall see in a moment) *whose* Evaluation it is that the text reports. To do so is not to negate the earlier point I made about the oblique relationship between linguistic representation of Problem-Solution patterns and the non-linguistic patterns we may find in our existence; we require no knowledge other than that supplied by the text in order to specify the participants associated with the components of the pattern. With that in mind, a fuller account of the pattern in Example 7.17 can be provided, as in Figure 7.7. The topology of Figure 7.7 is rather different from that of Figure 7.6 but that is partly a matter of convenience of representation (though the arrows do highlight slightly different aspects of the relationships among the parts). Arrows indicate logical direction, not the order in which information is communicated (as we have already seen).

I mentioned above that it was particularly important to attach Evaluation to the participant from whom it originated. In the case of this text, it will be apparent from Figure 7.7 that the Positive Evaluation comes from the same source as the Response. The text seems complete to us as readers, but it may not seem complete to us as sceptical scientists until we see some independent evaluation or else the detailed results of the tests carried out. The absence of any Evaluation from the writer might give us pause for thought.

What is slightly unusual in popular science writing is the norm in advertising; advertisers always positively evaluate their product or service. Sometimes, though, there may be more than one Evaluation. Consider the following example from the 1930s; as always, sentence numbering has been added.

7.18   (1) 'I've got to have a . . . *minor operation*'
        [picture omitted of a man in obvious discomfort talking
            to a sitting man, probably intended to be his boss]

(2) *More serious than most men realize . . . the troubles caused by harsh toilet tissue*

(3) In nearly every business organization a surprisingly large percentage of the employees are suffering from rectal trouble.

(4) This fact is well known to companies that require physical examinations of their personnel. (5) Yet even these same concerns are frequently negligent in providing equipment that will safeguard the health of their employees.

(6) Harsh toilet tissue, for instance.

(7) Any physician will tell you that mucous membrane can be seriously inflamed by the use of harsh or chemically impure toilet tissue.

(8) Some specialists estimate that 65 per cent of all men and women at middle age suffer from troubles caused or aggravated by inferior toilet tissue.

(9) Protection from rectal illness is just as important in the home as in business.

(10) Fortunately, women are more careful in matters of this kind than men.

(11) Already millions of homes are equipped with ScotTissue or Waldorf – the tissues that doctors and hospitals recommend.

(12) Extremely soft, cloth-like and absorbent, these safety tissues cannot harm the most sensitive skin. (13) They are chemically pure, contain no harsh irritants.

(14) Be safe . . . at home, at work. (15) Insist on ScotTissue or Waldorf. Scott Paper Company, Chester, Pa. (16) In Canada, Scott Paper Company, Ltd, Toronto, Ontario

[illustrations of ScotTissue and Waldorf toilet rolls with accompanying descriptive text omitted]

This advertisement, although more than 60 years old, has a number of the characteristic features of Problem-Solution advertisements. Notice, though, that there are two Positive Evaluations, one ascribed to doctors and hospitals, the other emanating from ScotTissue, as can be seen in Figure 7.8.

Figures 7.2 and 7.5 must now be seen as simplifications of the pattern possibilities, in that they do not include participant attribution. A more abstract representation of the possibilities is offered in Figure 7.9, though obviously this diagram does not attempt to pick up on the complications of recycling. It follows from Figure 7.9 that there may be more than one Response from different participants, and that there may be a range of Evaluations from participants and writer, as illustrated in the ScotTissue text.

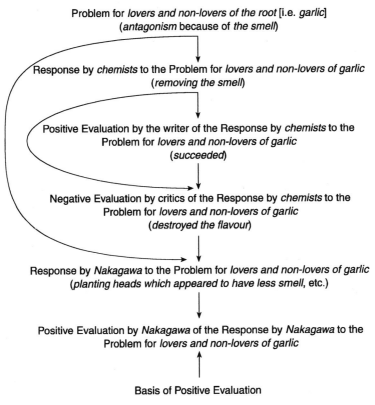

Figure 7.7 Participant attribution in *No smell garlic.*

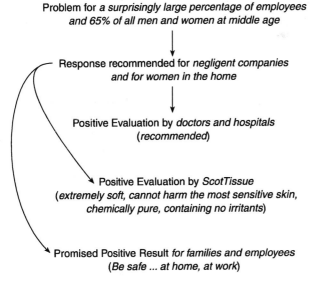

Figure 7.8 Overall Problem-Solution patterning of ScotTissue advertisement.

Problem for *x*

↓

Response by *y*^{n} to Problem for *x*

↓

Evaluation by *z*^{n} of Response by *y* to Problem for *x*

where *y* may or may not be the same as *x*
and *z* may or may not be the same as either *x* or *y*
and any or all of *x*, *y* and *z* may be the writer.

Figure 7.9 Participant attribution in the Problem-Solution pattern.

Interlocking patterns in narrative

There are a number of implications to this modification to our description but perhaps the most important is that it makes it possible to account for narratives with more than one central participant. Consider the following delightful verse tale by AA Milne:

7.19   *Bad Sir Brian Botany*
    Sir Brian had a battleaxe with great big knobs on;
       He went about the villagers and blipped them on the head.
    On Wednesday and on Saturday, but mostly on the latter day,
       He called at all the cottages, and this is what he said:
         'I am Sir Brian!' (*ting-ling*)
          'I am Sir Brian!' (*rat-tat*)
         'I am Sir Brian, as bold as a lion –
          Take *that!* – and *that!* – and *that!*'

    Sir Brian had a pair of boots with great big spurs on,
       A fighting pair of which he was particularly fond.
    On Tuesday and on Friday, just to make the street look tidy,
       He'd collect the passing villagers and kick them in the pond.
         'I am Sir Brian!' (*sper-lash!*)
          'I am Sir Brian!' (*sper-losh!*)
         'I am Sir Brian, as bold as a lion –
          Is anyone else for a wash?'

    Sir Brian woke one morning, and he couldn't find his battleaxe;
       He walked into the village in his second pair of boots.
    He had gone a hundred paces, when the street was full of faces,
       And the villagers were round him with ironical salutes.
         'You are Sir Brian? Indeed!
         You are Sir Brian? Dear, dear!
        You are Sir Brian, as bold as a lion?
         Delighted to meet you here!'

Sir Brian went a journey, and he found a lot of duckweed:
> They pulled him out and dried him, and they blipped him on the head.
They took him by the breeches, and they hurled him into ditches,
> And they pushed him under waterfalls, and this is what they said:
>> 'You are Sir Brian – don't laugh,
>>> You are Sir Brian – don't cry;
>> You are Sir Brian, as bold as a lion –
>>> Sir Brian, the lion, good-bye!'

Sir Brian struggled home again, and chopped up his battleaxe,
> Sir Brian took his fighting boots, and threw them in the fire.
He is quite a different person now he hasn't got his spurs on,
> And he goes about the village as B. Botany, Esquire.
>> 'I am Sir Brian? Oh, *no!*
>> I am Sir Brian? Who's he?
>> *I* haven't got any title, I'm Botany –
>> Plain Mr Botany (B).

This tale of a worker's revolution from my childhood is still, by narrative standards, a simple affair, but, unlike *My Love Story*, it has – in classical terminology – a protagonist and a (group) antagonist, and accordingly participant linking of the pattern elements becomes essential if we are to produce an adequate account of its structure.

The first thing to note is that the villagers have a Problem, evoked by *blipped them on the head*. The pattern for them is shown in Figure 7.10.

But Sir Brian also has a Problem once the villagers attack him, and his pattern looks similar, except that we have an extensive Situation comprising verses 1 and 2 (see Figure 7.11).

Problem for villagers (*blipped*, etc.)

↓

Response by villagers (ditto)

↓

Positive Result for villagers (*Sir Brian chopped up his battleaxe*)

Figure 7.10 The first Problem-Solution pattern in *Bad Sir Brian Botany*.

Situation for Sir Brian

↓

Problem for Sir Brian (*blipped*, etc.)

↓

Response by Sir Brian (*Sir Brian chopped up his battleaxe*)

↓

Implied Positive Result
for the former Sir Brian

Figure 7.11 The second Problem-Solution pattern in *Bad Sir Brian Botany*.

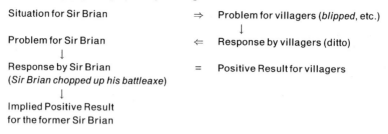

Figure 7.12 The combined Problem-Solution patterns in *Bad Sir Brian Botany.*

Of course the point is that these two patterns interweave, and make a single pattern, shown in Figure 7.12. The combination of arrows and equal signs in the centre column is meant to indicate that Sir Brian's Situation is the same as and leads to the villager's Problem, that the villagers' Response is the same as and leads to Sir Brian's Response, and so on. Once we allow for the interlocking of participant-linked Problem-Solution patterns, we are in the position to consider handling quite complex texts. Or we would be if this were the only pattern. But it is not, and in the next chapter a range of patterns will be described that are similar to the Problem-Solution pattern and share many of its properties.

Summary of the characteristics of Problem-Solution patterns

Before we examine other culturally popular patterns, it may be helpful to list the characteristics of the Problem-Solution pattern as described in this chapter, not least because most of them will also be found to be characteristics of the other patterns:

(a) The Problem-Solution pattern arises as a result of the writer answering a predictable series of questions. The order in which these questions are answered is, however, not fixed.

(b) The pattern is characteristically lexically signalled, either by means of inscribed signals (e.g. *solution*) or inscribed evaluations functioning as signals (e.g. *unfortunately*) or by means of evoking signals (e.g. *had no money*). One or more of these signals serves as a trigger for the pattern, in that it makes the pattern visible to the reader.

(c) The pattern may be preceded by a Situation which is recognised retro-spectively as providing a context for the pattern proper.

(d) In between Problem and Response there may be an intervening stage in which either a Plan or Recommendation or outline of what will count as a Response occurs.

(e) A Negative Result or a Negative Evaluation of the Response usually prompts a recycling of the pattern, and the pattern continues to recycle until such time as a Positive Result or Evaluation is reached. A Positive Result or Evaluation can always be overridden by an immediately following Negative Result or

Evaluation. The exception is when a Negative Result is felt to be so severe as not to admit further Response.

(f) The elements of the pattern are attributed to participants in the text, those participants including the writer and reader.

(g) Participant attribution permits the recognition of the interweaving of several different and co-existing patterns.

Bibliographical end-notes

Example 7.9 is drawn from *Mr Nosey* by Roger Hargreaves; Example 7.10 is drawn from *Big Dog. . . Little Dog: A Bedtime Story* by P. D. Eastman. The advertisement for MCIS (7.13) was current in national newspapers in the early part of 1998. Example 7.14 was taken from an advertisement for home wax treatments current in the mid-1980s. *My Love Story* (7.16) was written by my daughter when she was seven and printed in the Moor Green Primary School magazine. *No smell garlic* (7.17) appeared in *New Scientist*, 4 May 1978, p. 295. The advertisement (7.18) for ScotTissue was current in the 1930s; the advertising campaign of which it formed a part was a highly successful one. *Bad Sir Brian Botany* (7.19) is one of the poems by A. A. Milne in *When We Were Very Young*, first published in 1927 by Methuen & Co.

A large number of linguists have sought to describe the way knowledge is stored and utilised in the interpretation of text and the world, and they have all, it would sometimes seem, invented a new term to describe the phenomenon, as Widdowson (1984) has complained. The term 'schema' comes from Bartlett (1932) and probably is the most used, but the following terms have had currency also: frames (Goffman 1975), plans and scripts (Schank and Abelson 1977), ideational scaffolding (Adams 1979), global knowledge patterns (de Beaugrande 1980), scenarios (Sanford and Garrod 1981). Langer (1987), in an investigation of reading, concluded that readers activate a combination of genre knowledge, content knowledge and form knowledge when they make sense of text; although the boundaries between these types of knowledge are not clear-cut, this position seems sound.

The pattern here identified has been widely described. Grimes (1975) and Van Dijk (1977) make brief reference to it. Fuller descriptions can be found in Winter (1976, 1977), Hoey (1979, 1983), Jordan (1980, 1984, 1992), and Crombie (1985) all of whom describe it in terms very similar to those adopted here. Mann and Thompson (1986, 1988) and the story grammarians (e.g. Rumelhart 1975, Stein with Glenn 1979, with Policastro 1984, and on her own, 1982) have used related systems of description. Meyer has a similar and fully worked out description of long standing that has been particularly developed in connection with work on memory (e.g. Meyer 1975, 1992, with Rice 1982). Labov (1972, with Waletzky 1967, and Fanshel 1977) has used an influential method of description that has a number of features in common with that provided here.

8 Other culturally popular patterns

Introduction

I ended the previous chapter with a list of features associated with the Problem-Solution pattern. Almost all these characteristics also apply to the patterns I shall cover in this chapter, with only minor terminological changes. This chapter will take their applicability for granted and I will not seek to demonstrate for each new pattern that it is, for example, capable of recycling or is characteristically signalled. Where I do mention these features, it will be in order to introduce some new feature that it was not possible to bring in during the last chapter.

There were several reasons for giving the Problem-Solution pattern first. One was that it is one of the most frequently occurring (if not the most frequent); another was that it has been the most thoroughly investigated of all the patterns. Many of the patterns covered in the current chapter, on the other hand, have been little described and are either not mentioned in the literature or are only mentioned in passing. A third reason was that, as will become apparent, there are grounds for regarding it as more basic than the other patterns.

The limitations of Problem-Solution patterning

The first thing to note is that we do need other patterns. It would be easy to infer from some of what has been written, including perhaps some of my own contributions to the field, that the Problem-Solution pattern accounts for the majority of texts. This is not so. If we look at how it applies to the telling of *Goldilocks and The Three Bears* that was analysed from a hierarchical perspective in Chapter 4, we will see that it accounts for only a proportion of the text.

At first it looks as if the categories associated with Problem-Solution will account for this story very well. The first eight sentences form a complete, if uninteresting, pattern (Figure 8.1). The two types of Situation reflect two types of background information that can be supplied prior to the onset of a pattern. The first reports statements that have validity for a considerable time. Thus Father Bear is assumed to have been big for a indefinite period previously and, since nothing happens in the story to change his size (it isn't his porridge that gets eaten!), he is assumed to remain big throughout. Baby Bear has presumably been

General Situation (sentences 1–4)
Particular Situation (sentences 5–7)
↓
Problem (The porridge was rather hot)   ⎞
↓   ⎟
Response (the three bears went for a walk in the wood)   ⎬   (sentence 8)
↓   ⎟
Implied Positive Result (it cooled)   ⎠

Figure 8.1 Analysis of the first eight sentences of *Goldilocks and the Three Bears*.

tiny and little as long as he has been in (fictional) existence. On the other hand, the cooking of the porridge is reported as true just for this day. Adult writing displays the same kind of division. Dickens' *Barnaby Rudge* begins with statements about an inn that have validity over a long period and then offers statements about people in it on a particular night which have validity only for the occasion reported.

The Problem is somewhat subtly signalled by *rather x*. In an examination of 78 instances of *rather* + adjective or adverb (excluding comparative adjectives and adverbs), drawn from the *Guardian* newspaper, I found that almost 58% of the adjectives or adverbs were negative evaluations; only 24% were positive (the remainder being neutral). This means that *rather* has a preference for negatives (the technical term for this is that it has a negative semantic prosody). This, combined with the word *so* at the beginning of the next clause, means that we interpret the hotness as problematic rather than as an asset.

So far so good. The analysis continues to appear to work in the next chunk of text. Indeed, it is here that it seems most natural to apply it. Sentences 9–11 are again general Situation, these statements having general validity rather than validity only on this occasion, while sentences 12–17a provide particular Situation. The Problem is identified in the second half of sentence 17; she was *hungry*, an Aspect of her Situation requiring a Response. There then follows a recycling pattern as shown in Figure 8.2.

It would be easy to be satisfied with this analysis, but it has certain deficiencies that cannot be overlooked. In the first place, and not perhaps very importantly, *tast[ing] the porridge* hardly counts as an adequate Response to the Problem of being *hungry*; only when Goldilocks eats the third bowl of porridge *all up* can we presume that the Problem has been adequately solved. Secondly, and more seriously, there is too much heterogeneous material lumped together under the heading of Particular Situation. It seems to go beyond preparatory material and to provide us with a substantial chunk of story, compared, for example, with the brief Particular Situation pertaining to the Bears.

The third incident, with the three beds, follows a very similar path to that outlined for the porridge episode, though of course with only a brief Situation (see Figure 8.3). Here there is no excess of Situation and the unease I was expressing about the Responses does not apply. As a preliminary to going to sleep, Goldilocks' actions are appropriate.

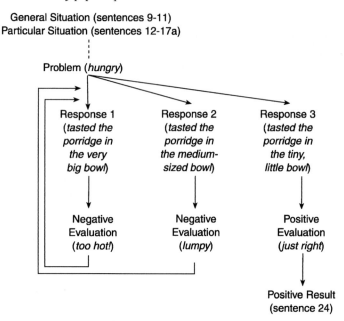

Figure 8.2 Analysis of the 'porridge' episode in *Goldilocks and the Three Bears*.

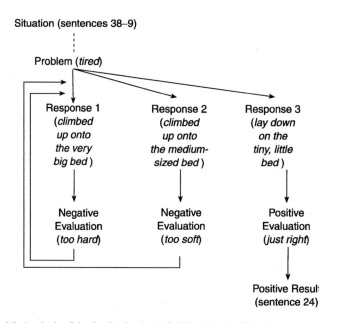

Figure 8.3 Analysis of the 'bed' episode in *Goldilocks and the Three Bears*.

However, there is a much bigger anomaly to worry about. We have an adequate analysis of Goldilocks' first piece of antisocial behaviour and an equally adequate analysis of her third piece of antisocial behaviour. But what do we do about the second? In all sorts of ways, the incident of her trying out the chairs and finding them variously comfortable until she finds Baby Bear's chair is parallel to the porridge and bed incidents. There is the rejection of the chairs of Father Bear and Mother Bear, expressed in very similar terms (*too high* and *too hard*), there is the exploitation of Baby Bear's belongings, and at the outset there is a very similarly worded Situation. *But crucially there is no Problem.* There is no trigger of the pattern whatsoever. We appear to move directly from Situation to Response, and this is simply not permissible within the terms laid down in the previous chapter. Clearly we will not have a satisfactory description of narrative patterning until we can account for the middle 'chair' episode.

Nor do the limitations of the Problem-Solution pattern end there. If we look at the last third of the story, from the return of the Bears to the escape of Goldilocks, we find that once again Problem-Solution only accounts for a small proportion of the text. The final few sentences (sentences 66–70), relating Goldilock's escape from the bears on discovery, fit well enough, with sentence 66 serving as Situation, sentence 67 as Problem (evoked by *bears* for those who know their wildlife and inscribed as *fright* for those who don't), sentence 68 as Response and sentence 69 as Positive Result (for all concerned). The final sentence underlines this Result and tells us to expect no more patterns to open up.

But what do we do with what is unquestionably the most famous part of the story – the Bears' repeated puzzlement about the mystery intruder – a part so famous that a sex comedy starring Dean Martin was once made entitled *Who's Been Sleeping in My Bed?* It is not an adequate answer to squeeze this episode into the Problem-Solution categories. In the first place, the questions they repeatedly ask are not conveniently categorisable as an aspect of Situation requiring a Response (the definition I have given for Problem), unless the term *requiring* in this definition is stretched. Secondly, there is no recognisable signal of Problem here nor is it easy to imagine one. Finally, a 'Response' to this 'Problem' would not answer the question 'What did they do about it?' Their enquiry does not require that anyone *do* anything at all.

What all this means is that the Problem-Solution pattern is only part of the answer to the question of how texts are organised. Applying it to a traditional tale such as *Goldilocks and the Three Bears* has shown it to account for almost exactly half the story. While that is still quite a lot, it means that we need to look for other types of pattern.

The Goal-Achievement pattern

One pattern that is readily attested can be illustrated by reference to the fabricated 'language teaching' narrative that I repeatedly manipulated in the previous chapter. Consider the following rather less vainglorious variant of that narrative:

8.1   (1) I am a teacher of English Language. (2) One day some students came to me wanting to be able to write novels. (3) I taught them text analysis. (4) Now they can't even write their names.

The tale of reversal is still intact, even perhaps strengthened, but the second sentence is no longer a Problem as defined. Students wanting to write novels can hardly be regarded as a problem even for the most jaundiced of teachers. What we have here is the trigger of a pattern that is closely related to the Problem-Solution pattern but has its own signals and operates slightly differently, namely the Goal-Achievement pattern, which can be represented by the questions:

What was the situation?
What goal did *x* want to achieve?
What method did *x* or *y* use to achieve it?
How successful was this in the opinion of *x*, *y* or *z*?/What was the result for *x*?

where *x*, *y* and *z* may be the same person(s) and one or more may be the writer.

The Goal-Achievement pattern is associated with narratives and the more straightforward advertisements; it is also associated with scientific writing, both popular and specialist. Its component parts are Situation, Goal, Method of Achievement and Evaluation and/or Result. The options it permits are the same as those for Problem-Solution. The major difference between this and the Problem-Solution pattern is that Goal is defined as 'an intended change in Situation'. The following authentic, if unlikely, advertisement illustrates the pattern straightforwardly; as always, I have added sentence numbering:

8.2   (1) How to rub your stomach away.
       (2) FREE REPORT
       (3) Here's a new method from China to flatten your stomach.
       (4) There are two principal components to this exercise. (5) The first part begins by... [details omitted].
       (5) To order your copy of HOW TO RUB YOUR STOMACH AWAY send your name, address and report title to Carnell plc

Sentence 1 defines the Goal and Sentence 2 is assumed to offer a Method cataphorically referred to in the phrase *How to*, which also serves to trigger the script/pattern in the reader. Sentence 3 then spells out the Method, signalled (self-evidently) by *method*. The same sentence repeats the Goal *to flatten your stomach*. Subsequent sentences give particulars of the Method, in a preview-detail relation, though these are omitted here. Sentence 5 invites the readers to make the Method their own.

In some respects, that is all that one needs to say about the Goal-Achievement pattern. It has its own signals (e.g. *want to, would like to, aim, objective, means, way, strategy, by V-ing*) though there are some shared signals – the last two in the previous list appear sometimes as signals of Response. Otherwise Goal-Achievement is like Problem-Solution in almost all the respects listed at the end of the previous chapter. We have already seen that the pattern arises as a result of the writer answering a predictable series of questions and that Situation, Plan and/or Recommended Method can optionally appear before and within the pattern. That it recycles when there is normal Negative Evaluation or Result is shown by a dull version of the 'language teaching' text:

8.3 (1) I am a teacher of English Language. (2) One day some students came to me wanting to be able to write novels. (3) I taught them text analysis. (4) This showed them how to identify the structure of novels but not how to write them. (5) So I taught them literary criticism. (6) This taught them how to interpret novels and place them in their historical and cultural contexts, but they still were unable to write them. (7) So . . . etc.

This and the previous version also demonstrate that participant attribution is as much a feature of the Goal-Achievement pattern as it was of the Problem-Solution pattern; thus, in Example 8.3, we have a Goal for some students, a Method adopted by the teacher and a Result for the students.

There is, however, an important respect in which the possibilities for Goal-Achievement patterns differ from those considered for Problem-Solution patterns, and this is that whereas it was shown to be perfectly possible to have an interlocking Problem-Solution pattern (as for *Bad Sir Brian Botany*), it is not theoretically possible to have interlocking Goal-Achievement patterns, as shown in Figures 8.4 and 8.5. It is, however, perfectly possible for a Goal-Achievement pattern to interlock with a Problem-Solution pattern (see Figure 8.6). An example of such interlocking is the following news item:

8.4 (1) If you want to order a Chinese takeaway, force your teenager to turn down his hi-fi, or if you need help with closing the window, what number do you call?

(2) For the people of Kent, the answer would appear to be 999.

(3) Of the 170,000 emergency calls made to Kent constabulary last year only about a quarter had anything to do with the police. (4) The vast bulk were for the trivial, the mundane and the absurd. (5) Many Kent residents also appear to view 999 as a cheap alternative to Directory Enquiries.

(6) The police have finally had enough. (7) In two weeks' time anyone who telephones 999 and asks a detective to inform their mother that they are going to be home late – as someone did earlier this month – will be given a verbal clip round the ear.

What we have is a more complex version of the pattern of organisation illustrated in Figure 8.6 where one participant's Means for achieving a Goal is another participant's Problem. Sentence 1 states a Goal (*want to*), something that may be

Figure 8.4 An impossible interlocking of Goal-Achievement patterns.

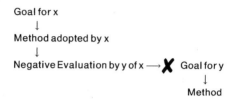

Figure 8.5 A second impossible interlocking of Goal-Achievement patterns.

Figure 8.6 A possible interlocking of Goal-Achievement and Problem-Solution patterns.

seen either as a Goal or a Problem (*force a teenager to turn down his hi-fi*) and a Problem (*need*). Sentence 5 adds a further Goal. In all but the last case the participant concerned is *you*; in the final instance the participant is *many Kent residents*. This mixed bag of Goals and Problems find their Method and/or Response in sentence 2 (*answer*), the participant being *the people of Kent*. It is at this point that we encounter the interlocking of the Goal-Achievement and Problem-Solution patterns. The Negative Evaluations in Sentences 3 and 4 mark the Method used by the people of Kent as Problem for the police. Sentence 7 then provides their Response to their Problem.

What all this demonstrates is that one text may represent the interleaving of different patterns, not simply of differently attributed patterns. Once we recognise this, we have to be alert to other ways that Goal-Achievement and Problem-Solution may combine. To start with a relatively simple case, here is another child's joke, very similar in some respects to the one analysed in Chapter 4:

8.5   (1) There was once three men, Fred, Bill and Joe, who entered a competition who could stay in a pigsty with lots of pigs for the longest amount of time. (2) First of all went in Fred, and he stayed in for 10 minutes, 20 minutes, half an hour. (3) 'Pooh stinky, fresh air!' (4) He came out. (5) Then went in Bill, and he stayed in for ten minutes, 20 minutes, half an hour, 40 minutes, 50 minutes, one hour. (6) 'Pooh stinky, fresh air!' (7) *He* came out. (8) Then went Joe, and he was like a tramp and was rather smelly. (9) He stayed in for 10 minutes, 20 minutes, 30 minutes, 40 minutes, 50 minutes, 60 minutes, one hour ten minutes, one hour 20 minutes, one hour 30 minutes, one hour 40 minutes, one hour 50 minutes, two hours. (10) The pigs came out. (11) 'Pooh stinky, fresh air!'

The dominant pattern in this joke is Goal-Achievement with each man setting out to achieve the Goal of staying in a pigsty the longest. In marked contrast to the previously analysed joke, the first two characters have irretrievably Negative Results (the laws of the joke denying them repeated attempts to better their time) and the third man has a Positive Result.

Even in a narrative like this, dominated by Goal-Achievement, Problem-Solution patterns can be detected. The reader might spot that embedded within each story there is in fact a mini-Problem-Solution pattern, which might be represented diagrammatically as in Figure 8.7. This organisation is then repeated for each of the subsequent episodes, with the important difference that in the third episode it is the pigs that have the Problem with their Response providing a Positive Result for Joe. We would want to say that the Goal-Achievement patterns dominate in the three episodes of the joke, but it is of interest that a full analysis needs the Problem-Solution pattern as well.

Another way the patterns may combine is that a Goal may have a self-evident Method of Achievement, which some Problem prevents from being used. An example is the following extract from a somewhat improbable but entirely genuine advertisement:

8.6   (1) Read the world's 100 Best Classics . . . in less than 2 hours
        (2) Like most of us, you've always wanted to read the world's great classics of literature. (3) But, because you have so much on, you just haven't been able to find the time. (4) And right now, you cannot see when you will have the time. (5) Now you can catch up on the world's greatest books – in just 60 seconds per book, thanks to a new guide called *The 100 Best Classics at a Glance.*

Sentence 2 describes a Goal for 'you' (*you've always wanted*). The obvious Method is to read them! But sentences 3 and 4 describe a Problem (lack of time) which

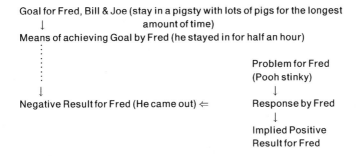

Figure 8.7 Analysis of first episode of 'pigsty' joke.

prevents the obvious Method being successful. Sentence 5 promises a Response to the Problem (*60 seconds per book*) which simultaneously permits the Achievement of the Goal. (We will return to sentence 1 later in the chapter.)

Goal-Achievement patterns are common in a wide variety of texts. They are, for obvious reasons, very common in advertisements and in certain kinds of scientific writing and specialist journalism. They also occur in narratives; in the British context, the traditional stories of Dick Whittington and Puss-in-Boots use Goal-Achievement as their dominant mode of organisation.

The Opportunity-Taking pattern

Goal-Achievement is an important pattern, particularly given its tendency to occur within Problem-Solution patterns. But recognition of its existence does not bring us the slightest bit closer to a fuller analysis of *Goldilocks and the Three Bears*. For that we need to turn to another pattern, closely related to Goal-Achievement, namely the Opportunity-Taking pattern.

As a way into this pattern, it is worth reflecting for a moment on the ways we interact. We can offer information (inform) and request goods and services (request); we can also offer goods and services (offer) and request information (question) (Halliday 1994). These types of speech action roughly correlate with certain types of pattern. Goal-Achievement patterns begin with some proposition not unlike a request. Goals and requests share the property of being something that some participant would like to see happen. (The correlation and where Problem-Solution fits into it will be considered in the final chapter.) This partial parallelism might invite us to expect a pattern that begins with some proposition not unlike an offer and a pattern that begins with a question or something like a question, and we indeed find both. The offer-like pattern is the Opportunity-Taking pattern and there are, in fact, two question-like patterns, one discussed later in this chapter ('The Gap in Knowledge-Filling pattern') and the other in Chapter 9. The Opportunity-Taking pattern often begins with an implicit offer which a participant reacts to. If we re-consider the Rumelhart and Ortony text with which the previous chapter began, we can see that it fits into this format:

8.7   Mary heard the ice cream man coming. She remembered her pocket money. She rushed into the house.

The first sentence reports an Opportunity, and the second and third report the (beginning of) the Taking of that Opportunity with the second sentence filling a Plan function like that noted for both the Problem-Solution and Goal-Achievement patterns. Indeed the pattern for Opportunity-Taking is very similar to those we have already considered. The questions it answers are:

What was the situation?
What opportunity arose for *x* within this situation?

What did *x* do about it?
What was the result for *x*?

It can be represented diagrammatically as in Figure 8.8.

As with the previous patterns, Opportunity-Taking occurs in a range of types of text. It is, however, particularly common in advertisements, newspaper offers (note the word!) and narratives. Here is a fairly straightforward advertisement example:

8.8 TURNER'S VENICE

(1) A UNIQUE OPPORTUNITY TO OBTAIN FOUR LIMITED LITHOGRAPHS FROM THE ARTIST'S FINAL TOUR OF VENICE
(2) A Special Offer to Collectors
(3) Reply now and you will receive a free colour brochure giving you a fascinating insight to Turner's Venice. (4) The publishers will immediately reserve a complete set of pictures for you.

Sentences 1 and 2 provide the Opportunity, signalled by *opportunity* and *offer*, and, indirectly, by *unique*, which has a strong tendency, along with words like *special*, *once in a lifetime*, *outstanding* and *unusual*, to co-occur with the Opportunity on offer; *special* in fact occurs in sentence 2. Sentence 3 describes how the Opportunity may be taken and reports a Positive Result in sentence 4.

The features we identified for Goal-Achievement apply here also. So patterns may nest inside each other in the ways described above. In Example 8.6, the first sentence is in fact an Opportunity. So the full patterning for that text is as in Figure 8.9. This diagram reflects an important function of Opportunity-Taking patterns. They often combine with Problem-Solution or Goal-Achievement patterns, with the Taking of the Opportunity doubling as Response to Problem

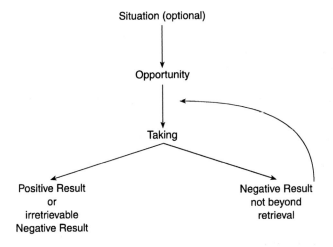

Figure 8.8 The organisation of the Opportunity-Taking pattern.

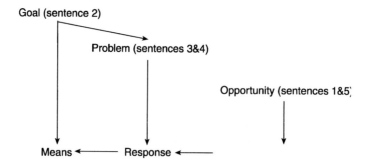

Figure 8.9 A fuller analysis of 'reading the classics' advertisement.

or Means of Achieving Goal. If we look again at *Bad Sir Brian Botany* (Example 7.19), we see that a fuller analysis would be as shown in Figure 8.10.

Another instance of the interlocking of Opportunity-Taking and Problem-Solution patterns is the following story from Genesis:

8.9   Early the next morning Abraham took some food and a skin of water and gave them to Hagar. He set them on her shoulders and sent her off with the boy. She went on her way and wandered in the desert of Beersheba. When the water in the skin was gone, she put the boy under one of the bushes. Then she went off and sat down nearby, about a bow-shot away, for she thought, 'I cannot watch the boy die'. And as she sat there nearby, she began to sob . . . Then God opened her eyes and she saw a well of water. So she went and filled the skin with water and gave the boy a drink.

This has a similar structure to that of *Bad Sir Brian Botany*, albeit simpler (Fig. 8.11).

The combination of Problem-Solution and Opportunity-Taking just illustrated may be common enough to be treated as a stable kind of pattern-complex. Notice that an Opportunity can be attributed, as in this instance and the advertisements

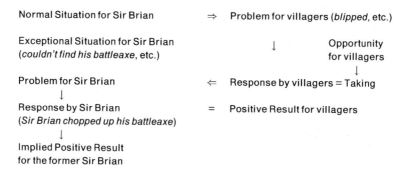

Figure 8.10 The combination of Problem-Solution and Opportunity-Taking patterns in *Bad Sir Brian Botany.*

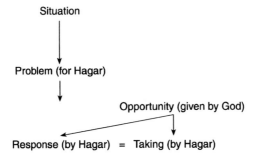

Figure 8.11 The combination of Problem-Solution and Opportunity-Taking patterns in the story of Hagar.

we have looked at, but it may be unattributed; this represents a subtle difference from the situation described for the previous two patterns.

All the examples I have given so far of Opportunity-Taking patterns in narrative have been in combination with Problem-Solution. But this is not a requirement. As an example of Opportunity-Taking patterning on its own, consider the following extract from *Alice's Adventures in Wonderland*.

8.10   Soon her eye fell on a little glass book that was lying under the table: she opened it, and found in it a very small cake, on which the words 'EAT ME' were beautifully marked in currants.

'Well, I'll eat it,' said Alice ... So she set to work, and very soon finished off the cake.

Here the context does not set the cake up as a possible Response (though Alice has her problems). Strictly speaking we have two Opportunities here. The book offers the Opportunity to be opened and the cake offers the Opportunity to be eaten.

Although Opportunity-Taking is like Goal-Achievement and Problem-Solution in many ways, and although, as I sought to show in my account of the advertisements, its signals are often of exactly the same type as those of the other patterns, the pattern is often triggered in a rather different way. Opportunity is characteristically signalled in narrative by an encounter with an object of unambiguous function. Thus we have had:

8.11   Mary heard the ice cream man coming.

8.12   Then God opened her eyes and she saw a well of water.

8.13   Soon her eye fell on a little glass book that was lying under the table: she opened it, and found in it a very small cake.

The first thing to note about this set of Opportunities is that they all include an explicit sensory encounter (*heard, saw* (twice), *her eye fell on*). The second point of note is that all the objects but the last have an unambiguous function. Ice cream men only function to sell ice cream, wells only function to provide water, books are to be opened (and read, normally) and cakes have no other function than to be eaten – part of the weirdness of Alice's experience is that the cake she encounters spells out the self-evident in currants.

With these points in mind, we can explain substantial chunks of the Goldilocks story:

8.14　(13) Soon Goldilocks came to the little house where the three bears lived.
(14) The door was open and she peeped inside. (15) No-one was there so she walked in.
(16) Goldilocks saw the three bowls of porridge and the three spoons on the table. (17) The porridge smelt good, and Goldilocks was hungry because she had not had her breakfast.
(18) Goldilocks picked up the very big spoon and tasted the porridge in the very big bowl. (19) It was too hot!

Doors have unambiguous functions – letting people in or keeping them out – and therefore this open door represents an opportunity for Goldilocks which she immediately takes. She then has a sensory encounter with porridge and spoons (!) (porridge and spoons of course admitting of no ambiguity regarding their functions) and again takes the Opportunity. Notice that in this instance we have another case where an Opportunity offers a Response to a Problem (*hungry*), though here we only learn of the Problem after the Opportunity has been encountered.

Further Opportunity-Taking patterns can be found in the episodes with the chairs and the beds:

8.15　(25) Then Goldilocks saw three chairs: a very big chair, a medium-sized chair and a tiny, little chair . . . (38) Next Goldilocks went into the bedroom.
(39) There she saw three beds; a very big bed, a medium-sized bed and a tiny, little bed.

Again, we have a similar structure to those cited above: Goldilocks saw X, where X has clear functions. Now we have explained the parallelism between the three episodes; the porridge, chairs and beds all represent Opportunities for Goldilocks which she takes, with the recycling characteristic of Problem-Solution and Goal-Achievement patterns.

It might be thought that the notion of signalling is being stretched when we talk of encounters with objects of unambiguous function. But support for this extension of the notion of signalling comes from study of a corpus of examples analysed with the help of WordSmith (Scott 1999). Firstly *saw* is often used to describe someone finding an Opportunity in contexts where the 'seeing' is likely to be, or must be, metaphorical, e.g.:

8.16   Actually, my first aspiration was to study law, but I *saw* a *booklet* about Standard Chartered, applied and got an interview.

8.17   She suddenly *saw* a career opening up ahead of her.

8.18   Being a hard-headed man of business he probably *saw* a *chance* to get some free advertising.

The booklet will have been seen physically, but it could equally have been described as 'picked up' or 'read' and the physical encounter is arguably not in the forefront of the expression. In the subsequent two cases there is no question of the seeing being literal. The fact that non-literal *saw* has become (part of) a signal in its own right is further evidence of the correctness of the original assumption that verbs of perception used literally, especially in conjunction with objects of unambiguous function, serve as signals of Opportunity-Taking. (However, we must be careful not to jump to the conclusion that all instances of *saw* are signals of Opportunity. A fortune-teller peering over a glass ball might well be signalling an Opportunity if (s)he said 'I see a tall dark stranger' but if (s)he said 'I see a dark shadow' (s)he would be understood as signalling a Problem.)

Nor is *saw* the only signalling item to receive support from corpus study. The phrase in the Goldilocks story *The door was open* turns out to be a signal of Opportunity in its own right, as in the following:

8.19   But even if Mr Milosevic manages at least to leave the door slightly open to compromise, there is growing evidence that he has begun to lose control of the same Serbian forces into which he breathed deadly life.

8.20   Door is open for Graf and a German double [Newspaper headline]

8.21   ... but his barnstorming style of close support for his back row may not dovetail with Best's preference for an expansive game. The door could open for Aadel Kardooni, of Leicester.

In each of these cases, the 'open door' is functioning as pure signal of Opportunity. The fact that it can so function supports the view that the literal 'open door' can do likewise.

The Desire Arousal-Fulfilment pattern

There is another pattern that often occurs with Opportunity-Taking or as an alternative to it, but which can be seen as having a separate status. This can again be illustrated with a story from Genesis, this time concerning Jacob:

8.22   (1) Now Laban had two daughters; the name of the older was Leah, and the name of the younger was Rachel. (2) Leah had weak eyes, but Rachel was lovely in form and beautiful. (3) Jacob was in love with Rachel and said, 'I'll work for you seven years in return for your younger daughter Rachel.'

(4) Laban said, 'It's better that I give her to you than to some other man. (4a) Stay here with me.' (5) So Jacob served seven years to get Rachel, but they seemed like only a few days to him because of his love for her.

(6) Then Jacob said to Laban, 'Give me my wife. (6a) My time is completed, and I want to lie with her.'

(7) So Laban brought together all the people of the place and gave a feast. (8) But when evening came, he took his daughter Leah and gave her to Jacob, and Jacob lay with her. (9) And Laban gave his servant girl Zilpah to his daughter as her maid servant.

(10) When morning came, there was Leah! (11) So Jacob said to Laban, 'What is this you have done to me? (11a) I served you for Rachel, didn't I? (11b) Why have you deceived me?'

(12) Laban replied, 'It is not our custom here to give the younger daughter in marriage before the older one. (12a) Finish this daughter's bridal week; then we will give you the younger one also, in return for another seven years of work.'

(13) And Jacob did so. (14) He finished the week with Leah, and then Laban gave him his daughter Rachel to be his wife. (15) Laban gave his servant girl Bilhah to his daughter Rachel as her maidservant. (16) Jacob lay with Rachel also, and he loved Rachel more than Leah. (17) And he worked for Laban another seven years.

There are some parts of this story we can account for with the patterns covered so far. Sentence 3, for example, describes a Goal and Means of Achieving the Goal for Jacob. Likewise sentence 10 by implication leaves Jacob with a Problem, with 12a offering a Recommended Response to his Problem. But neither of these patterns adequately describes the text. The story is a love story and love stories are not triggered by Problem statements, though these often follow; still less are they triggered by Goal statements or Opportunity statements, both of which are more suited to stories of seduction, though again they may well follow.

What characterises a love story is that it starts with a Positive Evaluation. Some participant is described in terms that make it apparent that s/he is attractive to another participant. This is in marked contrast to the Problem-Solution pattern, one of whose characteristic types of triggering signal is Negative Evaluation. The presence of Negative Evaluation triggers a pattern whereby the reader expects some participant to respond to the problematic situation signalled in this way. What we have in Example 8.22, however, is the opposite of this, in that the evaluation is positive rather than negative. A particular kind of Positive Evaluation (*lovely in form and beautiful*) has been used, and the effect of it is to raise in the reader an expectation that a participant will react to this positive situation in a particular and precise way (*Jacob was in love with Rachel*). This, then, becomes the defining element of a pattern in much the way that Problem, Goal and

Figure 8.12 The Desire Arousal-Fulfilment pattern.

Opportunity serve as defining elements for their patterns. The questions being answered in texts of this kind are the following:

> What was the situation?
> Who or what within this situation was particularly attractive?
> What effect did this have on *x*?
> What did *x* do about it?
> What was the result?

The pattern can be represented diagrammatically as shown in Figure 8.12.

In Example 8.22, then, sentence 1 describes the general Situation. Sentence 2 triggers the pattern by positively evaluating the appearance of Rachel (*lovely in form and beautiful*); in this Situation element Rachel is described as an Object of Desire. Sentence 3 describes the immediate effect – the Arousal of Desire (*Jacob was in love with Rachel*) – and a Plan for Desire Fulfilment. Sentence 5 describes the carrying out of the Plan with initially Negative Results. Recycling then occurs, with the agreement to serve another seven years (sentences 12, 13 and 17) as the new Attempt at Desire Fulfilment and sentence 16 as the Positive Result.

In two respects the Desire Arousal-Desire Fulfilment pattern differs slightly from the patterns we have considered previously. In the first place, the second element of Situation is compulsory and must contain certain, quite specific, features. Indeed in many respects it is more like Problem or Goal or Opportunity. Second, the rules of recycling are less clear. On the one hand, a Negative Result sometimes leads to the abandonment of the Attempt; on the other, in erotic writing (which covers everything from Mills & Boon to altogether raunchier material), Positive Result may also lead to recycling! If the first kiss is described as exciting, the participant will characteristically seek to kiss the Object of Desire again.

The label 'Object of Desire' is chosen for two reasons. First, the person desired is the Object of someone else's observations not the Subject of his/her own actions, and the existence of the pattern appears to assert that being an Object of Desire licenses the action of another in seeking to fulfil his or her desire at the Object's expense. A second ideological implication of the pattern, connected with the first, arises from the fact that love stories and erotic narratives are not the only kind of text that are organised in this way. Consider the following example:

8.23   (1) Lexmark Printers. (2) So good, you'll want to stay together forever.

(3) It's definitely a love thing. (4) 'Nice curves,' said *Business Week* and promptly gave the Lexmark Color Jetprinter 2030 a Gold Medal in its prestigious Annual Design Awards. (5) The top of the range Color Jetprinter 7000 boasts 1200 × 1200 dpi, laser quality print clarity and amazing 8 ppm speed. (6) *PC Pro* awarded it six out of six for value for money. (7) Try any printer in the Lexmark inkjet range yourself and you'll soon appreciate the features that inspire such adoration. (8) Every model is easy to use, totally reliable and delivers unsurpassed standards of print quality, brightness and contrast. (9) The 2030 and 2050 can also be expanded to six-colours, producing brilliant photo-realistic pictures. (10) Amazingly, these objects of desire start at only £119. (11) That means you can invest in one and still easily afford to buy it flowers or treat it to a holiday. (12) If you're ready for a little romance, call 01628 481500, e-mail us at inkjet@lexmark.com or ask for a demonstration at any leading retailer.

This advertisement is more self-conscious about using the pattern than most, but it is like many advertisements in describing the products in terms that are appropriate for Objects of Desire (*nice curves, amazing speed, totally reliable*) (even exceptionally referring to them in sentence 10 as *objects of desire*) and then inviting the reader to attempt Fulfilment of their Desire (sentence 12).

What this advertisement draws our attention to is that Object of Desire need not be a person. The ideological implications are that the Desire Arousal pattern treats people like objects and gives to objects a value above their station.

Advertisements are not the only type of text that makes use of the pattern to describe desire for objects; narratives routinely do so too. There is more to the story of Adam and Eve than I am about to describe, but a part of the narrative is organised around the Desire Arousal-Fulfilment pattern:

8.24   When the woman saw that the fruit of the tree was good for food and pleasing to the eye, and also desirable for gaining wisdom, she took some and ate it.

First, we have signals of positive evaluation (*good for food, pleasing, desirable*), the last of which specifically alerts us to the pattern being used. We also have reference to perception, a signal that overlaps with Opportunity-Taking but which occurs regularly in conjunction with Desire Arousal when the thing perceived is evaluated positively rather than simply presented as something of unmistakable function.

Two types of signal characterise the Desire Arousal-Fulfilment pattern. The first of these are the items of positive evaluation already mentioned. Not any positive evaluations will do, though, and the conditions under which they operate as signals are not entirely clear. If what is being described is already possessed by the participant or is an object that no one could, or would want to, possess, then the signalling properties of the positive evaluation are overruled. Thus *it was a beautiful night* and *These eyes were looking at us. It was two beautiful polar foxes* both describe objects beyond possession.

Some signals of Object of Desire are shared with other situations, e.g. *beautiful, lovely*. Others are more specialised, e.g. *sexy, attractive, tasty,* and overwhelmingly function as signals of Object of Desire. While *attractive* seems to be the most common adjective in Lonely Hearts Columns (Marley, 2000), in a corpus comprising newspaper text its most common use is in business – *an attractive offer, an attractive investment.* These texts are, however, still often organised in terms of the Desire Arousal-Fulfilment pattern. Interestingly *sexy* is now often used in contexts outside the love story (or erotic narrative) (e.g. *astronomy is really sexy these days*) though it remains to be investigated whether these instances are occurring in patterns of Desire Arousal-Fulfilment. These specialised positive signals contrast with the negative evaluations that signal Problem-Solution, yet they seem to function like opposites which meet in the middle, because both patterns characteristically result in difficult situations for the participant. The Desire Arousal statement can indeed be regarded as a specialised type of Problem, in that it can be defined as an Aspect of the participant's Situation that Requires a Response. On the other hand, Attempt at Desire Fulfilment can be defined in terms very similar to those used to define Goal – an intended change in situation.

Often the positive evaluations either imply or explicitly refer to the use of some sense. Thus the apple in Example 8.24 is described as *pleasing to the eye*; in Example 8.23, *nice curves* implies a viewer (or a feeler). In the following aborted Desire-Arousal pattern (aborted in that the word *envy* tells us to have low expectations of Fulfilment) the use of taste leads directly to the Desire Arousal:

8.25   Not long ago I prepared Ruth a lunch of microwaved baked potatoes, fish fingers and a grating of cheddar. Potatoes and fish got mashed together while still hot, then mixed with the cheese before cooling and serving. I tasted it to check the temperature, and was stricken with pangs of envy.

The second kind of signal of Desire Arousal is one that particularly applies when the pattern is used to report narratives of love or lust, namely the description of parts of a person's body that are not functional in terms of recognition e.g. *bum, breasts.* Thus we have sentences such as the following:

8.26   Ushering them into the kitchen, I cannot help noticing that Sabrina's bum sticks out in the satisfactory pneumatic style.

This is, of course, a further instance of Jim Martin's distinction between 'inscribed' evaluations and 'evoked' evaluations. Given certain stereotypical views of what makes people attractive to each other, such as the tallness of a man, the size of a woman's bosom, the squareness of a man's jaw and the size of a woman's eyes (to name only a few), it is possible for a writer to evoke the idea that a person represents an Object of Desire by judicious use of these stereotypical attributes. (This, of course, has – or should have – nothing to do with what actually makes a person desirable.)

Sometimes the Desire Arousal-Fulfilment pattern interlocks with a Problem-Solution pattern, as in the following instance from the Joseph narrative in Genesis:

8.27   (1) Now Joseph was well-built and handsome, and after a while his master's wife took notice of Joseph and said, 'Come to bed with me!' (2) But he refused ... (3) And though she spoke to Joseph day after day, he refused to go to bed with her or even to be with her. (4) One day he went into the house to attend to his duties, and none of the household servants was inside. (5) She caught him by the cloak and said, 'Come to bed with me!' (6) But he left his cloak in her hand and ran out of the house ... (7) She kept his cloak beside her until his master came home ... (8) When his master heard the story his wife told him, saying, 'This is how your slave treated me,' he burned with anger. (9) Joseph's master took him and put him in prison, the place where the king's prisoners were confined.

We can notice in this passage a number of the features already noted. Firstly, *well-built* is strictly not a Positive Evaluation (unless the residual Positive Evaluation in *well* is attended to), but it nevertheless *evokes* a Positive Evaluation. On the other hand, *handsome* directly inscribes the evaluation. The verb phrase *took notice of*, in addition to triggering the Desire Arousal-Fulfilment pattern, also alerts us to the act of perception that underlay the triggering. However, a full analysis of this story requires reference to the Problem-Solution pattern as well. A diagrammatic representation of the interlocking of the two patterns is shown in Figure 8.13.

If we now return to the extract from *Goldilocks and the Three Bears* given as Example 8.14, we can now add a small modification to our original analysis of the 'porridge' episode. The first clause of sentence 17 contains the positive evaluation *good* along with a verb of perception *smelt*; it is therefore clearly marking the porridge as an Object of Desire and reporting Desire Arousal in Goldilocks. This means that sentences 16 and 17 must now be seen as having triggers of three separate patterns.

8.28   (16) Goldilocks saw the three bowls of porridge and the three spoons on the table [OPPORTUNITY]. (17) The porridge smelt good [DESIRE AROUSAL], and Goldilocks was hungry because she had not had her breakfast [PROBLEM].

The actions described in sentence 18 of Example 8.14 represent the beginning of the attempt simultaneously to Take the Opportunity, Fulfil the Desire and Respond to the Problem. It is perhaps an indication that the description has become over-complicated that this can be so. Yet it is also the case that all the following three versions of the text are acceptable:

8.29   (16) Goldilocks saw the three bowls of porridge and the three spoons on the table. (18) Goldilocks picked up the very big spoon and tasted the porridge in the very big bowl. (19) It was too hot!

8.30   (17) The porridge [that the Bears had left to cool] smelt good. (18) Goldilocks picked up the very big spoon and tasted the porridge in the very big bowl. (19) It was too hot!

8.31   (17) Goldilocks was hungry because she had not had her breakfast. (18) Goldilocks picked up the very big spoon and tasted the porridge [that Father Bear had left to cool] in the very big bowl. (19) It was too hot!

All three tellings are acceptable; therefore it is not the case that any of the descriptive approaches we have adopted are redundant.

The Gap in Knowledge-Filling pattern

We can now account for everything in the Goldilocks story until the three Bears come home. From that point, though, the description remains inadequate. I now

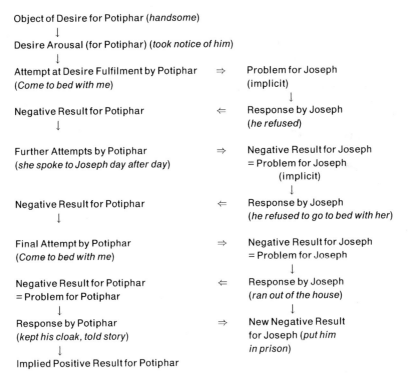

Figure 8.13 Interlocking Desire Arousal-Fulfilment and Problem-Solution patterns in the Joseph and Potiphar story in *Genesis*.

need to introduce another pattern of organisation – the Gap in Knowledge-Filling pattern. This is a hard pattern to illustrate in a short space because it rarely occurs in brief texts. It can be found in great numbers of academic papers, however, as well as detective stories of a particular kind. I shall illustrate it first with extracts from an article on applied linguistics and from a theoretical linguistics textbook and then with a complete popular science article.

The following extracts are taken from an article by Alastair Sharp published in the English for Special Purposes journal *The ESPecialist*.

8.32   (1) In a study by Weir (1988), college and university subject teachers indicated that clarity of expression was (not surprisingly) an essential feature of academic writing... (2) A number of researchers have suggested that although academics may recognise such features of good writing and demand it from their students, they do not necessarily praise it in their colleagues ... (3) The ELT profession endeavours, theoretically, to offer examples of good practice and clarity in writing. (4) Are ELT professionals, however, impressed by impenetrable prose from their colleagues, even if they criticise it when it is produced by their students?

[There then follows an account of the choosing of a suitable readability formula and of a questionnaire designed to elicit from ELT professionals their views of anonymised extracts from ELT writings. He reports the results of this and then goes on to comment as follows.]

(5) It is recognised that the scale of this survey is limited. (6) However, it does indicate that ELT professionals *are* impressed by less penetrable prose. (7) They may expect clarity from their students, but may be less concerned about what is produced by colleagues.

What we have here are the answers to the following questions:

What was the Situation? (answered in sentences 1 and 3)
What gap in our knowledge arose within that situation?
(answered in sentences 2 and 4?)
What did Alaistair Sharp do to fill the gap? (the omitted material answers this question)
What was the result? (sentences 5–7)

As with all the other patterns, recycling is perfectly possible. Consider the following abbreviated passage from Stephen Levinson's *Pragmatics*:

8.33   (1) The relatively restricted sense of the term *pragmatics* in Anglo-American philosophy and linguistics, and correspondingly in this book, deserves some attempt at definition. (2) Such a definition is, however, by no means easy to provide, and we shall play with a number of possibilities... (3) Let us therefore consider a set of possible definitions of pragmatics. (4) We shall find that each of them has deficiencies or difficulties of a sort that would equally hinder definitions of other fields, but at least in this way, by assaults from all flanks, a good sketch of the general topography can be obtained.

(5) Let us start with some definitions that are in fact less than satisfactory. (6) One possible definition might go as follows: pragmatics is the study of those principles that will account for why a certain set of sentences are anomalous, or not possible utterances . . . (7) Although an approach of this sort may be quite a good way of illustrating the kind of principles that pragmatics is concerned with, it will hardly do as an explicit definition of the field – for the simple reason that the set of pragmatic (as opposed to semantic, syntactic or sociolinguistic) anomalies are presupposed, rather than explained.

(8) Another kind of definition that might be offered would be that pragmatics is the study of language from a *functional* perspective, that is, that it attempts to explain facets of linguistic structure by reference to non-linguistic pressures and causes. (9) But such a definition, or scope, for pragmatics would fail to distinguish linguistic pragmatics from many other disciplines interested in functional approaches to language, including psycholinguistics and sociolinguistics.

Sentence 1 of Example 8.33 provides a Gap in Knowledge, and sentences 2 and 3 represent a 'plan' for filling the Gap of the kind we have observed with the other patterns. Sentence 4 negatively evaluates the attempts to fill the gap in advance as does sentence 5. Sentence 6 represents the first actual attempt to fill the Gap. Having already been negatively evaluated in advance in sentence 5 it is then negatively evaluated again in sentence 7, and a basis for that evaluation is provided. This forces the pattern to recycle and a second attempt at filling the Gap is offered at sentence 8, which is in turn rejected in sentence 9. And so the pattern continues for many pages.

The Gap in Knowledge-Filling pattern is used in narratives as well as scientific and academic writing. The traditional folk-tale of the Elves and the Shoemaker tells the story of a poor shoemaker who is about to go out of business but is mysteriously rescued by an unseen agent who converts the pieces of leather he leaves out every night into perfectly made pairs of shoes. Having started as a Problem-Solution text, the text now turns into a Gap in Knowledge text, with the shoemaker taking steps to discover who his mysterious benefactors are. Closer to hand, metaphorically speaking, we have our Goldilocks story as another illustration. In the final episode the Bears repeatedly articulate Gaps in Knowledge. Father Bear's reiterated gaps will serve as representative of all the stated gaps.

8.34   (49) Father Bear looked at his very big porridge bowl and said in a very loud voice, 'Who has been eating *my* porridge?' . . .

(52) Next Father Bear looked at his very big chair. (53) 'Who has been sitting in *my* chair?' he asked in a very loud voice . . .

(58) Next the three bears went into the bedroom. (59) Father Bear looked at

his very big bed. (60) 'Who has been lying on *my* bed?' he asked in a very loud voice.

Then, finally, Baby Bear fills the Gap by looking at his bed:

8.35   (63) Baby Bear looked at his tiny, little bed.
(64) 'Here she is!' he cried, making his tiny, little voice as loud as he could.
(65) 'Here is the naughty girl who has eaten *my* porridge and broken *my* chair! (65a) Here she is!'

And we now have a complete analysis of Goldilocks, at least in terms of culturally popular patterns.

A final return to *Death and the Compass*

In *Death and the Compass* Borges uses three of the patterns we have been considering in this chapter: the Gap in Knowledge-Filling pattern, the Goal-Achievement pattern, and the Opportunity-Taking pattern. Only Desire Arousal-Fulfilment is unused of the patterns I have been describing. The dominant pattern on first reading is that of Gap in Knowledge-Filling. The first murder presents a Gap, and Lönnrot attempts to fill the Gap by investigating the religious aspects of the case:

8.36   'No need to look for a three-legged cat here,' Treviranus was saying as he brandished an imperious cigar. 'We all know that the Tetrarch of Galilee owns the finest sapphires in the world. Someone, intending to steal them, must have broken in here by mistake. Yarmolinsky got up; the robber had to kill him. How does it sound to you?'
'Possible, but not interesting,' Lönnrot answered. 'You'll reply that reality hasn't the least obligation to be interesting. And I'll answer you that reality may avoid that obligation but that hypotheses may not. In the hypothesis you propose, chance intervenes copiously. Here we have a dead rabbi; I would prefer a purely rabbinical explanation, not the imaginary mis-chances of an imaginary robber.'

Here we have an example of the recycling noted as a possibility for all the patterns. The murder represents a Gap, in response to which Treviranus offers a possible Filling, which is negatively evaluated by Lönnrot ('chance intervenes copiously') as having left the Gap unfilled; the latter detective then identifies what will count as an adequate Filling, in so doing signalling the pattern with the word *explanation* ('I would prefer a purely rabbinical explanation'). Subsequent murders, because of their symmetry, are seen as comprising a single Gap rather than accumulation of Gaps. When the map with the equilateral triangle is sent to Lönnrot, he is able – apparently – to fill the Gap:

8.37   The three locations were in fact equidistant. Symmetry in time (the third of December, the third of January, the third of February); symmetry in space as well . . . Suddenly he felt as if he were on the point of solving the mystery.

The word *mystery* confirms the pattern, and *solving* shows that the Gap is being filled. The use of *solving* as a signal for the pattern is evidence, if it were needed, of the essential kinship of the patterns I have been describing. Interestingly just as a Gap in Knowledge-Filling pattern may 'borrow' a Problem-Solution signal, so Problem-Solution patterns often 'borrow' the characteristic Gap in Knowledge-Filling signal *answer*.

Once Red Scharlach starts his re-telling of the story, the Gap in Knowledge-Filling pattern is at one and the same time completed – all the mysteries are explained – and shown to be false. Treviranus' original explanation of the first murder is revealed to have been correct and the Gap thereafter to have been of Lönnrot's own making. The 'real' patterns are a Goal-Achievement pattern:

8.38   'On those nights I swore by the God who sees with two faces and by all the gods of fever and of the mirrors to weave a labyrinth around the man who had imprisoned my brother. I have woven it and it is firm: the ingredients are a dead heresiologist, a compass, an eighteenth-century sect, a Greek word, a dagger, the diamonds of a paint shop.'

and an Opportunity-Taking pattern:

8.39   'The first term of the sequence was given me by chance . . . Ten days later I learned through the *Yidische Zaitung* that you were seeking in Yarmolinsky's writing the key to his death . . . I knew that you would conjecture that the Hasidim had sacrificed the rabbi; I set myself the task of justifying that conjecture.'

We can represent the patterning of the text as in Figure 8.14. The question mark against the Negative Evaluation for Lönnrot may look odd, given that the effect of his mistaken Filling of the Gap is that he dies, but, as Borges himself points out in the introduction to the story quoted in Chapter 3, 'he did succeed in divining the secret morphology behind the fiendish series'.

Seen from the perspective of a second reading, the Gap in Knowledge-Filling pattern is not inherent to the text. The pattern only exists because Lönnrot – and we – create it. In Chapter 6 we looked at the way *Death and the Compass* might be analysed using a matrix and saw that each path through the matrix produced a radically different effect – detective story, mystery, thriller, revenge story could all be produced. On the basis of this, I argued that the differences amongst alternative tellings of the same 'happening' were so considerable that it makes no sense to talk of them all sharing the same story. Such a conclusion might be supported after analysing *Death and the Compass* in terms of culturally popular

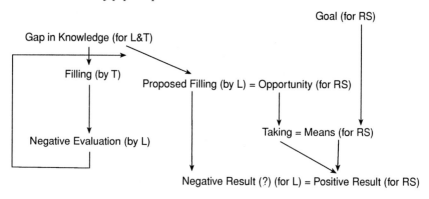

Figure 8.14 A simplified representation of the patterning in *Death and the Compass*.

patterns; Borges seems to be alerting readers to the evanescent nature of the patterns we have been describing: one moment the pattern is there, the next it no longer applies, and the effect is to make one unsure what story one is actually analysing. Depending on which pattern we attend to, the story looks different. Borges is in effect questioning the stability of any analysis one might provide of any text and reminding us of how important the reader's participation is in the creation of meaning and structure in text. Indeed Lönnrot and the reader are alike in making a pattern out of what they receive. Lönnrot takes the information he is given by Red Scharlach and finds symmetries and culturally popular patterns within it, but the patterns and symmetries have come in part from within him and the information is capable of a quite different reading such as that which his fellow detective, Treviranus, supplies. Likewise the reader receives text from Borges (or his translator) and finds patterns and symmetries within it only to have those symmetries and patterns destabilised as s/he reads. In short Borges reminds us that text is the site of an unreliable and variable interaction between reader and writer and it is to that textual interaction that we again turn in the final chapter of this book, looking at two patterns that seek to replicate the interactivity of face-to-face talk.

One pattern or many?

Clearly all the patterns we have been considering have much in common and there may be many circumstances in which distinguishing them is unnecessary. We may choose to talk of the SPRE pattern, and see S as Situation in all the patterns, including Object of Desire in the Desire Arousal pattern, P as Problem, Goal, Gap in Knowledge, Opportunity or Desire Arousal, and R as Response, Means of Achievement, Filling of Gap, Taking of Opportunity or Attempt to fulfil the Desire. E would be Evaluation for all these patterns. Doing so brings a greater degree of abstraction to the analysis, which for some purposes may be good, but it also takes us further from the text, and from the detail of the lexical realisation, and in the end that could be self-defeating. The route of greater abstraction/

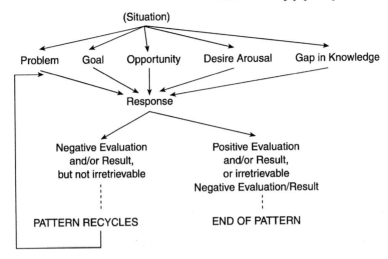

Figure 8.15 The options available in a SPRE pattern.

generality should therefore only be taken when the minutiae of the text under examination are not relevant to the matter being investigated. It can be recognised, though, that it is in the trigger that the various patterns differ and there may be no great benefit in distinguishing the different kinds of R; it would not affect the description much therefore to posit a set of patterning options that looked like Figure 8.15.

Some implications for language learning

The implication of the schema/script perspective for reading and in particular for pre-reading activities is that if a reader does not share a schema/script with the writer, s/he will not find it easy to read the text. One of the defects of statistical measures of readability is that they compute difficulty in terms of sentence length and word length but cannot take account of the possible presence or absence of shared schemata/scripts. A newspaper text may be simply worded in short sentences and still be largely unintelligible because a precise and detailed schema that the reader lacks is being accessed. An important function of pre-reading activities is to supply a missing schema or missing knowledge from an existing schema.

The reading and writing implications of the range of SPRE patterns are various. In the first place, conformity to the pattern when writing is likely to make organising the text easier and will almost certainly make the text easier to read. Experience with teaching communications skills in the early years of my career showed that quite often highly intelligent students found it hard to organise their thoughts when they settled down to write and at the very least would lose valuable time trying to find a way into their subject. The various SPRE patterns serve as ready-made templates and, while it is emphatically not the case that all good writing has to conform to them, it can benefit a learner writer to have a pattern to stick to.

More generally, if a learner comes from a cultural tradition with different rhetorical expectations they may need to be shown how the various patterns operate. If on the other hand they come from traditions containing a similar or the same pattern, they need to be encouraged to transfer their expectations from one tradition to another. All students need to be able to recognise pattern triggers and key signals elsewhere in the pattern. Use of the pattern can encourage better prediction skills in reading.

A particular strategy that can be used is for the learner to be encouraged to hunt for signals of the patterns. This strategy works a little like that described at the end of Chapter 3. The learner, armed with a set of characteristic signals, scans the text looking for the first sentence that contains a trigger of Problem, Goal, Opportunity, Desire Arousal or Gap in Knowledge and then reads that sentence. Then s/he scans down until a Response signal is found; this sentence is also read. An Evaluation is then sought; if it is positive the reader checks that a negative evaluation does not immediately follow. Of course if it does, then the process continues; otherwise the learner stops at that point. This strategy allows the learner to make principled selections from the text, and teaches a valuable vocabulary in the process, but it is, of course, dependent on the text having one of the patterns in question.

From the writing perspective the various patterns may help learners shape their texts. Sometimes even quite experienced writers plunge into the middle of their scientific or business reports, jumping straight to the Response before spelling out the Problem, Gap in Knowledge or Goal; while this can sometimes be effective, as in Example 7.17, unless it is handled with skill such an ordering is likely to result in the text being hard to follow or even incomprehensible. I know of one pharmaceuticals company who had to repeat vital tests because the reports of those tests neglected to tell the reader what was being tested for. Learner writers can usefully be encouraged to step back from their texts and consider what their readers are likely to need in order to appreciate fully the importance of the Responses or Recommended Responses they wish to report.

Some writing suffers from undersignalling or mis-signalling. Undersignalling occurs when a reader is unable to identify a clear trigger of a pattern and so is uncertain whether the pattern is being used or not. A good writer does not use signals heavily but does give clear indications of the different stages of the pattern to his or her readers. The signalling vocabulary is valuable vocabulary and deserves to be given some priority in language teaching. Mis-signalling occurs when the signalling item triggers expectations that are not met. This is a common fault in learner writing.

From a practical teaching point of view, several of the specific patterns are of special importance. The Goal-Achievement pattern and the Gap in Knowledge-Filling pattern just described are particularly valuable for people learning to read and/or write in English in an academic context, since both patterns are widely used in academic writing. Goal-Achievement and Opportunity-Taking are both widely used in business English. Only the Desire-Arousal pattern has relatively little functional importance from a writing perspective, though it occurs widely in the kinds of leisure text that learners of English might read and, of course, slightly indirectly, account for many advertisements.

Bibliographical end-notes

The advertisement for the book 'How to Rub Your Stomach Away' (8.2) appeared in national newspapers at the beginning of 1997. The extract from a news story (8.4) is by Jason Bennetto and appeared in *The Independent* on 10 September 1997, p. 1. The joke (8.5) was told by my daughter, Alice, and transcribed by me. The advertisement for *100 Classics at a Glance* (8.6) appeared in national newspapers during 1997. The advertisement for Turner's lithographs (8.8) was current in the summer of 1997. The extracts from the book of Genesis (8.9; 8.22; 8.24) are Genesis 21.14–16, 19, Genesis 29.16–30 and Genesis 3.6, respectively. Example 8.10 is drawn from *Alice's Adventures in Wonderland* by Lewis Carroll. The advertisement for Lexmark (8.23) was current in national newspapers mid-1997. Examples 8.27 and 8.27 were drawn from the British National Corpus. The Borges' quotations are, as before, from Donald A. Yates' translation.

Most of the patterns listed in this chapter have been little discussed. The Goal-Achievement pattern has its basis in Winter (1971, 1974)'s instrument-achievement relation. Some of Jordan (1984)'s discussion of Problem-Solution patterns contains within it an assumption of the possibility of Goal-Achievement patterns. The Opportunity-Taking and Desire Arousal-Fulfilment patterns were both proposed in Hoey (1997b) as a result of a study of erotic writing for a volume on Language and Desire. The Gap in Knowledge-Filling pattern was first recognised by Diana Adams-Smith (1986); it has obvious affinities with the first stage of Swales' model of moves for article introductions (1981, 1990). There is now a need to relate and integrate these two distinct but clearly related ways of talking about text.

9 When the pattern turns into a dialogue

Introduction

We arrived at the end of the previous chapter with a range of patterns that share a number of properties, some of which may be worth itemising at this juncture. First, all the patterns are brought to a conclusion or else re-activated by a Positive or Negative Evaluation and/or Result. Second, all the patterns are characteristically signalled either by inscribed or evoking lexical choices. Finally, all the posited patterns have some provoking initiation which logically and sequentially leads to some reaction; in every case the reaction is actor-oriented, even if the original initiation is not attributed to any individual. Thus a Gap in Knowledge, for example, is frequently a Gap for all participants and for readers as well, but the Filling of that Gap will be attributed to some specific participant. Likewise a Problem may be articulated as universally felt but the Response will be the reaction of a particular participant. In this chapter, however, I will introduce a pattern with some of these properties – the capacity for recycling, the initiation – but with others mutated or missing. In the act of considering this pattern, we will be reminded of the interactive nature of text and alerted to the limitations of the approach that has been adopted for its description in this book.

Question-Answer patterns

There is a pattern that superficially looks a lot like the Gap in Knowledge-Filling pattern and, equally superficially, seems to share a great deal with the patterns discussed in Chapters 7 and 8, and that is the Question-Answer pattern. As its features are described, its resemblance to the Gap in Knowledge-Filling pattern and the other patterns we have been considering will quickly fall away. The main elements of the pattern are Question, Answer, and Positive/Negative Evaluation, the last being obligatory when the Answer is ascribed to someone other than the author but optional (and in fact uncommon) when the Answer is the author's own. Whereas the other patterns are found both in long and short texts, this pattern rarely occurs in short texts, presumably because, as was noted in Chapter 2, *all* sentences can be seen as answers to unstated questions, and therefore choosing to make a question explicit would be heavy-handed if the question's currency did not extend over a considerable part of the text.

As an example of the way the pattern operates, consider Example 9.1, which represents a greatly abbreviated version of the first chapter of a textbook on political philosophy, discussed from a quite different perspective in Hoey (1991a). Sentence numbers do not indicate continuity; there are a number of places indicated in the text where there are significant omissions.

9.1   (1) What, then, is the advantage which we may hope to derive from a study of the political writers of the past? (2) A view prevalent in earlier ages would have provided a simple answer to this question. (3) A work of politics, it would have been said, is the handbook of an art, the art of governing. (4) Just as a man of superior knowledge or skill in the art of carpentry may compile a work in which his knowledge is made available to those who aspire to be good carpenters, so a man of superior wisdom in the art of politics may set down his knowledge in a book for the instruction of those whose business it is to found, govern, or preserve states. (5) If this is what political theory is there is no difficulty in determining what advantage may be expected from the study of great political works. (6) They will be consulted by those who have to govern states.

(7) Some of the greatest political writers have believed themselves to be offering such a system of practical instruction, and many students of their works in the past have undoubtedly sought, and may have found in their pages that practical guidance which they have professed to offer. (8) But this is certainly not the advantage which a modern reader can be promised from a study of their works. (9) This entire conception of politics as an art and of the political philosopher as the teacher of it rests upon assumptions which it is impossible to accept. (10) If it were correct, the writers of political theory would need to be themselves past masters in the art of governing, and statesmen would need to apprentice themselves to them in order to learn their job. (11) But we find that this is not so. (12) Few political philosophers have themselves exhibited any mastery of the art of governing, and few successful statesmen have owed their success to the study of political writings. [There then occur 11 sentences discussing this point in more detail, omitted here.]

(13) If political theory is not a body of science for the instruction of statesmen, what is it? (14) There is a doctrine, the 'dialectical materialism' of Karl Marx, which gives a fundamentally different account of its nature. (15) According to this doctrine, political theory is not prior, but posterior, to political fact. [This point is expanded upon in 21 sentences omitted here.]

(16) The Marxist theory thus completely reverses the relation of priority between political theory and political fact which was implied in the theory which I began by mentioning; and it is clear that a very different estimate of the value of studying political theory will follow, according as we adopt one or the other of these two conflicting views of its nature. (18) According to the

former of them, it will be almost the most important study which a man can undertake, and an indispensable qualification for all who claim a share in the direction of public affairs. (19) According to the latter, since theory can in no case determine how a man will act, the study of it has no importance, and only an academic interest.

(20) I will not conceal my own opinion that, while the former doctrine errs by rating the study of this study too high, the latter errs by rating it too low. [In the original there then follow 55 sentences, omitted here, that give reasons for this judgement, which include the author's view that the historical conditions in which the political philosophers grew up would affect their theories.]

(21) But if what I have said of political theory is admitted to be true the question presents itself with hardly diminished force: What is the use of studying the political theories of the past? (22) If each is tied so closely to the conditions of the age from which it sprang how can it be relevant to the conditions of our own?

(23) First it may be answered that this very discrepancy is part of their value. (24) Only by help of the contrast with other civilizations can we become aware that the principles upon which our own is founded are peculiar and unique. [This point is then expanded upon in six sentences, omitted here.] (25) We are thus made conscious that our own civilization is a unique form of civilization, and not to be identified with civilization in general. (26) No doubt this truth may be recognized by those who have made no special study of the history of thought. (27) Indeed, the recognition is implicit in the usage, now growing common, by which men are becoming accustomed to use the designation 'Western' or 'Modern' or 'Christian' Civilization, in place of 'civilization' simply. (28) This adoption of a proper name in place of a general term implies in itself a recognition of the fact that the civilization thus designated is peculiar and unique. (29) But a study of past theories is necessary for the understanding of all that is implicit in the recognition; it enables us to see the present with something of the same objective vision with which we look at the past.

(30) But this is not the main value of the study. (31) The works of which this book and its companion volumes contain selections, ranging from Plato to the present time, are not simply foreign. (32) They represent stages of a single tradition of thought, at the end of which we stand. (33) They are products of civilizations which are not alien to our own, but are the sources of our own. (34) When we study the works of these writers, we are studying ideas which have been assimilated into our own ways of thinking, however much they may have been altered in the process. [This point is then exemplified in 78 sentences, omitted here.]

(35) I have mentioned only a few of the countless channels through which past civilizations operate in forming the mentality of modern civilization. (36) Because this mentality is, in the ways which I have indicated, derived in a peculiar degree from historical sources, an historical study is indis-

pensable to the understanding of it. (37) We cannot comprehend it fully until we have comprehended the elements which have gone to make it up, and have become acquainted with the forces which have stamped its character. (38) The value of the study of the great political philosophies of the European tradition is that it can give this comprehension and acquaintance in one important field of human thought. [This point is expanded in a further seven sentences, omitted here.]

(39) Perhaps the study may have a further use. (40) It may promote a deeper understanding of all that is involved in being civilized, and remove the temptation to suppose that a civilized man is merely a tame man, differing from the savage only in the way in which the domesticated animal differs from the wild one. [A final sentence is omitted.]

I have reduced to 40 sentences a chapter of 15 pages length, yet it will be apparent that the pattern of the text is apparently very similar to those described in previous chapters. The pattern begins with a Question (sentence 1) to which an Answer is given in sentences 2–7; this is then Rejected (Negatively Evaluated) in sentences 8 and 9, with a Basis for the Rejection provided by sentences 10–12. The Question is then reiterated in sentence 13. (Something similar occurs in Problem-Solution patterns whenever a Response is negatively evaluated, since Negative Evaluation is one of the signals of Problem, as we saw in Chapter 7.) A second Answer then follows in sentences 14–19, for which the author provides a Rejection in sentence 20; this Evaluation is followed by an extended Basis not given here. Sentences 21 and 22 repeat and reformulate the Question. Now the writer gives his own Answers – three in fact – in sentences 23–29, 30–38 and 39–40, each, bar the last, with accompanying justification. These justifications serve the function of providing Bases for unstated Positive Evaluations; the writer can be presumed to be in favour of his own answers. The pattern can be represented diagrammatically as in Figure 9.1, which has an obvious similarity to those we were considering in previous chapters for Problem-Solution and the other patterns.

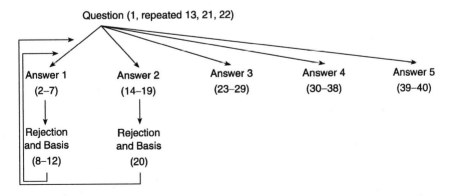

Figure 9.1 The organisation of Chapter 1 of *Master of Political Thought*, Vol. 1.

Nor is this the only point of similarity between this and previous patterns. The Question can be defined as an Aspect of Situation requiring a Verbal Response; this brings it directly into line with the definition of Problem given in Chapter 7, and Answer can be defined as Verbal Response. Of course, these definitions would serve equally well as characterisations of the components of the basic exchange pair Question-Answer in conversation, a matter to which I shall be forced to return later.

Again, as with previous patterns, there are signals in plenty, although they are not primarily lexical. To begin with, we recognise that sentence 1 is Question because of the interrogative (a syntactic matter), the question mark (a punctuation matter) and the conjunct *then* (a lexico-grammatical matter). This conjunct, in addition to tying the paragraph into its immediate context (omitted in Example 9.1), seems to mark out those rhetorical questions that are the starting-point for the Question-Answer pattern, as opposed to those unanswered rhetorical questions that occasionally occur in a certain kind of text and which do not provoke any pattern. There is also, importantly, use of repetition to mark the relationship of Question to Answers. Figure 9.2 shows one of a number of connections that can be found between the first version of the Question and the first Answer. The second Answer in sentence 15 relates to the restatement of the Question in sentence 13, while later sentences connect back to the original formulation. In both cases, repetition links the Questions and Answers. The connections between sentences 13 and 15 are shown in Figure 9.3 and one of the connections between the later sentences of the Answer and the original formulation of the Question are given in Figure 9.4. Similar diagrams could be produced connecting sentences 29, 34, 38 and 39 with sentence 1, all illustrating the repetition that connects Question and Answer.

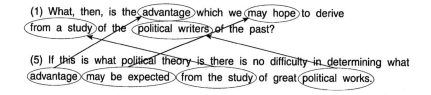

Figure 9.2 Cohesive links between question (1) and answer (5) in *Master of Political Thought* text.

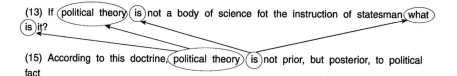

Figure 9.3 Cohesive links between second answer and reformulated question in *Master of Political Thought* text.

(1) What, then, is the (advantage) which we may hope to derive from a (study) of the (political) writers of the past?

(16) The Marxist theory thus completely reverses the relation of priority between political   theory   and political fact which was implied in the theory which I began by mentioning; and it is clear that a very different estimate of the (value) of (studying) (political) theory will follow, according as we adopt one or the other of these two conflicting   views

Figure 9.4   Cohesive links between one of the sentences of the second answer and the original question in *Master of Political Thought* text.

The interrogative structures, question marks and repetition between Question and Answer are all signalling devices special to the Question-Answer pattern. Although, however, sentence 2 refers to *a simple answer to this question*, sentence 21 to the *question* and sentence 23 to its being *answered*, there is not much evidence of lexical signalling of the kinds found for previous patterns; it should be remembered that the thin trawl just given is from a complete chapter of which Example 9.1 represents only the skeletal outline.

Despite this, the similarities between this and the patterns discussed in Chapters 7 and 8 are strong. In the first place, we have recycling, evidenced in Figure 9.1, and this capacity for recycling points to there being a similar dynamic within the pattern whereby a rejected Answer is felt not to provide closure for the text and the pattern must continue until Sisyphus reaches the top of the hill. Put abstractly, in diagrammatic terms identical to those used in Chapter 7, the possibilities would seem to be those shown in Figure 9.5.

Another similarity with the other patterns lies in the way the elements are attributed. Questions themselves are characteristically left unattributed, much as is the case for Gaps in Knowledge, with which superficially the Question-

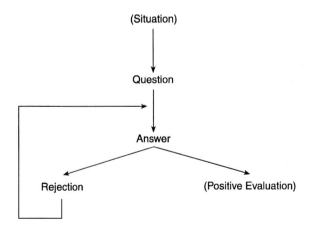

Figure 9.5   The basic question-answer pattern.

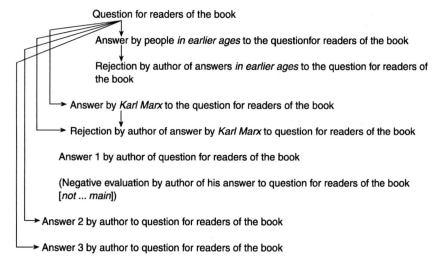

Figure 9.6 Pattern of organisation of the political philosophy textbook with attribution added.

Answer pattern has much in common. But the remaining elements are attributed, as for all the other patterns. So the organisation of Example 9.1 is more accurately represented as Figure 9.6.

I have laid great stress on the apparent similarities between the Question-Answer pattern and the other patterns we have examined, but my own signalling – my own attempts as writer to lead you to make accurate predictions about the remainder of my text – has been unequivocal throughout: the similarity is illusory. Let us then now look at what makes the Question-Answer pattern problematic.

Why Question-Answer is different

The first dissimilarity from the other patterns is that Positive Evaluation is supposed to bring a pattern to a close and so the pattern should not repeat itself after sentence 29. Yet the writer twice signals that he is overriding the reader's expectations of closure. After the first Answer, we are told that this 'is not the main value of the study'. This functions in the same way as a Negative Evaluation – indeed *not main* might even be regarded as Negative – and leads the reader to expect another, main, value. More subtly, the third Answer is introduced tentatively – *perhaps, may*. This signals that this is an afterthought, not a replacement of the earlier Answer. In no other pattern is such overriding possible – except under one condition, to be mentioned in the next paragraph.

The second dissimilarity relates to the impossibility of an intermediate stage between Question and Answer. Between Problem and Response there is the possibility of an optional stage labelled 'Plan' by the story grammarians; often in authentic texts this takes the form of Recommendation. A similar middle stage is possible for all the other patterns. Only with Question-Answer am I unable to attest such a stage. However, all the patterns discussed in the last two chapters have the option of stopping at Recommendation. Advertisements routinely describe a Problem, a Goal or an Opportunity and then suggest a Recommended Response or Recommended Means of fulfilling the Goal or a Recommendation that the reader take the Opportunity. The same is true of certain kinds of business reports. Further, in these kinds of text the option of providing more than one Recommendation is always open, and while the writer is likely to weight the options s/he is under no obligation to evaluate negatively any of the Recommendations made (though of course s/he may).

This parallel between Answer and Recommendation is on the face of it odd, in that a Recommended Response is a staging post on the way to a full Response whereas an Answer is complete in itself. What accounts for it is that a Response, a Means, the Taking of an Opportunity, the Filling of a Gap in Knowledge and an Attempt to fulfil a Desire are none of them speech acts – they are reports of actions. Recommending and Answering, however, are both speech acts (Austin 1962, Searle 1969). Although some narratives feature characters who recommend a course of action to other characters, the great majority of recommendations found in Problem-Response texts and the like are addressed to the audience, and this, too, is true of Answers: I recommend that you . . .; I answer your question thus: . . .

A third important characteristic of the Question-Answer pattern separating it from the other patterns is that there is no logical sequence relationship between Question and Answer. The major elements of all the other patterns are connected in a cause-consequence relation. Because Joe has a problem, Joe does something about it. Because Joe has a goal, Joe adopts some means of achieving that goal. Because an opportunity presents itself, Joe takes the opportunity. Because there is a gap in Joe's knowledge or understanding, Joe takes measures to fill it. Because Joe desires Jo, Joe acts in such a way as to get Jo. (In some cases a purpose relation more accurately reflects the connection, but that does not materially affect the argument.) Hoey (1983) provides detailed criteria for the interpretation of cause-consequence signalling as Problem-Response signalling. However, it seems contrived (even if not impossible) to attempt to paraphrase the relation between Question and Answer in terms of a causal relationship: 'because there is a question, Joe answers it' (??).

Intimately connected with the last point is the fact that the signalling of the Question-Answer pattern is primarily achieved through repetition, as we have seen. What makes this problematic is that, as noted in Chapter 2 and 3 and in Winter (1974) and Hoey (1983), systematic repetition is associated with Matching relations such as Contrast, Similarity and General-Particular; indeed a *wh*-question might be seen as a general statement containing a request that some generality be particularised. Thus Question-Answer is a matching pattern, not a sequence pattern.

The relationship of Question-Answer patterns to Claim-Response patterns

There is, however, one respect in which Question-Answer patterns differ from their near neighbours that is so striking that it makes the other differences pale into relative insignificance. This is that, under some circumstances, the Question can be omitted. As an illustration of this, consider the following version of the first half of Example 9.1 (given as Example 9.2) in which the questions and the lexical signals associated with them have been omitted:

9.2 (3) A work of politics, it would [once] have been said, is the handbook of an art, the art of governing. (4) Just as a man of superior knowledge or skill in the art of carpentry may compile a work in which his knowledge is made available to those who aspire to be good carpenters, so a man of superior wisdom in the art of politics may set down his knowledge in a book for the instruction of those whose business it is to found, govern, or preserve states. (5) If this is what political theory is there is no difficulty in determining what advantage may be expected from the study of great political works. (6) They will be consulted by those who have to govern states.

(7) Some of the greatest political writers have believed themselves to be offering such a system of practical instruction, and many students of their works in the past have undoubtedly sought, and may have found in their pages that practical guidance which they have professed to offer. (8) But this is certainly not the advantage which a modern reader can be promised from a study of their works. (9) This entire conception of politics as an art and of the political philosopher as the teacher of it rests upon assumptions which it is impossible to accept. (10) If it were correct, the writers of political theory would need to be themselves past masters in the art of governing, and statesmen would need to apprentice themselves to them in order to learn their job. (11) But we find that this is not so. (12) Few political philosophers have themselves exhibited any mastery of the art of governing, and few successful statesmen have owed their success to the study of political writings.

(14) There is a doctrine, the 'dialectical materialism' of Karl Marx, which gives a fundamentally different account of [the] nature [of political theory]. (15) According to this doctrine, political theory is not prior, but posterior, to political fact.

(16) The Marxist theory thus completely reverses the relation of priority between political theory and political fact which was implied in the theory which I began by mentioning; and it is clear that a very different estimate of the value of studying political theory will follow, according as we adopt one or the other of these two conflicting views of its nature. (18) According to the former of them, it will be almost the most important study which a man can undertake, and an indispensable qualification for all who claim a share in the direction of public affairs. (19) According to the latter, since theory can

in no case determine how a man will act, the study of it has no importance, and only an academic interest.

(20) I will not conceal my own opinion that, while the former doctrine errs by rating the study of this study too high, the latter errs by rating it too low.

In my judgement (and I hope in yours), Example 9.2 is an intelligible and not unnatural text, despite the absence of the Questions. The same certainly would not be true of most Problem-Response texts that were missing their Problems nor of most Goal-Achievement texts that were missing their Goals. It is not just that they would cease to be Problem-Response and Goal-Achievement patterns – after all, Example 9.2 is no longer a Question-Answer text, despite its acceptability as text – it is that they would cease to be intelligible (or at very least they would be differently intelligible). The same is true of the other patterns, except sometimes the Opportunity-Taking pattern.

The claim I am making about Example 9.2 is that it means the same as Example 9.1 but is not analysable in terms of the Question-Answer pattern. Importantly, this is not the same as saying that it is not patterned at all. There is in fact a pattern that would account for Example 9.2, but it is a pattern of a rather different kind from those considered in previous chapters. A book is always a selection of what one might say, and this book is no exception. There are Sequence patterns and there are Matching patterns, and this book has focused on the former. All the patterns handled in Chapters 7 and 8 are instances of Sequence patterns, in that the dominant relations out of which they are constructed are Sequence relations; on the other hand, the only Matching pattern that has been discussed in any detail is the Colony pattern, where the components of a colony are related to each other by weak Matching relations of Similarity. There are, however, many other Matching patterns which space has not permitted coverage of (some of these are discussed in Hoey, 1983); one such possibility is the Claim-Response pattern and this is the pattern of which Example 9.1, bereft of its Questions, is now an instance.

The Claim-Response pattern, also known as the Hypothetical-Real pattern (Winter 1974, 1986/1994, 1996; Williames 1984) has the basic components shown in Figure 9.7. This perhaps over-complex diagram does not represent all the options. It is not possible to identify optional and compulsory elements for this pattern; a text may include or omit any of the elements in the above. What the diagram purports to show are some of the more common options available to a writer using this pattern. Thus a Claim may be denied and then corrected with or without Reasons being given for the Claim, the Denial or the Correction. A Claim may also be affirmed, in which case Reasons will characteristically be given for the Affirmation, or, perhaps more commonly, the Affirmation will reveal itself to have been a feint and be followed by a Denial. Fabricated examples illustrating various of the possible permutations include:

9.3   Joe's an old friend of mine [Situation]. People say he's stupid [Claim], but that's rubbish [Denial]. He's got a degree in Psychology [Reason for Denial].

9.4   People say Joe's stupid [Claim]. But he's actually very clever [Correction]. He's got a degree in Psychology [Reason for Correction].

9.5   Joe's not stupid [Denial]. He's clever [Correction]. After all, he's got a degree in Psychology [Reason for Correction].

9.6   People say Joe's stupid [Claim]. He certainly seems to be [Affirmation]. He's always muddling things up [Reason for Affirmation].

9.7   Joe's an old friend of mine [Situation]. People say's Joe's stupid [Claim]. That's because he's always forgetting things [Reason for Claim]. He's not stupid, though [Denial]. He's actually very bright [Correction]. For a start, he's got a degree in Psychology [Reason for Correction].

9.8   People say Joe's stupid [Claim]. I suppose he is in some ways [Affirmation]. He gets things terribly muddled on occasion [Reason for Affirmation]. But in other respects he's far from stupid [Correction]. For a start, he's got a degree in Psychology [Reason for Correction].

One important point about this list of possibilities is that the Claim element is as optional as the rest. It no more defines the pattern than any other element, in marked contrast to the Sequence patterns we have been considering elsewhere.

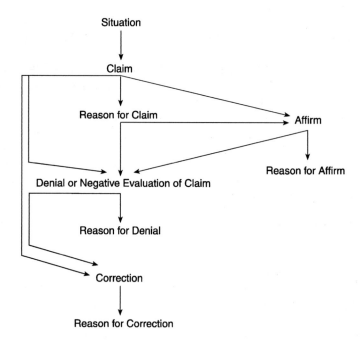

Figure 9.7 The optional stages in Claim-Denial and Claim-Affirmation patterns.

The pattern can as readily start at Denial. The explanation for this lies in the Matching nature of the pattern; Matching relations are neither tied to a particular order nor is there need for a trigger.

Letters to newspapers often make use of the various Claim-Response patterns, for the obvious reason that letters are often a reaction to something written in an earlier issue of a newspaper. In such circumstances the claim may be referred to rather than fully re-articulated. An example of Claim-Denial where the Claim is fully articulated is the following extract from a letter to the *Guardian*:

9.9   (1) I have in my possession a copy of a press release from Sir Aaron Klug, the president of the Royal Society dated April 1996 – a month after it was officially admitted that BSE was probably the cause of the new variant CJD. (2) In it he stated that 'the sheep form of the disease, called Scrapie, is known not to infect humans.' (3) We know no such thing. (4) What we know is that we do not know whether Scrapie can infect humans and cause CJD, a very different matter.

Dr Helen Grant
London

Here we have a Situation (sentence 1), a Claim (sentence 2), a Denial (sentence 3) and a Correction (sentence 4). It will be noticed that, as with the Sequence patterns, we have attribution. The Claim in sentence 2 is explicitly attributed to Sir Aaron Klug. The Denial and Correction are attributed to the author named at the foot of the letter. We also have the characteristic signalling by repetition connecting Claim, Denial and Correction. This is shown in Figures 9.8, 9.9 and 9.10.

An example of a Claim-Response pattern making use of the Claim-Affirmation possibility, where the Claim is referred to rather than re-articulated, is the following letter to *The Independent*:

9.10   (1) It was refreshing to read similar views to my own on Aberdeen. (2) I have been living in Aberdeen for the last four years as a student of English at the university and this place has nearly killed me and drove me to the verge of alcoholism! (3) I come from West Belfast – not the most scenic of areas – but Aberdeen makes it look lovely.

Colm Michael Quinn
Aberdeen

Sentence 1 refers to a Claim (*views . . . on Aberdeen*) which the remainder of the sentence and sentence 3 affirm; the Claim is not explicitly articulated presumably since it can be inferred from what follows. Sentence 2 provides a Reason for the Affirmation.

Armed with the various forms of Claim-Response pattern, we can now return to the version of the 'political philosophy' text that had had its Questions removed,

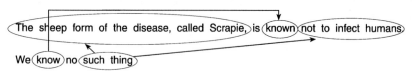

The sheep form of the disease, called Scrapie, is (known) not to infect humans

We (know) no (such thing)

Figure 9.8 Repetition between Claim and Denial in 'Scrapie' letter.

(We)(know) no such thing

What (we)(know) is that (we) do not (know) whether Scrapie can infect humans and cause CJD, a very different matter.

Figure 9.9 Repetition between Denial and Correction in 'Scrapie' letter.

The sheep form of the disease, called (Scrapie) is (known) not to (infect) (humans)

What we (know) is that we do not (know) whether (Scrapie) can (infect) (humans) and cause CJD, a very different matter.

Figure 9.10 Repetition between Claim and Correction in 'Scrapie' letter.

given as Example 9.2. We can now see that it is unproblematically analysable in terms of Claim-Denial(-Correction) (see Figure 9.11).

Had I modified the second half of Example 9.1 in the same vein, eliminating the reiteration of Question, the pattern would have continued with Basis of the second Denial and the writer's three Corrections corresponding to the three Answers in the original.

What I am saying is that we have a regular relationship between Question-Answer patterns and the Claim-Denial version of the Claim-Response patterns; this relationship can be represented as in Figure 9.12. Notice that the attribution of Correction to the author eliminates the possibility of multilayering.

Claim in former ages (sentences 3–7)
↓
Denial (sentences 8 and 9)
↓
Basis of Denial (sentences 10–12)

Claim by Karl Marx (sentences 14–19)
↓
Denial (sentence 20)

Figure 9.11 An analysis of the political philosophy passage in terms of Claim-Denial.

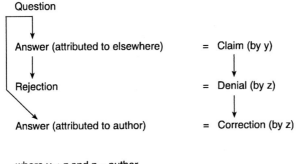

Figure 9.12 The relationship of the Question-Answer and Claim-Response patterns.

A cline of patterns

The association of Question-Answer with Claim-Response is not the only association with other patterns that Claim-Denial can boast. Under the right circumstances Claim-Denial may associate with Problem-Solution patterns also. This can be illustrated in a succession of texts published over a seven-day period in *The Independent.* The first of these texts was a long article by Linda Tsang on sexual harassment, published on 26 October 1999. Simplifying somewhat, this text describes a general Problem for women solicitors (that they are sexually harassed on occasion by their firm's clients) and then gives several individual Responses, including sharp rebuffs that result in the loss of the clients, before describing a more general Response in the form of a harassment help line for women solicitors. This text provoked the following response (somewhat abridged), three days after the original article

9.11   (1) As a young female professional, I was worried by Linda Tsang's article
'The solicitors who get solicited' (26 October). (2) If we have reached the
stage where young women cannot cope with a man's hand on their knee in
a taxi, then the human race is doomed ... (3) Men are given to making
sexual advances and indeed life would be very dull if they did not, but
surely it is not beyond the wit of a female lawyer or barrister to use some
feminine charm skilfully to deflect such advances, or even (political
incorrectness here) turn the situation to her advantage. (4) A client who
fancies you is surely a client you can soon have eating out of your hand ...
(5) So come on girlies, stop swooning and try a more spirited approach.

Dr Elaine Duncan
Birmingham

First, we have a Claim-Denial pattern. Sentence 1 alludes to Linda Tsang's claim, recapping it in the *if*-clause in sentence 2. It also denies the Claim, with a Reason

(1)	(2)	(3)	(4)	(5)	(6)
Problem	Problem	Problem		Question	Question
Response	Response	Recommended Response	Claim	Answer	Answer
Positive Evaluation	Negative Evaluation	Negative Evaluation	Denial	Negative Evaluation	(Positive Evaluation)
	Response	Recommended Response	Correction	Answer	
	Positive Evaluation	Positive Evaluation	(Positive Evaluation)	(Positive Evaluation)	

Figure 9.13 Cline of patterns from Problem-Solution to Question-Answer.

for Denial occurring (somewhat facetiously) in the main clause of sentence 2. Sentence 3 offers a Correction with sentence 4 offering a Reason for this Correction. But we also have a Problem-Solution pattern, with the title of Linda Tsang's article and the nominal group *a man's hand on their knee in a taxi* defining the Problem and sentences 3 and 4 offered as Response. Sentence 5, which reiterates the Correction, turns the Response into a Recommended Response. (Perhaps unsurprisingly, this text provoked another letter four days later in the same paper in which Dr Duncan's advice was reported and then negatively evaluated (denied), thereby recycling the Problem-Solution pattern; the later author notes that 'the solution lies in having women present in the working world in equal numbers to men'.)

What these letters show is that we have a cline running from Problem-Solution to Question-Answer (Figure 9.13). Each of these patterns has its own characteristics but clearly there is sufficient overlap to make it impossible to police borders between patterns.

Where patterning and interaction meet

I have been saying throughout this book that text is the site of an interaction between writer and reader. The Question-Answer and Claim-Denial/Affirmation patterns seem to point to a further form of textual interaction, that between the author and someone other than the reader. To explore this a little, we need to consider the model of spoken exchange structure provided by Sinclair and Coulthard (1975). The model was developed to account for classroom interaction, but has been usefully adapted to describe everyday conversation by Francis and Hunston (1992). Exchanges in the Sinclair-Coulthard model have three parts, an initiation (I), a response (R) and feedback (later renamed follow-up (F), by Coulthard and Brazil 1979/1992). These functions in the exchange are met by moves which are made up of one or more acts. Moves have been the subject of some disagreement and are not relevant to my argument here. Acts can be defined as the minimum speech actions performed by speakers. A minimal exchange is the following:

9.12	Teacher:	Do you know what we mean by accent?	I	elicitation
	Pupil:	It's the way you talk	R	reply
	Teacher:	The way we talk.	F	accept
		This is a very broad comment		evaluate

(from Sinclair and Coulthard 1975, 48)

Here we have a straightforward IRF structure with the F component consisting of two acts.

Now consider what happens when the pupils do not get it right first go. The class is looking at road signs:

9.13	Teacher:	This I think is a super one	I	starter
		Isobel		nomination
		Can you think what it means?		elicitation
	Pupil 1:	Does it mean there's been an accident further down the road?	R	reply
	Teacher:	No [with level intonation]	F	evaluate
	Pupil 2:	Does it mean a double bend ahead?	R	reply
	Teacher:	No [again with level intonation]	F	evaluate
		Look at the car	(I)	clue
	Pupil 3:	Slippery roads?	R	reply
	Teacher:	Yes. It means be careful because the road's very slippery	F	evaluate
				comment

(data from Sinclair and Coulthard 1975, 54)

What is apparent here is that the Negative Evaluation of the teacher sets up a recycling of the exchange, with the exchange continuing to provoke responses until a Positive Evaluation is forthcoming from the teacher. If that does not sound familiar, you must have skipped the previous two chapters! In particular the parallels with the Question–Answer pattern are striking. If we compare the possibility just illustrated for exchange structure with one of the possibilities for the Question–Answer pattern indicated in Figure 9.5, we get the parallels shown in Figure 9.14. It is immediately apparent that the only difference between the two types of organisation is that the exchange structure is an account of moment-by-moment decisions taken by a number of participants in real time, while the Question–Answer pattern is a record of an exchange, true or fictional. The two systems merge in the following example:

9.14 (1) 'What's a Sacrament?' Margaret wanted to know.
(2) 'It's a little bit hard to explain,' said Mummie. (3) 'It's something you can see that means something you can't see.'
(4) Ronnie and Margaret looked puzzled. (5) 'Something you can see that

means something you can't see?' repeated Margaret. (6) 'I don't understand that at all.'

(7) 'Well, it's like this,' said Mummie. (8) 'Every Sacrament has two parts – the part you can see, and the part you can't. (9) When Baby John was baptized today, all you saw was the water. [2 sentences omitted] (10) Well, Baptism means "washing". (11) You could see the water, but you couldn't see the heavenly washing of Baby's soul. (12) And you couldn't see the Holy Spirit either, when He came to Baby John to help him be good. (13) That's what I meant by the part you could see and the part you couldn't. (14) Every Sacrament is like that. (15) It is the way God works. (16) He takes a common ordinary thing like water, and He uses it for something else.'

(17) 'I see', said Margaret thoughtfully.

How do we analyse this? It should be apparent that we could either describe it in terms of the I-R-F(neg.)-R-F(pos.) structure or the Question-Answer-Negative Evaluation-Answer-Positive Evaluation pattern, and the descriptions would just be terminological variants. There are two conclusions to be drawn from this. The first conclusion must be that there is no difference between reading a dialogue such as Example 9.14 and reading or hearing interactions such as those reported in Examples 9.12 and 9.13. The non-speaking members of the class in Examples 9.12 and 9.13 are in little different position from the transcribers of the tape; both had to process the talk as text, making connections between utterances, making predictions about what might happen and identifying patterns as they develop, in these and many other educational cases, Question-Answer patterns. Similarly the transcribers and we as readers of the transcription are in the same boat as each other: we are attempting to make connections and find pattern in the talk in a quest to find the (transcribed) talk coherent. So the processes involved in understanding spoken dialogue are the same as those involved in understanding written monologue.

The second conclusion is that not only is text a site of interaction between author and reader, but it may be where a writer records earlier interactions, or fictionally represents interactions, involving one or more participants other than

Question	I	elicit
Answer	R	reply
Negative Evaluation	F	evaluation (negative)
Answer	R	reply
Positive Evaluation	F	evaluation (positive)

Figure 9.14 A comparison of a possible Question-Answer pattern with a possible exchange structure.

the writer and reader themselves. Taken superficially such a conclusion is blindingly obvious; one only has to open any novel to see the fictional record of interactions. But the point I am making goes beyond this. I am claiming that there is no difference between a Question-Answer pattern reflected in recorded dialogue like Example 9.14 and a Question-Answer pattern in a philosophical discourse such as Example 9.1. I am claiming in fact that all the patterning we have been considering in this and the last two chapters may be seen as a record of, and derivative from, the structures found in spoken discourse and social behaviour.

Once we see this, other patterns can be reinterpreted as records of interaction. Opportunity-Taking is a record of an offer followed by an acceptance, and in the case of advertisements it is still an offer and the interaction is not a record of an interaction but part of an exchange with the reader. Gap in Knowledge is a record of someone's question and their attempt to answer it. Less obviously a Goal-Achievement pattern records a request that some participant has made to him- or herself and the participant's attempt to comply with that request. Problem-Solution, with which we started, can be understood as a record of the demand made upon someone by something in the world and their attempt to conform to that demand. Desire Arousal-Desire Fulfilment is more complex in that there are elements of request ('desire'), offer ('smelt good'), and demand ('need').

A short conclusion

I began this book unconventionally; I shall end it less so. I have attempted in this book to show that text is not an object of study but exists only as part of an interaction between an author/writer and a reader who ideally will have the characteristics hypothesised for the text's audience. I have suggested that writers and readers engage in a kind of dance whereby the writer seeks to anticipate the questions that a reader will want answered and the reader seeks to predict the questions that the writer will try to answer. These questions may be small-scale or large-scale. Sometimes texts are highly specialised with regard to the questions that they answer, answering the same question over and over again; these are the colony texts. In the case of mainstream texts, the achieved text represents only one ordering of the questions that the writer chooses to answer, as the matrix perspective shows. Seen from such a perspective, also, the well-maintained boundary-line between narrative and non-narrative text seems to break down. Further evidence for believing the boundary to be vague can be found in the existence of culturally popular patterns which apply promiscuously to narrative and non-narrative text alike. These were shown to be configurations of questions that writers and readers agree should be answered, and represent an economical way of facilitating communication. Finally, in this chapter, this model was argued to be an interim position on the way to a truly interactive description. The future of analysis of text may depend not simply on describing textual interaction in the terms described here but on taking seriously the effect of interaction on text and within text. And this in turn means that we need to revisit existing descriptions of spoken discourse as well as rethinking existing descriptions of written discourse. There is still a great deal of work to be done on textual interaction, questions to be answered, gaps to be filled, problems to be solved, opportunities to be taken. I have initiated; I leave it to you to respond.

Bibliographical end-notes

Example 9.1 is an abridged version of chapter 1 of *Masters of Political Thought* (Volume 1) by Michael F. Foster. Example 9.9 appeared in the *Guardian* in October 1999. Example 9.10 appeared in *The Independent* on 2 November 1999. Example 9.11 is an abridged version of a letter published in *The Independent* on 29 October 1999. The instances of classroom talk (9.12 and 9.13) were both taken from Sinclair and Coulthard (1975). Example 9.14 was drawn from *Ronnie and the Sacraments* by Mrs A. C. Osborn Hann, 1947, published by The National Society and SPCK.

An earlier version of the argument presented in this chapter can be found in Hoey (1986b). Susan Thompson (1997) shows how questions are used in spoken monologue – an important half-way position between the written monologues and spoken dialogues that we have been considering here.

The hypothetical-real relation was described by Winter (1974). He argued that it was one of the two most fundamental relations in text (Winter 1986/1994), the other being situation-evaluation. His last paper before his death dealt with the denial-correction (Winter 1996). I adopt the term 'claim' rather than 'hypothetical' because it allows me to talk of a 'claim by x'. However the term 'hypothetical' has the advantage that it picks up a wider range of textual phenomenon. Thus:

People say Joe is stupid. But he speaks five languages

and

Joe may be stupid. But he speaks five languages

are both, in Winter's terms, hypothetical-real relations. The first sentence of the latter fits less neatly into the category of 'claim' (although I should so label it). Carol Marley (personal communication) has noted that the modality that signals hypothetical/claim in examples such as the second is closely related to a question. Williames (1984) argues that hypothetical-real is not a relation like matching contrast or cause-consequence but a pattern like Problem-Solution. I follow Williames in this.

The classic statement of exchange structure is Sinclair and Coulthard (1975), an abridged version of which appears in Coulthard (1992), which also contains other key papers on the subject. Levinson (1983) presents a critical position on this work.

Bibliography

Abraham, S. (1993) Writing to Learn: Knowledge and Knowledge-Transforming in Undergraduate Writing. Unpublished PhD thesis, University of Birmingham.

Adams, M. J. (1979) 'A schema-theoretic view of reading' in R. O. Freedle and A. C. Collins (eds.) *New Directions in Discourse Processing*. Norwood, NJ: Ablex, pp. 1–22.

Adams-Smith, D. (1986) Aspects of Register Variation in Seven Popular Science Articles and the Research Papers from which They were Derived. Unpublished MA dissertation, University of Birmingham.

Al-Sharief, S. (1998) 'Analysing interaction in texts: a framework'. *Liverpool Working Papers in Applied Linguistics*, 4.1, 1–32.

Arcay Hands, E. (1996) 'Los patrones léxicos de M. Hoey en textos escritos en español'. *Revista Venezolana de Linguistica Applicada*, 2.1, 27–76.

—— (1998) 'Lexical patterns in Venezuelan Spanish academic texts'. *Opción: Revista de Ciencias Humanas y Sociales*, 14.25, 32–47.

—— and L. Cosse (1998) *Análise Multidimensional de Ensayos Académicos*. Valencia, Ven: Ediciones de Rectorado, University of Carabobo.

Austin, J. L. (1962) *How to Do Things with Words*. London: Oxford University Press.

Australian Nature Conservation Agency and Mutitjulu Community Inc. (1990) *The Mala Walk and the Mutitjulu Walk: An Insight into Uluru*. Uluru: Australian Nature Conservation Agency in association with the Mutitjulu Community, Uluru.

Ballard, D. L., R. J. Conrad and R. E. Longacre (1971a) 'The deep and surface grammar of interclausal relations'. *Foundations of Language*, 7, 70–118.

—— (1971b) 'More on the deep and surface grammar of interclausal relations'. *Language Data*, Asian-Pacific Series, No 1. Ukarumpa, Papua New-Guinea: Summer Institute of Linguistics Publications.

Bartlett, F. (1932) *Remembering*. Cambridge: Cambridge University Press.

de Beaugrande, R. (1980) *Text, Discourse and Process: Towards a Multi-disciplinary Science of Texts*. London: Longman.

Beekman, J. (1970) 'Propositions and their relations within a discourse'. *Notes on Translation*, 37.

Beekman, J. and J. Callow (1974) *Translating the Word of God*. Michigan: Zondervan Press.

Beekman, J., Callow, J. and M. Kopesec (1981) *The Semantic Structure of Written Communication* (circulated within S.I.L. but not formally published).

Bell, A. (1991) *The Language of News Media*. Oxford: Blackwell.

Berber Sardinha, A. P. (1995) 'A preliminary study into patterns of lexis of business texts', in B. Warvik *et al* (eds.), *Organization in Discourse: Proceedings from the Turku Conference, Anglicana Turkuensia*, 14, pp. 157–66.

—— (1997) Automatic Identification of Segments in Written Text. Unpublished PhD thesis, University of Liverpool.

Berkenkotter, C. and T. Huckin (1995) *Genre Knowledge in Disciplinary Communication.* Hillsdale, NJ: Erlbaum Associates.

Bhatia, V. (1983) *An Applied Discourse Analysis of English Legislative Writing.* Birmingham: University of Aston Language Studies Unit.

—— (1993) *Analysing Genre: Language Use in Professional Settings.* London: Longman.

Biber, D. (1988) *Variation Across Speech and Writing.* Cambridge: Cambridge University Press.

Bourne, J. (1998) 'Constructing 'linguistic maturity': Interactions around written text in the primary classroom'. *Studia Anglica Posnaniensia*, 23 (special ed.: Festschrift for Kari Sajavaara), pp. 61–71.

Bowcher, W. (in preparation) Play-by-Play Talk on Radio: An Enquiry into Some Relations between Language and Context, PhD Thesis, University of Liverpool.

Brazil, D. (1985) *The Communicative Value of Intonation.* Discourse Analysis Monographs. Birmingham: ELR, University of Birmingham.

Brown, P. and S. Levinson (1987) *Politeness: Some Universals in Language Usage.* Cambridge: Cambridge University Press.

Caldas, C. R. (ed.) (1987) *Narrative Studies.* Special issue of *Ilha do Desterro*, Vol. 18, Florianopolis: University of Santa Catarina.

Caldas-Coulthard, C. R. (1988) Reported Interaction in Narrative: A Study of Speech Representation in Written Discourse. Unpublished PhD thesis, University of Birmingham.

—— (1993) 'From discourse analysis to critical discourse analysis: the differential representation of women and men speaking in written news' in J.McH. Sinclair, M. Hoey and G. Fox (eds.), *Techniques of Description: Spoken and Written Discourse* (a festschrift for Malcolm Coulthard). London: Routledge, pp. 196–208.

—— and M. Coulthard (eds.) (1996) *Texts and Practices: Readings in Critical Discourse Analysis.* London: Routledge.

Carter, R. (1998) *Vocabulary: Applied Linguistic Perspectives* (2nd edn.). London: Routledge.

Chatman, S. (1978) *Story and Discourse: Narrative Structure in Fiction and Film.* Ithaca, NY: Cornell University Press.

Christie, F. and J. R. Martin (eds) (1997) *Genre and Institutions: Social Processes in the Workplace and the School.* London: Cassell.

Connor, U. (1996) *Contrastive Rhetoric: Cross-cultural Aspects of Second-Language Writing.* Cambridge: Cambridge University Press.

—— (1998) 'Contrastive rhetoric: developments and challenges'. *Studia Anglica Posnaniensia*, 23 (special ed.: Festschrift for Kari Sajavaara), pp. 105–16.

—— and R. Kaplan (eds) (1987) *Writing across Languages: Analysis of L2 Text.* Reading, Mass.: Addison Wesley.

Cook, G. (1992) *The Discourse of Advertising.* London: Routledge.

Coulthard, M. (1990) 'Matching relations in Borges' 'la Muerte y la Brujula': an exercise in linguistic stylistics'. *Lenguas Modernas*, 17, 57–62.

—— (1992) 'On the importance of matching relations in the analysis and translation of literary texts'. *Ilha do Desterro*, 27: special issue: *Text Analysis/Análise de Texto* (ed. J. L. Meurer), pp. 3–44.

—— (ed.) (1992) *Advances in Spoken Discourse Analysis.* London: Routledge.

—— (ed.) (1994) *Advances in Written Text Analysis.* London: Routledge.

—— and D. Brazil (1979) *Exchange Structure.* Discourse Analysis Monographs. Birmingham: ELR, University of Birmingham, reprinted in abridged form in Coulthard (ed.), (1992), pp. 50–78.

Crombie, W. (1985) *Process and Relation in Discourse and Language Learning*. Oxford: Oxford University Press.

Crystal, D. and D. Davy (1969) *Investigating English Style*. London: Longman.

Darnton, A. (1987a) Episodes in the Development of Narrative Awareness in Children. Unpublished M.Litt thesis, University of Birmingham.

—— (1987b) 'Inter-episodic relationships in children's narrative', in C. R. Caldas (ed.), *Narrative Studies*. Special issue of *Ilha do Desterro*, Vol. 18, Florianopolis: University of Santa Catarina.

—— (1998) This Way Through the Woods: New Directions in Narrative Analysis. Unpublished PhD thesis, University of Liverpool.

Dijk, T. Van (1977) *Text and Context: Explorations in the Semantics and Pragmatics of Discourse*. London: Longman.

—— (1988) *News as Discourse*. Hillsdale, NJ: Lawrence Erlbaum.

Dudley-Evans, T. (1994) 'Genre analysis: an approach for text analysis for ESP', in M. Coulthard (ed.) *Advances in Written Text Analysis*. London: Routledge, pp. 219–28.

—— (1995) 'Genre models for the teaching of academic writing to second language speakers: advantages and disadvantages'. *Journal of TESOL France*, 2.2, 181–92.

Eco, U. (1979) *The Role of the Reader: Explorations in the Semiotics of Texts*. Bloomington: Indiana University Press.

Edge, J. (1986) Towards a Professional Reading Strategy for EFL Teacher Trainees. Unpublished PhD thesis, University of Birmingham.

Emmott, C. (1997) *Narrative Comprehension: A Discourse Perspective*. Oxford: Clarendon Press.

Fairclough, N. (1989) *Language and Power*. London: Longman.

—— (1992a) *Critical Language Awareness*. London: Longman.

—— (1992b) 'Discourse and text: linguistic and intertextual analysis within discourse analysis'. *Discourse and Society*, 3.2, 193–217.

Fowler, H. W. (1965) *Fowler's Modern English Usage* (2nd edn.). London: Oxford University Press.

Fowler, R. (1991) *Language in the News: Discourse and Ideology in the Press*. London: Routledge.

—— B. Hodge, G. Kress and T. Trew (1979) *Language and Control*. London: Routledge and Kegan.

Francis, G. (1986) *Anaphoric Nouns*. Discourse Analysis Monographs. Birmingham: University of Birmingham.

—— (1989) 'Aspects of nominal-group lexical cohesion'. *Interface: Journal of Applied Linguistics*, 4.1, 27–53.

—— (1994) 'Labelling discourse: an aspect of nominal-group lexical cohesion' in M. Coulthard (ed.), *Advances in Written Text Analysis*. London: Routledge, pp. 83–101.

—— and S. Hunston (1992) 'Analysing everyday conversation' in M. Coulthard (ed.), *Advances in Spoken Discourse Analysis*. London: Routledge, pp. 123–61.

Freund, E. (1987) *The Return of the Reader: Reader-Response Criticism*. London: Methuen.

Genette, G. (1972) *Discours de récit* (in *Figures III*). Paris: Editions du Seuil; published in English as *Narrative Discourse* (1980), translated by Jane E. Lewin Oxford: Basil Blackwell.

—— (1982) *Palimpsestes: La Litterature au Second Degré*. Paris: Seuil.

Georgakopoulou, A. and D. Goutsos (1997) *Discourse Analysis: An Introduction*. Edinburgh: Edinburgh University Press.

Goffman, E. (1975) *Frame Analysis: An Essay on the Organization of Experience*. Harmondsworth: Penguin.

—— (1981) *Forms of Talk*. Philadelphia: University of Pennsylvania Press.

Goodman, K. (1967) 'Reading: a psycholinguistic guessing game'. *Journal of the Reading*

Specialist, 4, 126–35.

—— (1973) 'On the psycholinguistic method of teaching reading', in F. Smith (ed.), *Psycholinguistics and Reading*. NY: Holt, Rinehart and Winston, pp. 158–76.

Graustein, G. and W. Thiele (1979) 'An approach to the analysis of English texts'. *Linguistische Studien*, A55, 3–15.

—— (1980) 'Zur Struktur der Bedeitung von englischen Texten'. *Linguistische Arbeitsberichte*, 26, 12–28.

—— (1981) 'Principles of text analysis'. *Linguistische Arbeitsberichte*, 31, 3–29.

—— (1987) *Properties of English Texts*. Leipzig: VEB Verlag Enzykapadie Leipzig.

Grice, H. P. (1967) *Logic and Conversation*. Unpublished MSS of the William James Lectures, Harvard University.

—— (1975) 'Logic and conversation' in P. Cole and J. L. Morgan (eds), *Syntax and Semantics 3: Speech Acts*. N.Y.: Academic Press, pp. 41–58.

—— (1978) 'Further notes on logic and conversation' in P. Cole (ed.), *Syntax and Semantics 9: Pragmatics*. N.Y.: Academic Press, pp. 113–28.

Grimes, J. (1972) 'Outlines and overlays'. *Language*, 48.3, 513–24.

—— (1975) *The Thread of Discourse*. The Hague: Mouton.

Hall, R. (ed.) *The Eleventh LACUS Forum*. Columbia, South Carolina: Hornbeam Press.

Halliday, M. A. K. (1994) *An Introduction to Functional Grammar* (2nd edn.). London: Edward Arnold.

—— and R. Hasan (1976) *Cohesion in English*. London: Longman.

—— (1985) *Language, Context and Text: Aspects of Language in a Social-semiotic Perspectives*. Geelong: Deakin University Press (republished by OUP, 1989).

Hasan, R. (1984) 'Coherence and cohesive harmony', in J. Flood (ed.), *Understanding Reader Comprehension*. Delaware: International Reading Association, pp. 181–219.

—— (1989) 'Part B' in M. A. K. Halliday and R. Hasan (1989) *Language, Context and Text: Aspects of Language in a Social-Semiotic Perspective* (2nd edn.). Oxford: Oxford University Press.

—— (1995) 'The conception of context in text', in P. Fries and M. Gregory (eds), *Discourse in Society: Systemic Functional Perspectives*. Norwood, NJ: Ablex, pp. 183–283.

Hinds, J. (1983) 'Contrastive thetoric: Japanese and English'. *Text*, 3.2, 183–95.

—— (1987) 'Reader versus writer responsibility: a new typology', in U. Connor and R. Kaplan (eds), *Writing across Languages: Analysis of L2 Text*. Reading, Mass.: Addison Wesley, pp. 141–52.

Hodge, R. and G. Kress (1993) *Language as Ideology* (2nd edn.). London: Routledge.

Hoey, M. (1979) *Signalling in Discourse*. Discourse Analysis Monographs, Birmingham: ELR, University of Birmingham.

—— (1983) *On the Surface of Discourse*. London: George Allen and Unwin, republished (1991) by English Studies Unit, University of Nottingham.

—— (1985a) 'The statute as discourse and the lawyer as linguist', in R. Hall (ed.), *The Eleventh LACUS Forum*. Columbia, South Carolina: Hornbeam Press, pp. 255–62.

—— (1985b) 'The paragraph boundary as a marker of relations between the parts of a discourse' *M.A.L.S. Journal*, 10, 96–107.

—— (1986a) 'Undeveloped discourse: some factors affecting the adequacy of children's non-fictional written discourse', in J. Harris and J. Wilkinson (eds), *Reading Children's Writing*. London: Allen and Unwin, pp. 74–92.

—— (1986b) 'Overlapping patterns of discourse organization and their implications for clause relational analysis of Problem-Solution texts', in C. R. Cooper and S. Greenbaum (eds), *Studying Writing: Linguistic Approaches*. London: Sage, pp. 187–214.

—— (1986c) 'The discourse colony: a preliminary study of a neglected discourse type', in M. Coulthard (ed.) *Talking About Text: Studies Presented to David Brazil on this Retirement*. Birmingham: English Language Research. Univesity of Birmingham, pp. 1–26.

—— (1987) 'The importance of comparison and contrast in narrative organisation', in C. R. Caldas (ed.), *Narrative Studies*. Special issue of *Ilha do Desterro*, Vol. 18, Florianopolis: University of Santa Catarina.

—— (1988) 'The discourse properties of the criminal statute', in C. Walter (ed.) *Computer Power and Legal Language*. NY: Quorum, pp. 69–88 (reprinted in G. Nixon and J. Honey (eds) *An Historic Tongue: Studies in English Linguistics in Memory of Barbara Strang*, London, Routledge, pp. 145–66).

—— (1991a) *Patterns of Lexis in Text*. Oxford: Oxford University Press.

—— (1991b) 'Another perspective on coherence and cohesive harmony' in E. Ventola (ed.), *Functional and Systemic Linguistics: Approaches and Uses*. Berlin: Mouton De Gruyter, pp. 385–414.

—— (1991c) 'The matrix organisation of narrative and non-narrative text in English', in *Proceedings of the 5th Symposium on the Description and/or Comparison of English and Greek*. Thessaloniki: Aristotle University, pp. 216–53.

—— (1993) 'A common signal in discourse: How the word *reason* is used in texts', in J. McH. Sinclair, M. Hoey and G. Fox (eds), *Techniques of Description: Spoken and Written Discourse* (a festschrift for Malcolm Coulthard). London: Routledge, pp. 67–82.

—— (1994a) 'Signalling in discourse: a functional analysis of a common discourse pattern in written and spoken English', in M. Coulthard (ed.), *Advances in Written Text Analysis*. London: Routledge, pp. 26–45.

—— (1994b) 'Patterns of lexis in narrative: a preliminary study', in S.-K. Tanskanen and B. Warvik (eds), *Topics and Comments: Papers from the Discourse Project*. *Anglicana Turkuensia*, 13, 1–40.

—— (1995) 'The lexical nature of intertextuality: a preliminary study' in B. Warvik, S.-K. Tanskanen and R. Hiltunen (eds) *Organization in Discourse: Proceedings from the Turku Conference*, *Anglicana Turkuansia*, 14, pp. 73–94.

—— (1996a) 'The discourse's disappearing (and reappearing) subject: An exploration of the extent of intertextual interference in the production of texts', in K. Simms (ed.), *Language and the Subject*. Amsterdam: RoDoPi, pp. 245–64.

—— (1996b) 'Cohesive Words: A Paper of Consequence', in J Svartvik (ed.), *Words: Proceedings of an International Symposium*, Kungl., Vitterhets Historie och Antikvitets Akademien. Konferenser 36, Stockholm, pp. 71–90.

—— (1997a) 'The interaction of textual and lexical factors in the identification of para-graph boundaries', in M. Reinhardt and W. Thiele, (eds), *Grammar and Text in Synchrony and Diachrony in Honour of Gottfried Graustein*. Vervuert Verlag, Germany, pp. 141–67.

—— (1997b) 'The organisation of narratives of desire: A study of first-person erotic fantasies', in K. Harvey and C. Shalom (eds), *Language and Desire: Encoding Sex, Romance and Intimacy*. London: Routledge.

—— (2000) 'A matrix perspective on narrative text', in T. Virtanen and I. Maricic (eds), *Perspectives on Discourse: Proceedings from the 1998 and 1999 Discourse Symposia at Växjö*. Växjö: Växjö University Press.

Hon Ching Fu (1998) Genre Awareness in Children. Unpublished PhD Thesis, University of Liverpool.

Hopkins, A. and T. Dudley-Evans (1988) 'A genre-based investigation of the discussion sections in articles and dissertations'. *English for Specific Purposes*, 7, 113–21.

Iser, W. (1978) *The Act of Reading: A Theory of Aesthetic Response.* Baltimore: Johns Hopkins University Press (orig. pub. in German, 1976).

Johns, T. F. (1980) 'The text and its message: an approach to the teaching of reading strategies for students of development administration', in H. von Faber (ed.), *Pariser Werkstattgespräch 1978: Leseverstehen im Fremdsprachenunterricht* Munich: Goethe Institut/ British Council, Paris, reprinted in M. Coulthard (ed.), (1994) pp. 102–16.

Jones, S. (1998) 'Approaching antonymy afresh'. *Liverpool Working Papers in Applied Linguistics,* 4.1, 71–85.

—— (1999) Investigating Antonymy in Text. Unpublished PhD Thesis, University of Liverpool.

Joos, M. (1961) *The Five Clocks.* New York: Harcourt, Brace and World.

Jordan, M. P. (1980) 'Short texts to explain Problem-Solution stuctures – and vice versa'. *Instructional Science,* 9, 221–52.

—— (1984) *Rhetoric of Everyday English Texts.* London: George Allen and Unwin.

—— (1985) 'Some relations of surprise and expectation in English' in B. Hall (ed.), *The Eleventh LACUS Forum.* Columbia, South Carolina: Hombeam Press.

—— (1988) 'Some advances in clause relational theory', in J. D. Benson and W. S. Greaves (eds), *Systemic Functional Approaches to Discourse.* Norwood NJ: Ablex.

—— (1990) 'Clause relations within the anaphoric nominal group', in M. P. Jordan (ed.), *The 16th LACUS Forum.* Lake Bluff, IL: LACUS.

—— (1992) 'An integrated three-pronged analysis of a fund-raising letter', in W. C. Mann and S. A. Thompson (eds), *Discourse Discription: Diverse Linguistic Analyses of a Fund-Raising Text.* Amsterdam: John Benjamins, pp. 171–226.

Kaplan, R. (1966) 'Cultural thought patterns in intercultural education'. *Language Learning,* 16, 1–20.

—— (1972) *The Anatomy of Rhetoric: Prolegomena to a Functional Theory of Rhetoric.* Philadelphia: Center for Curriculum Development.

—— (1977) 'Contrastive rhetoric: some hypotheses'. *ITL,* 39/40 61–72.

—— (1987) 'Cultural thought patterns revisited' in U. Connor and R. Kaplan (eds), *Writing across Languages: Analysis of L2 Text.* Reading, Mass.: Addison Wesley.

—— (1988) 'Contrastive rhetoric and second language learning: notes towards a theory of contrastive rhetoric' in A. C. Purves (ed.), *Writing across Languages and Cultures: Issues in Contrastive Rhetoric.* Newbury Park: Sage.

—— R. L. Jones and G. R. Tucker (eds.) (1982) *Annual Review of Applied Linguistics III: Contrastive Rhetoric.* Rowley: Newbury House.

Kasher, A. (1991) 'On the pragmatic modules: a lecture'. *Journal of Pragmatics,* 16, 381–97.

Kay, H. and T. Dudley-Evans (1998) 'Genre: what teachers think'. *ELT Journal,* 52.4, 308–14.

Kopytko, R. (1995) 'Against rationalistic pragmatics'. *Journal of Pragmatics,* 23, 475–91.

—— (1998) 'Relational pragmatics'. *Studia Anglica Posnaniensia,* 23, (special ed.: Festschrift for Kari Sajavaara), pp. 195–211.

Kress, G. (1991) 'Critical discourse analysis'. *Annual Review of Applied Linguistics,* 11, 84–100.

Labov, W. (1972) *Language in the Inner City.* Oxford: Blackwell.

—— and D. Fanshel (1977) *Therapeutic Discourse.* N.Y.: Academic Press.

—— and J. Waletzky (1967) 'Narrative analysis: oral versions of personal experience', in J. Helm (ed.), *Essays on the Verbal and Visual Arts.* Seattle: University of Washington Press, pp. 25–42.

Langer, J. A. (1987) 'The construction of meaning and the assessment of comprehension: an analysis of reader performance on standardized test items', in R. O. Freedle (ed.), *Advances in Discourse Processes Vol. 12.* Norwood, NJ: Ablex, pp. 225–44.

Lee, D. (2000) Modelling variation in Spoken and Written Language: The Multi-Dimensional Appoach Revisited. Unpublished PhD Thesis, University of Liverpool.

Levinson, S. C. (1983) *Pragmatics*. Cambridge: Cambridge University Press.

Longacre, R. E. (1968) *Discourse, Paragraph and Sentence Structure in Selected Philippine Languages*. S.I.L. Publications in Linguistics and Related Fields, No 21, Vols. 1 and 2. Dallas, Texas: Summer Institute of Linguistics Publications.

—— (1972) *Hierarchy and Universality of Discourse Constituents in New Guinea Languages: Discussion and Texts*. Washington, DC: Georgetown University Press.

—— (1974) 'Narrative versus other discourse genres' in R. Brend (ed.), *Advances in Tagmemics*. Amsterdam: North-Holland Publishing Co., pp. 357–376.

—— (1976) *An Anatomy of Speech Notions*. Lisse: Peter de Ridder Press.

—— (1979) 'The paragraph as a grammatical unit', in T. Givón (ed.), *Discourse and Syntax*. NY: Academic Press, pp. 115–34.

—— (1983) *The Grammar of Discourse*. NY: Plenum Press.

—— (1989) *Joseph: A Story of Divine Providence. A Text Theoretical and Textlinguistic Analysis of Genesis 37 and 39–48*. Winona Lake: Eisenbrauns.

—— (1992) 'The discourse strategy of an appeals letter', in W. C. Mann and S. A. Thompson (eds), *Discourse Description: Diverse Linguistic Analyses of a Fund-Raising Text*. Amsterdam: John Benjamins, pp. 109–30.

McCarthy, M. (1991) *Discourse Analysis for Language Teachers*. Cambridge: Cambridge University Press.

Maier, E. and E. Hovy (1993) 'Organizing discourse structure relations using meta-functions', in H. Horacek and M. Zock (eds), *New Concepts in Natural Language Generation: Planning, Realization and System*. London: Pinter, pp. 69–86.

Mann, W. C. and S. A. Thompson (1986) 'Relational propositions in discourse'. *Discourse Processes*, 9, 57–90.

—— (1988) 'Rhetorical structure theory: toward a functional theory of text organization'. *Text*, 8.3, 243–81.

—— (eds.) (1992) *Discourse Description: Diverse Linguistic Analyses of a Fund-Raising Text*. Amsterdam: John Benjamins.

Mann, W. C., C. Matthiessen and S. A. Thompson (1992) 'Rhetorical structure theory and text analysis', in Mann and Thompson (eds.), pp 39–78.

Marley, C. (1995) 'A little light on *The Heart of Darkness*', in J Payne (ed.), *Linguistic Approaches to Literature: Papers in Literary Stylistics*. Discourse Analysis Monographs, Birmingham: ELR, University of Birmingham, pp. 74–101.

—— (2000) 'Interaction in written dating advertisements', in M Coulthard *et al.* (eds.), *Working with Dialogue*. Tübingen: Niemeyer Verlag, pp. 293–305.

Martin, J. R. (1989) *Factual Writing: Exploring and Challenging Social Reality*. Oxford: Oxford University Press.

—— (1992) *English Text: System and Structure* Amsterdam: John Benjamins.

—— (1997) 'Analysing genre: functional parameters', in F. Christie and J. R. Martin (eds), *Genre and Institutions: Social Processes in the Workplace and the School*. London: Cassell, pp. 3–39.

Mauranen, A. (1993a) 'Contrastive ESP rhetoric: Metatext in Finnish-English economics texts'. *English for Specific Purposes*, 12, 3–22.

—— (1993b) *Cultural Differences in Academic Rhetoric*. Frankfurt: Peter Lang.

—— (1998) 'Another look at genre'. *Studia Anglica Posnaniensia*, 23, (special ed.: Festschrift for Kari Sajavaara), pp. 303–15.

Meyer, B. J. F. (1975) *The Organization of Prose and Its Effects on Memory*. Amsterdam: North-Holland.

—— (1992) 'An analysis of a plea for money', in W. C. Mann and S. A. Thompson (eds), *Discourse Description: Diverse Linguistic Analyses of a Fund-Raising Text*. Amsterdam: John Benjamins, pp. 79–108.

—— and G. E. Rice (1982) 'The interaction of reader strategies and the organization of text'. *Text*, 2, 155–92.

—— (1984) 'The structure of text' in P. D. Pearson and M. Kamil (eds), *Handbook of Research in Reading*. NY: Longman.

Moi, T. (ed.) (1986) *The Kristeva Reader*. Oxford: Blackwell.

Morgan, J. L. and M. Sellner (1980) 'Discourse and linguistic theory', in R. J. Spiro, B. Bruce and W. Brewer (eds), *Theoretical Issues in Reading Comprehension*. Hillsdale, NJ: Lawrence Erlbaum, pp. 165–200.

Morley, J. (1998) *Truth to Tell: Form and Function in Newspaper Headlines*. Bologna: CLUEB.

Myers, G. (1999) 'Interaction in writing: principles and problems', in C. N. Candlin and K. Hyland (eds), *Writing: Texts, Processes and Practices*. London: Longman.

Nystrand, M. (1986) *The Structure of Written Communication: Studies in Reciprocity between Writers and Readers*. Orlando: Academic Press.

—— (1989) 'A social interactive model of writing'. *Written Communication*, 6.1, 66–85.

O'Halloran, K. (1999) Mystifying Discourse: A Critique of Current Assumptions and an Alternative Framework for Analysis. Unpublished PhD Thesis, Institute of Education, University of London.

Paltridge, B. (1996) 'Genre, text type, and the language learning classroom'. *ELT Journal*, 50.3, 237–43.

Peng W. (1998) Lexical Patterning, Key Words and the Theme-Rheme System. Unpublished PhD Thesis, University of Liverpool.

Pike, K. (1967) *Language in Relation to a Unified Theory of the Structure of Human Behaviour* [1954–9], 2nd revised edn. The Hague: Mouton.

—— (1981) 'Grammar versus reference in the analysis of discourse', in *Tagmemics, Discourse and Verbal Art*. Michigan: University of Michigan Press.

Pratt, M. L. (1977) *Toward a Speech Act Theory of Literary Discourse*. Bloomington: Indiana University Press.

Prince, G. (1973) *A Grammar of Stories*. The Hague: Mouton.

Purves, A. C. (ed.) (1988) *Writing across Languages and Cultures: Issues in Contrastive Rhetoric*. Newbury Park: Sage.

Rimmon-Kenan, S. (1983) *Narrative Fiction: Contemporary Poetics*. London: Methuen.

Roe, P. (1977) *Scientific Text*. Discourse Analysis Monographs. Birmingham: ELR, University of Birmingham.

Rumelhart, D. E. (1975) 'Notes on a schema for stories', in D. G. Bobrow and A. Collins (eds), *Representation and Understanding: Studies in Cognitive Science*. NY: Academic Press, pp. 211–36.

—— (1977) 'Understanding and summarising brief stories', in D. LaBerge and S. J. Samuels (eds), *Basic Processes in Reading: Perception and Comprehension*. Hillsdale, NJ: Lawrence Erlbaum.

—— (1980) 'On evaluating story grammars'. *Cognitive Science*, 4, 313–16.

—— and A. Ortony (1977) 'The representation of knowledge in memory', in R. C. Anderson *et al.* (eds), *Schooling and the Acquisition of Knowledge*. NY: Halsted Press.

Salager-Meyer, F. (1990) 'Discoursal movements in medical English abstracts and their linguistic exponents: a genre analysis study'. *Interface*, 4.2, 107–24.

—— (1992) 'A text type and move analysis study of verb tense and modality distribution in medical English abstracts'. *English for Specific Purposes*, 93–113.

Sanford A. J. and S. C. Garrod (1981) *Understanding Written Language: Explorations in Comprehension beyond the Sentence.* Chichester: Wiley.

Schank R. C. and R. P. Abelson (1977) *Scripts, Plans, Goals and Understanding.* NY: Halsted Press.

Scott, M. (1999) *WordSmith Tools, Version 3.* Oxford: Oxford University Press.

Scott, N. (1998) Normalisation and Readers' Expectations: A Study of Literary Translation, Unpublished PhD Thesis, University of Liverpool.

Searle, J. R. (1969) *Speech Acts.* Cambridge: Cambridge University Press.

Shalom, C. (1997) 'That great supermarket of desire: attributes of the desired other in personal advertisements', in K. Harvey and C. Shalom (eds), *Language and Desire* London: Routledge, pp. 186–203.

Shepherd, T. (1988) Matching Relations in Narrative Discourse. Unpublished MA dissertation, Universidade Federal do Paraná.

—— (1993) A Linguistic Approach to the Description of Repeated Elements in Fringe Narratives: Principles of Organization of Prose and Filmic Text. Unpublished PhD Thesis, University of Birmingham.

—— (1997) 'Towards a description of a typical narratives: a study of the underlying organisation of *Flaubert's Parrot*'. *Language and Discourse*, 5, 71–96.

Sinclair, J.Mc.H and M. Coulthard (1975) *Towards an Analysis of Discourse: The English Used by Teachers and Pupils.* London: Oxford University Press, reprinted in abridged form in M. Coulthard (ed.), (1992) pp. 1–34.

—— M. Hoey and G. Fox (eds.) (1993) *Techniques of Description: Spoken and Written Discourse* (a festschrift for Malcolm Coulthard). London: Routledge.

Smith, F. (1978) *Understanding Reading.* NY: Holt, Rinehart and Winston.

Sperber, D. and D. Wilson (1995) *Relevance: Communication and Cognition* (2nd edn.). Oxford: Blackwell.

Stein, N. L. (1982) 'The definition of a story'. *Journal of Pragmatics*, 6, 487–507.

—— and C. C. Glenn (1979) 'An analysis of story comprehension in elementary school children', in R. O. Freedle (ed.), *New Directions in Discourse Processing (Advances in Discourse Processes, 2).* Norwood, NJ: Ablex, pp. 53–120.

—— (1982) 'Children's concept of time: the development of a story schema', in W. Friedman (ed.), *The Developmental Psychology of Time.* NY: Academic Press, pp. 255–81.

—— and M. Policastro (1984) 'The concept of a story: a comparison between children's and teachers' viewpoints', in H. Mandl, N. L. Stein and T. Trabasso (eds), *Learning and Comprehension of Text.* Hillsdale, NJ: Erlbaum, pp. 113–55.

Stubbs, M. (1997) 'Whorf's children: Critical comments on critical discourse analysis', in A. Ryan and A. Wray (eds), *Evolving Models of Language: British Studies in Applied Linguistics*, 12, 100–16.

Suleiman, S. R. and I. Crosman (1980) *The Reader in the Text: Essays on Audience and Interpretation.* Princeton: Princeton University Press.

Sutherland, S. (1985) A Description of Description: A Study of Information Patterning in Descriptive Discourse and Its Implications for the EFL Classroom. Unpublished MA dissertation, University of Birmingham.

Swales, J. (1981) *Aspects of Article Introductions* (Aston ESP Monographs 1). Birmingham: Aston University.

—— (1990) *Genre Analysis: English in Academic and Research Settings.* Cambridge: Cambridge University Press.

Tadros, A. (1985) *Prediction in Text.* Discourse Analysis Monographs, Birmingham: ELR, University of Birmingham.

—— (1993) 'The pragmatics of text averral and attribution in academic text', in M. Hoey (ed.), *Data, Description, Discourse*. London: HarperCollins, pp. 98–114.

—— (1994) 'Predictive categories in expository text' in M. Coulthard (ed.), pp. 69–82.

Tanskanen, S-K. (2000) *Collaborating Towards Coherence*. PhD Thesis, University of Turku, Finland.

Thompson, G. and P. Thetela (1995) 'The sound of one hand clapping: the management of interaction in written discourse'. *Text*, 15.1, 103–27.

Thompson, S. E. (1997) *Presenting Research: A Study of Interaction in Academic Monologue*. Unpublished PhD Thesis, University of Liverpool.

Thorndyke, P. M. (1977) 'Cognitive structures in comprehension and memory of narrative discourse'. *Cognitive Psychology*, 9.1, 77–110.

Toolan, M. (1988) *Narrative: A Critical Linguistic Introduction*. London: Routledge.

Urquhart, A. (1978) 'Operating on learning texts', in L. Selinker *et al.* (eds), *English for Academic and Technical Purposes*. Rowley, Mass: Newbury House, pp. 211–22.

Ventola, E. (1987) *The Structure of Social Interaction*. London: Frances Pinter.

Vestergaard, T. and K. Schrøder (1985) *The Language of Advertising*. Oxford: Basil Blackwell.

Warvik, B, S-K. Tanskanen and R. Hiltunen (eds), *Organization in Discourse: Proceedings from the Turku Conference, Anglicana Turkuensia*, 14.

Wessels, E. M. (1993) *Bonding and Related Measures of Coherence in Student Academic Writing*. Unpublished MA dissertation, University of South Africa.

White, P. R. R. (1999) *Telling Media Tales: The News Story as Rhetoric*. Unpublished PhD Thesis, University of Sydney.

Widdowson, Henry (1979) *Explorations in Applied Linguistics*. Oxford: Oxford University Press.

—— (1984) *Explorations in Applied Linguistics 2*. London: Oxford University Press.

—— (1996) 'Reply to Fairclough: Discourse and interpretation: Conjectures and refutations'. *Language and Literature*, 5.1, 57–69.

—— (1998) 'Review article: The theory and practice of critical discourse analysis'. *Applied Linguistics*, 19.1, 136–51.

Williames, J. (1984) *An Enquiry into the Interactive Nature of Written Discourse: The Example of the Newspaper Argument Letter*. Unpublished MA dissertation, University of Birmingham.

Winter, E. (1971) 'Connection in science material: a proposition about the semantics of clause relations' in *CILT Reports and Papers No 7: Technology in a Second Language*. London: Centre for Information on Language Teaching and Research, pp. 41–52.

—— (1974) *Replacement as a Function of Repetition: A Study of Some of its Principal Features in the Clause Relations of Contemporary English*, Unpublished PhD Thesis, University of London.

—— (1976) 'Fundamentals of information structure: pilot manual for further development according to student need' mimeo. The Hatfield Polytechnic.

—— (1977) 'A clause-relational approach to English texts'. *Instructional Science* (special edn.), 6, 1–92.

—— (1979) 'Replacement as a fundamental function of the sentence in context'. *Forum Linguisticum*, 4.2, 95–133.

—— (1982) *Towards a Contextual Grammar of English*. London: George Allen and Unwin.

—— (1986) 'Clause relations as information structure: two basic text structures in English', in M. Coulthard (ed.), *Talking about Text: Studies presented to David Brazil on his retirement*. Discourse Analysis Monographs No 13, Birmingham: ELR, University of Birmingham, pp. 88–108, reprinted with emendations in M. Coulthard (ed.), (1994) pp. 46–68.

—— (1992) 'The notion of unspecific versus specific as one way of analysing the information of a fund-raising letter', in W. C. Mann and S. A. Thompson (eds), *Discourse Description: Diverse Linguistic Analyses of a Fund-Raising Text*. Amsterdam: John Benjamins, pp. 131–70.

—— (1994) 'Clause relations as information structure: two basic text structures in English' in M. Coulthard (ed.), *Advances in Written Text Analysis*. London: Routledge, pp. 46–88.

—— (1996) 'Denial and correction as the most fundamental Clause Relation'. Paper given to conference *Developing Discourse-Awareness in Cross-Cultural Contexts*, University of Warsaw.

Index